W9-CCD-724

Praise for *An Appalachian Childhood*

By nature, Brady has two very important qualities in abundance - she is a seeker and a superb storyteller. Brady not only follows her own path, but with machete in hand, she clears the whole damn road herself! Brady's childhood was not comfortable - needs were not met without a physical, mental, and often spiritual struggle - but through that strife you see how this exceptional character was built. What comes through the pages more than anything else is this enormous sense of gratitude for her life and the people she's been fortunate enough to share it with. There are no bitter undertones or sickly sweet moments, just simple, honest, vivid storytelling from a fascinating woman light years ahead of her time and place. Brady's writing encourages us to shake off our laziness and societal constraints - that hard work can have its own rewards, that falling fast asleep from sheer exhaustion in the warm loving embrace of your grandmother might just be as good as it gets.

-Holly Thompson, Menlo Park, CA

I was immediately transported back in time, smelling Grandma's cornbread, seeing the March flowers blooming, feeling the red Georgia dirt beneath my bare feet and the cold mountain creek water, hearing the katydids and whippoorwills, picking wild Yates apples, breaking beans on the porch for a day of canning, tasting sweet homemade jelly on hot biscuits, walking down that dusty road to catch the school bus. I could read the writing on the wall, literally newspapers covered the walls of the house. These stories will be enjoyed by anyone who reads this book. Maybe it will spark a memory from their own childhood long ago. But for a handful of folks who know and live in North Georgia, this book is a great gift, to see the Burnt Mountain area of the past through this storyteller's eyes. She has created a legacy that her family will cherish for many generations. I thoroughly enjoyed this memoir, and am eagerly awaiting the second half to be published.

-Susan Tidwell, Ellijay, GA

This is one of the most beautiful true-life stories, written by an extraordinary writer.

-Julie Dene, Artist, London, England

I really loved Grandma Dean's book. Her energy and drive have been so inspiring to our young Team Members.

-Scott Sherman, Store Team Leader, Whole Foods Market, Cupertino, CA

I'm savoring every visual and story in this memoir. I can hear Deany Brady saying the words and feel as if I'm there, experiencing the full rich memories through her gift of storytelling.

-Neddie Barnett, Menlo Park, CA

An Appalachian Childhood is a real gem! I loved it!!

-Linda Hambrick, Amsterdam, The Netherlands

Brady has had such an interesting life and I think she was a girl/woman ahead of her time. Her book completely consumed me.

-Carrie Farrell, Menlo Park, CA

Deany Brady's memoir, *An Appalachian Childhood*, is filled with some of the most compelling life stories we have read.

-Jim and Cathy Treftz, Sunnyvale, CA.

This is a wonderful, warm, and tender personal account of a difficult yet loving family life in the heart of Appalachia.

-Dr. Lillian Stern, Philadelphia, PA

I'm supposed to be putting my kids to bed but I can't put down this book!

-Donna Lowman, Ellijay, GA

AN APPALACHIAN CHILDHOOD

DEANY BRADY

Text copyright © 2013

Odean W. Brady

All Rights Reserved

I dedicate this book to Mr. Hagan, my inspiring, wise, and loving friend and mentor, who believed in me with such enthusiasm. I hope he would be proud of this effort.

Nothing great was ever achieved without enthusiasm.

--- Ralph Waldo Emerson, "Circles"

Let us rise up
and be thankful,
for if we didn't
learn a lot today,
at least we
learned a little,
and if we didn't
learn a little, at
least we didn't
get sick, and if
we got sick, at
least we didn't
die; so let us all
be thankful.

--- Buddha

If the only prayer you
ever said in your whole
life was, "Thank you,"
that would suffice.

--- Meister Eckhart

Acknowledgements

Lynn Murphy read my chapters in the beginning, loved them, and encouraged me to write more during our many writing dinners together. Thank you, my friend.

Harriet Scott Chessman, my editor, lovingly and patiently helped me develop this memoir over the course of two years. She has encouraged me to bring the images, voices, and scenes of my girlhood into these pages. The magnitude of my gratitude to Harriet can never be fully expressed.

My lifelong dream of writing a book gained a more tangible form through the tireless, in-depth creative teaching of Ellen Sussman, in her "Novel in a Year" course. I thank my lucky stars for Ellen's teaching and inspiration.

I am profoundly indebted to my parents and my grandma, who nurtured me with such love, and who encouraged me to finish high school -- something that so few children in Appalachia were able to do.

My daughter Jeriann, always my first and most important reader, has lovingly nudged me to write this memoir and has generously contributed her insights and deep understanding of me. My dear son-in-law David has quietly offered his support (and not only with my computer). I have always been cheered on by my brother Gene, my late sister Colleen, and their dear families. And this book is my "hug" to my precious grandson Brady. Now he can know his grandma's story.

I hold in my heart joyful appreciation for the many parents of students in my daughter's second-grade classroom, Room G-3, at Laurel School in Menlo Park, California, where I have volunteered since 1996. They have added much to making the past seventeen years of my life some of my best. These dear parents and their sweet children have given me a fresh reason to live and write, starting when I arrived in the Bay Area after losing my ninety-six-year old father in Appalachia.

My heartfelt appreciation goes to London artist Julie Dene. In planning my front book cover, I sent Julie the only photograph I have of myself as a child -- a picture of a small Odean in a group of other children standing close together, their arms around each other -- and I asked her if she could create an image of me as a child, on my own. I was elated beyond words to see the result of her exquisite work. I thought a miracle had occurred, until I discovered that Julie Dene is a direct descendant of J. M. W. Turner.

Introduction

My six-year-old grandson and I are lounging together on a big rock protruding into the creek that flows through our Appalachian farm. My daughter Jeriann lies near us on the grassy bank. All of us are enjoying our annual visit to Ellijay, Georgia, my birthplace.

"Grandma Deany, are you as old as Santa Claus?" Brady asks.

I am dumbfounded, not so much by the unflattering guess at my age, as by the fact that I remember asking almost the same question of my Grandma on these rocks when I was a child myself.

Glancing at Brady's and my feet as we dabble them in the water, I can almost see my Grandma's rough, worn feet, with the painful corns on her toes. Beside hers are mine, with tiny toes wiggling, eager to begin my journey. I lived near this spot for most of my childhood, in a two-room shack on a hilly farm. It was a difficult life, but one filled with loving parents and the rich blessing of my Grandma and my Great-Grandpa. My sister Colleen was almost two years old when I was born, and my brother Gene was born when I was nine.

I dreamed all my childhood of a better life for my family and myself, and finally, twenty years after my birth here, I found my way first to Miami, and then to a happy marriage in New York City, where I lived with my husband Jerry Brady and our daughter Jeriann in the Penthouse of the Delmonico Hotel on Park Avenue. During my New York years, Jerry and I enjoyed friendships with many people in show business – a lively group of actors, singers and entertainers, including Frank Sinatra and the comedian Milton Berle. Our best friends were the television host Ed Sullivan and

11

his wife. My life became more heavenly than even I could have dreamed, until tragedy forced me to grow in different directions.

Over the years, I have told Jeriann these stories. She has often asked me to write them down, and this is what I have finally done. *An Appalachian Childhood*, the first half of my two-book memoir, tells the story of my first twenty years, as I grew up in Appalachia during the 1930's and 40's – a way of life that has changed, and in many aspects vanished. In writing about my childhood farm life, I hope to pay tribute both to my hard-working family and to the world of small communities like ours in those hills. More large houses dot the hills now, just like the mansion of the Coca-Cola Lady I write about here, who bought my family's jelly and produce. Fewer people wash their laundry in the creek these days, or send their littlest children to crawl under the house to fetch the hens' eggs. Fewer children tote water in buckets and sleep in the same bed with a grandmother and siblings. And I have a feeling that fewer stories are told by the light of a fire on winter evenings.

The second half of my memoir, *Higher than Yonder Mountain,* tells the story of my Miami and New York years, and the challenges that led me back to Appalachia to start over. I live now with Jeriann and her family in California, and I feel lucky to have the chance to make these yearly visits to my childhood home in the hills of Georgia.

As I glance down at my grandson sitting beside me on the rock, I place my arm around his small, square shoulders and let my cheek brush his. The creek water touches our feet and plays with our toes as it flows on.

Deany Brady

Sunnyvale, California

and Ellijay, Georgia

My mother, Mamie Lawing, taken in the winter of 1925
before she and Daddy married on July 11, 1925

My father, William Arthur Warren, taken on the porch
of his family home in the winter of 1925

Chapter 1

An Appalachian Birth

I was born on a stifling hot day, August 15th, 1927, in the Appalachian mountains of North Georgia, to Arthur William Warren and Mamie Lawing Warren. Daddy guessed the temperature on that day would have been 110 degrees during the midday hours.

"But since there wasn't no thermometer to measure it," he always said, "ain't no way I could be sure how hot it was."

My Mommy's version of my birth was blurry, and my Grandma's version always sounded sketchy and tiresome to me, because she punctuated her story with so many details about her busy day, including very little about the grand entrance into the world of Odean Warren. My Grandma described how, during those long hours of Mommy's struggle to birth me, a stream of well-meaning neighbors "dropped in to sit a spell," so that in addition to Grandma's regular daily chores, she had to prepare meals around the clock for the doctor, relatives and neighbors.

My Daddy's version was my favorite. During my childhood, he told it to me on nearly every birthday, and years later, when I happened to be home in August, he would tell it again, relishing each detail. He always spoke slowly and with a deliberateness that made his listeners feel as if he were processing his thoughts on the spot, so that when he spoke, his words would come out as unfiltered truth. Thinking on a subject, he would scratch his head of thick, dark brown hair, which he kept clipped short on the sides and the back, but long and slicked back above his forehead.

Daddy's story started with the fact that Mommy had been severely ill during the entire nine months of her pregnancy. In spite of constant nausea, however, she had continued to do chores each day, both in the fields and in our two-room house.

"On a small farm like ours, you know," Daddy would say, "she could not be spared. Though of course," he would add with the hint of a smile, "the lack of money to buy kerosene oil for the lamp sometimes worked in her favor, by forcing her to go to bed with the chickens."

I was to discover later in my life something Daddy did not include in this story. My Mommy suffered from emotional difficulties stemming from her own birth to an unmarried fifteen-year-old girl -- my Grandma. The father had been the preacher's son, and it was unclear whether this pregnancy had come out of a rape or a consensual relationship. The story changed, depending on who told it. I remember Grandma saying that my Mommy's father had "up and left her, and gone out West someplace." My Mommy had heard people call her a "bastard" all her life, or else she had sensed them whispering this behind her back. She had never felt accepted, as a child and a young girl, in her community. This situation had created an emotional wound that gave her pain until her last breath in her eighty-second year, and I am certain that it increased her anguish in stressful times like childbirth.

Two days of labor in the sweltering heat had left Mommy lying limply on the bed, semi-conscious between bouts of pain. Often during those birth day storytelling times, at this point Daddy seemed to be feeling Mommy's exhaustion, and he would pause a few seconds as if the memory were unbearable.

Then, with renewed energy, he would add how lucky my Mommy had been to have a doctor. Most births in the neighborhood happened without any doctor's help at all.

The doctor had constant help from neighborhood women too. I could just picture the way more neighbors started to gather in and around our house, as some of the women went home to send other family members to take their places. Word was getting around that Mommy would not live, and the neighbors were most doubtful that I could survive either. Daddy allowed as how the neighborhood women keeping vigil were careful to give him gentle but straightforward warnings to prepare himself should all not go well on this day of my birthing.

Miss Bessie Wright said to my Daddy, "Arthur, you have got to be strong for your little Colleen here, and Miss Ethie and Uncle Dock [my Grandma and Great-Grandpa] all need you so badly. We can't question the ways of the Good Lord."

Possibly the neighbors did not feel that my failure to begin breathing would be such a great loss, since my parents could scarcely feed and take care of the one toddler they already had. (At this point Daddy always paused to assure me that the loss of his little Cottontail would have been an unbearable tragedy for the family, a moment I cherished in his story.)

I could just see the dawn of my birth day making its way through little round holes in the ceiling, as early light and soft breezes flowed generously through the cracks in the walls. The doctor and his helpers must have welcomed this freshness.

My Great-Great-Aunt Ibby's task was to hold the kerosene lamp. When needed, she would position herself so that she could lean on the footboard of Mommy's bed. In this way she could stretch her arms forward, holding the lamp so the doctor could do his work. Her tiny specs would slide down her long, crooked nose and lodge on the very tip of it. Beads of sweat on her face sparkled in the lamplight before breaking into tiny streams of warm water, which dripped onto the sheets.

Perhaps Aunt Ibby's mind was going back in time to the night her young niece Ethie, my Grandma, had given birth to my Mommy on this same bed. On that night Ibby's hands had let her hold the lamp more steadily. Now, as I was being born, she may have looked at the thin straw mattress under my Mommy and thought of how her writhing and turning had made it flat as a board. She may have reflected that this straw mattress cover had been refilled over twenty-five times since she had held the lamp for my Mommy's birth. Maybe Ibby was happy to think that soon the mattress would be filled again, since the harvest was coming up. Each August, when the wheat threshers came through, they left enough fresh, bouncy straw to fill all the beds in the community.

I often interrupted Daddy at this point in his story. I liked to steer him toward my own part in it.

"Daddy, tell me again – why did you name me Odean?'"

"Oh, your Great-Great-Aunt Ibby named you. She had heard that in England, the great country across the waters where our family originated, they had a theater named 'Odean,' and she liked the sound of it. Your Mommy and I loved Aunt Ibby and wanted to please her, even though she often made us feel she was a cut above us, since she'd had the good fortune to move from our mountains to Marietta, Georgia."

Ibby was certainly a great talker. As I was being born, Daddy said, she found many chances to express her gratitude for the good luck her son Arthur had had in being able to find a job in a chair factory in Marietta. Her son had been able to bring her there to live with his family. Now she came back to the mountains only in the summer months, when it was much too hot in the city. As she constantly reminded whoever might be listening, she always had a place to stay with her brother, Eli Whitney (Dock) Lawing, my Great-Grandpa.

18

When Daddy told this part of the story, he always gave instances of how Ibby just had to brag about having been able to rise above our simple life.

"I've been 'specially glad to be here this summer," she would say, "what with Mamie being so sick with the baby coming. It's lucky I'm not in our house in Marietta right now. I am glad to be of help to you all."

Daddy would wryly add that he had been sleeping on the floor all that summer, so Ibby could have his place on the bed beside my Mommy.

Like most people her age at that time, Ibby could not read. She took great pride, however, in the fact that her granddaughter Doreen was "getting a good education in the city, even all the way through high school."

Ibby's way of talking on and on, half to herself, was politely ignored by all in the birthing room, especially when she would commence boasting in a soft voice.

"Last spring," she said at one point, "Doreen was reading to me the words of a great man over in England, across the waters. The words he said was so purty. He must have been educated real good. I liked the sound of his name – Churchill. It made me think of a white church on a hill."

"Ibby was a good soul," Daddy would say, "even though her bragging about how good it was to have had the privilege of living in Marietta could get under your skin."

Then he would describe a conversation he and Mommy had overheard. It was a conversation between my Great-Grandpa Eli ("Dock") and Ibby about the family farm.

"During the early years of Mamie's and my marriage," Daddy would say, "we heard Ibby say to her younger brother, 'Eli,' – you know she never called him Dock – 'Eli, I have often thought about this, and I reckon our Ma, being ninety-five years old when she died, must have been a little crazy in her head to have deeded all this farm to you instead of giving some of it to me, her youngest daughter.'

"'Ibby, dear sister Ibby,' your Great-Grandpa said, 'our Ma gave me the farm because she was so smart in her head that she could see into the future and she knew you'd be living in luxury in the city, while she figured I would be the one to have to survive life here on this poor rocky hillside farm.'

"Ibby seemed to think about that a moment," Daddy said, "and then she nodded. 'I reckon so,' she said."

Here Daddy would pause a few seconds and chuckle as he remembered Mommy's Grandpa, whom he had loved so dearly.

Daddy figured Aunt Ibby must have been getting a little dizzy now, over my birthing, because she set the lamp on a table and asked a neighbor to take her place by Mommy's bed. Holding to the wall to brace herself, she moved to the door leading to the side room, which was a combined kitchen on one side and bedroom on the other. She held to the doorframe as she let her crooked little arthritic foot touch down on the lower floor, a distance of about two feet. Once in the kitchen, she carefully made her way over to a cane-bottomed chair and sat at the "eating table."

"Ethie, my child – my only niece –," she said to my Grandma, "you have been a blessing to this family. You took care of Eli's and my Ma until she died and now you are helping take care of Mamie and Arthur's little Colleen." As she said this, Ibby took a long look at my Grandma's face, adding, "Though you look like you're about to get tuckered out now. Can I help with something?"

My Grandma handed Ibby green beans to string, and Ibby sat comfortably and strung the beans slowly as she watched her niece do the cooking. When she declared she felt steady on her feet again, Ibby wandered over beside my Grandma, to help her boil water and prepare food.

Near my Mommy's and my bed, my Aunt Rosie sat, looking sleepy. She was Daddy's sister, seven years older than he was. Often she felt it was her duty to exercise a sharp tongue and to reprimand Daddy when he occasionally cursed. In church she epitomized the "hard-shelled Baptist" of those days because of her frantic shouting, mingled with hallelujahs and amens.

Aunt Rosie was a large woman, and the front posts of her narrow cane-bottomed chair must have pressed painfully, cutting into the flesh of her sprawling thighs. Because of her size, she could not move around easily, so she just sat most of the time and assessed the goings-on of my birth with a keen eye. She made it plain to the neighbor women that she did not approve of this new baby about to be born.

"Arthur and Mamie could barely take care of their one child, let alone another one," she said at one point, shaking her head.

She then breathed a long, irritated sigh, as she rolled her eyes around and upward to the mantel, where the mantel clock sat slowly ticking away the hours. This was the clock Daddy had inherited from their father. Squinting her eyes to stare at the clock's dingy face, she said she could barely make out the time to be 10:00 in the morning. My Daddy figured that Rosie was thinking, "Pa should have knowed that Arthur would never have a house that didn't leak when it rained, and would let the clock ruin." She could never understand why Pa had bequeathed that clock to Daddy instead of to her. "He must have been drunk on that corn liquor he made when he done such a foolish thing."

Aunt Rosie's attention was brought back to the room by little curly-haired Colleen bouncing through the house and coming to lean on her round knees. She patted the child's head and breathed another weary sigh. Daddy said she looked like she was thinking again what she had spoken earlier that day, that she wished the baby would hurry and come on out so she could go back to her own house, which was across a mountain and in another valley. Rosie had a tired husband there who needed her to cook the midday meal for him and her two sons, who were ten and twelve years old.

Through the years I often heard my mother say, "Rosie never tires of telling Arthur and me how blessed we were that the Good Lord saw fit to give her and her husband Berry boys instead of girls." She would mimic Aunt Rosie by rolling her eyes upward and the corners of her mouth downward as she declared, in Rosie's voice, "When boys fool around you can't tell it, but girls, they get pregnant."

Years later, Mommy would tell my sister Colleen and me that Aunt Rosie always thought it was her duty to try to persuade us to live virtuously, by her own shining example, since her sister-in-law, our Mommy, was a bastard.

A few other neighbor women were waiting at Mommy's bedside for the birth, but Daddy, being a careful storyteller, did not know them well enough to venture to give me an account of their thoughts.

The doctor had been at our house since the day before. We lived in such a remote area that he dared not leave. He told Daddy that if he wished, he could pay him for his twenty-four-hour house call by giving him some green corn growing on our mountain patch of ground, so Daddy left to pull fresh ears of corn from the stalks.

At this point in his story, Daddy usually digressed to tell me how he understood we might have come to speak of sweet corn as "roastin' ears." The local people slid those two words together

22

into one word, "roastneers." He would then tell the cherished story of Mommy's Great-Great-Grandfather, who had coined this word back in the Civil War. Daddy liked the sound of that word "roastneer," and I always felt proud at this point in the story to think that my own ancestor – the father of my Great-Grandpa Eli – had created a new word, whether or not you could find it in a dictionary.

About three o'clock in the afternoon on the day of my birth, Daddy returned from the field and placed several dozen ears of roastneers in the doctor's buggy. As he often added quietly, "I always meant to pay the doctor more in dollars, but I never had any extry money."

When Daddy looked up, he saw my Great-Grandpa Eli coming from the house toward the barn. Daddy said he could tell there was good news, because the chronic limp in Grandpa's right leg was hardly noticeable as he rushed toward Daddy, yelling, "Arthur, the baby's here. Mamie is alright and the baby ain't dead neither."

With hunched shoulders, carrying his black bag, the weary doctor came from the house just then, and made his way to his buggy. Daddy helped him hitch his horse while the doctor discussed how Mommy and I were recovering.

As the doctor talked, he kept looking wistfully at Daddy's two mules. For the whole day and night he'd been helping Mommy birth me, he'd kept coming out of the house to stand at the pasture fence to admire those mules, who were in a green meadow by the stream.

"Well, the doctor smiled at me and shook my hand warmly as he got into his buggy. Then he took one more look at my dandy pair of little gray mules."

In my early years, I was impatient with Daddy and all that small talk about the doctor constantly going outside to admire the mules. I felt the doctor should have been giving Mommy and me his undivided attention.

Sometimes I would interrupt to ask, "Daddy, why did the doctor go outside so often to look at your mules?"

Daddy would smile then, and get back on track.

"Dr. Chastain looked like his body felt so good as it sank into the cushioned seat of his buggy. Then he picked up the reins and called to his horse to git, and the buggy began to ease down the hill."

I always pictured the springs of the buggy gently moving up and down under the doctor as it took him out of sight on the narrow curved mountain road. That memory of his last grateful vision of the doctor seemed to remain vivid with Daddy, as he held it in his heart for all the years that followed.

I could just picture Daddy coming inside then, taking slow steps on the creaky old floor as he entered the room. He walked a narrow path among the women, who were now sitting quietly, recovering from the efforts they had exerted during the morning. As Daddy reached my mother's almost lifeless body lying under a flour-sack sheet, he bent over and placed his rough, calloused hand near her still, pale lips. He felt a scarce movement of warm air gently reach the palm of his hand.

"It felt like an angel's kiss," my Daddy would say, an expression that always struck me with its contrast to his rough, mountain man appearance.

Then he moved over to me in the bed at the adjacent corner of the room. The women had washed me and placed me under a blanket.

At that moment one of the neighbors whispered in Aunt Rosie's ear, "It's got the biggest head."

Overhearing this comment, my Daddy stood tall and stared at them as he emphatically declared, "Yes, by God, and plumb full of sense!"

Turning to go outside, he stooped a little, as was his habit, to clear the low door that led out to the narrow front porch. There he began to help my grandma fill brown paper "pokes" with vegetables she had gathered from the garden. That was their way of showing appreciation to each one who had helped. Grandma and Daddy kept ignoring the neighbor women's polite protests of "We don't want no pay."

No more mention was made about me as the women picked up their pokes of vegetables and headed for their homes. As they were leaving, their conversation was just murmured comments among themselves about how Arthur and Mamie could always grow the sweetest, best vegetables. They also inquired of Daddy how his crops were standing up through this hot, dry summer. These were expressions of genuine concern, because they knew that little creature, odd-looking as I was, would have to be fed.

Ending his story, Daddy would look at me with a self-satisfied grin and then, shaking his head, he would add mischievously, "And you know what? At the end of that day, I decided that if me and Mamie ever had another child, I would try to plan the next birth just after the threshers filled the straw mattress and not as it was for you – just before the mattress got filled with fresh straw."

To that, Mommy would remark dryly, "I'd appreciate that, Arthur."

Chapter 2

My Special Day with Daddy

One of my earliest and happiest memories is being with my Daddy beside a large hole in the ground, near a big blue lake. I may have been about four years old. The hole he was digging with his mules and mattock sat on top of Burnt Mountain, a distance of five miles from where my family lived in a valley on the east side of the mountain.

That summer Daddy had been working a few hours a week high up in the private community of Tate Mountain Estates, where the summer homes of wealthy Atlanta and Palm Beach families were being built around the lake. Those hours were infrequent, because working for someone else was not to Daddy's liking. He felt strongly that his rightful place was tending the little hillside farm he and Mommy had inherited from Mommy's side of the family. The big hole Daddy was digging would later hold the basement of a large rock mansion, the home of Willaford Ransom Leach and his wife, whom I always addressed as Mrs. Leach. Mrs. Leach was the granddaughter of the druggist, Asa Candler, who developed the drink he named Coca Cola.

As I would discover when I was older, that summer resort had been named for Sam Tate, on whose property the Tate Marble Quarries had been discovered. Those quarries would in future be named The Georgia Marble Company, whose marble would be bought by many foreign countries. Some of our neighbors, after returning from World War II, would proudly tell us they had seen Georgia Marble in buildings in Tokyo.

I would discover too that Burnt Mountain had gained its name from the fires that had been set to hasten the departure of the Cherokee people, who had originally made their home in a wide area amid the mountains and hills of northwest Georgia. The burning of their territory was part of the Cherokee Removal, which had ultimately led to the thousand-mile march from Tennessee to Oklahoma in 1838, known as the Trail of Tears. Once I had discovered this sad chapter in our history, I could sense the presence of the families who had been killed or forced to leave. As an older child, I felt that the howling winds in the pines were the ghosts of the Indians, crying.

On that summer day, however, I thought of this place high up on Burnt Mountain as heaven. I sat on an old quilt under the shade of a big oak tree, near where Daddy was digging the hole. It was a blissful day for me, since I was free from daily chores at home. The lake glittered in the sun, through the trees. I had spent the morning happily occupied, building myself a luxurious mansion with sticks, small stones, and thick green and brown oak leaves, which made beautiful soft carpets.

I based my mansion on one I had heard about a few days earlier. I had been poring over the newspaper that papered our walls, when I had come across the picture of a huge house. When I asked Mommy who owned that house, she stopped folding a pile of clothes and came to stand beside me.

First, she slowly spelled out two big words under the picture: "B U C K I N G H A M P A L A C E." Then she told me, "That house is in a land across the waters, called England. I hear tell that the man and woman who live there have got two little girls about the same age as you and Colleen."

Grandma called from where she sat in her rocker, "There's a picture of the two girls on the wall behind the stove in the kitchen." Evidently, I was not the only member of the family to get the news of the world from reading the walls!

I scrambled to get up and go to the kitchen. Grandma followed, saying it was time to stir the dried beans she had simmering in the black pot on the wood stove.

Peering through her specs at the picture of two well-dressed girls, she said, "I make out their names to be Elizabeth and Margaret."

My Grandma added, "So much grease has popped out from frying on the stove that the words are smeared."

As I built my mansion on the quilt, I spread out the rock walls to make the house even bigger. Remembering the princesses' names, I decided Colleen would be Elizabeth and I would be Margaret. I made a big fancy room for my Grandma, Colleen and me to sleep in. Then I began to furnish our room with elegant furniture and stuffed chairs, like those in the newspaper pictures of Shirley Temple's home. I also placed a big looking-glass on the wall. I made real windows that brought in a world of light.

Throughout the day, Daddy worked the mules single-handedly. First he worked John and then, once John would be dripping with sweat, Daddy would switch and work Jean, while he let John cool under the shade of a big oak. When he felt John was rested and cool enough, he would work him again.

I especially liked to watch Daddy dig with the mattock – a tool like a pickax. Grasping the wooden handle of it with both hands, he lifted the cutting edge skyward. With the mattock poised high over his right shoulder, he would let it pause an instant as I watched the sun reflect on its shiny blade. It looked to me as if he was giving directions to his arms, as he did to the mules, demanding that they thrust the tool powerfully into the ground.

Down came the sharp tool, yet the rocks and tough tree roots hindered its movement into the soil. Up and down, up and down, again and again the mattock went, with the sun reflecting off its shiny blade.

Daddy wore his faded, patched overalls with a long-sleeved plaid shirt. He thought that the long sleeves shaded his arms from the sun and kept him cooler. On his head he wore a lopsided straw hat, which covered a head of thick brown hair. His hair was always slicked back with lard into an Elvis-like style – long before Elvis.

Once when he swung upward, the mattock slipped from his hands and landed with a loud thud on a rock several feet behind him.

"Ah, damn it!" he said.

I am sure my presence kept his verbal outburst from becoming a sinful curse that used God's name. As Daddy impatiently retrieved the tool, I could see his anger at himself for having let one careless move temporarily interrupt his steady rhythm.

Soon he took a mule and hitched it to the scoop, a metal arm that looked like a large shovel. With the scoop, he could haul dirt and rocks out of the pit. With precision, he would urge each mule with verbal commands while gently pulling the reins with his left hand, indicating the directions he wanted the animal to follow. Simultaneously, with his right hand he would press the scoop down to let it fill itself as it moved forward. Then Daddy and the mule would drag the filled scoop to a wooded area at the edge of the yard, and there he would lift the heavy scoop and dump the dirt and rocks. While the mule took a few breaths of air, Daddy separated the rocks from the dirt with his large calloused hands. The biggest rocks would be used for the outside walls of the mansion. As Daddy separated out the rocks, I would come over to the dumping site and select small rocks and pebbles for my mansion.

When my shadow became small, I began to think about lunch. I saw Daddy pull from his pocket, in his overall bib, the old watch that had belonged to his daddy.

"It's time for dinner," he called out to me. The noontime meal was dinner. "You hungry, honey bunch?"

"Yeah, I'm hungry," I called back.

He unhitched the mule he was working and tied its bridle rein to a tree near where the other one was standing in the shade. He took his knife from his pocket and cut enough tender grass to fill my arms. Hugging the grass close, I gave each mule a bundle. Daddy also gave them the dried hay and two ears of corn we had brought along in a burlap bag attached to the harness of one mule.

While I listened to Jean and John chomp the corn and munch on the grass and hay, Daddy walked to the Drunkard's Spring and brought back a quart of water for us to drink with our lunch of large biscuits stuffed with scrambled eggs. He also brought a big bucket of water for the mules to share. Then he sat down on the ground in the shade beside me, took off his straw hat, and with a thin, worn rag wiped the mixture of dirt and sweat from his forehead.

Grandma had given him this fresh cloth from her rag bag that morning as we were leaving. She kept the rag bag supplied with clean old sugar-sack pillowcases and other such cloths to be used as handkerchiefs. Sometimes she tore a fresh piece of cloth, but often the cloths had already been torn, because she or my Mommy would wash the rags each week and use them for as long as they would hold together. I remember the first time I told my daughter about Grandma's rag bag, she cried out, "Mother, you were born before Kleenex!"

30

Once Daddy was ready, I handed him a biscuit and began eating mine. Having lived in my rock mansion all morning, I thought my scrambled egg sandwich a bit soggy and plain. (Years later, though, living in New York and dining on caviar and such at the swank restaurants, I would sometimes wish I could trade that fancy food for the sandwiches Mommy and Grandma always packed in the old rusty-edged lard bucket.)

After we ate, I watched the movement of Daddy's chest as he lay silently a little while on the quilt. His breathing seemed peaceful and calm, a contrast to his grunts and sighs during the morning hours. I listened to the birds singing as they flew into the shady branches of the oak tree above us. They seemed to like singing to Daddy and me.

Perhaps a half hour later, Daddy shook his body and raised himself to a sitting position on the quilt. Once he was standing, he twirled his battered straw hat to let the dust fall off, and then placed it on his thick hair. After softly patting my head, he hitched John again to the scoop.

As he moved toward the mule he looked back at me and said, "I gotta get busy. Honey bunch, you can go back to sleep now."

I was startled. He had not noticed -- he had not even seen my mansion. He did not understand that I had not been sleeping one minute. I had been very busy building something extraordinary. It was more than a mansion – it was a castle.

Hours later, I paused in my imaginative play and noticed the sun was slowly sliding down the sky, almost touching the tops of the trees on the far side of the lake. I was glad to see Daddy unhitching the mule from the scoop. It was time for us to start our five-mile trip back to our house in the valley below. Daddy lifted me and placed me on the back of John, the more gentle mule. I held onto the gadgets protruding from the gear at the bottom of the mule's neck. My bare legs slid on the warm slushy sweat on the mule's back, as Daddy helped me position myself securely on the leather and chains that crisscrossed around the mule's belly.

Being a very modest man and considering that we might meet a car coming up the mountain, Daddy carefully pulled my skirt down to about mid-calf of my legs. Then his large work-hardened hand gave a pat on the mule's rump, as he said gently, "Let's go, boy." John instantly began moving in the direction of home, as Daddy followed close behind, leading Jean. I knew that no matter how painfully tired Daddy's legs were, he would never put his grown-up body on the back of a tired animal. The steady clop of hoofs and the jangle of gear chains accompanied our weary selves.

I thought about my graceful castle all the way down the mountain, hoping it would stay safe under the oak tree. If I could go back another day with Daddy, I could add a whole new section, maybe, with twigs for couches and moss for rugs. I felt as if the castle was my true home, and I already missed it.

The protruding bones of the mule's back rubbed sharply against my tender tailbone. Frequently, the movement of the mule's body as he went down sharp inclines caused the gear to shift and become entangled with my legs. A car passing us on the dry dusty road sent clouds of dust into my eyes, leaving burning sensations and tears, as well as causing me a coughing spasm.

"You alright, hon?" I heard Daddy call from behind. The dust was so dense that I could not see him.

"Yeah," I answered. "You alright, too?"

"I shore am, just fine, only hungry. I hope Mamie and your Grandma gonna have a good supper ready when we get home." He sounded happy at that thought.

Twilight had almost faded into total darkness as we approached the barn. Daddy lifted me off the mule and held onto my arm while I walked around gingerly.

"My legs feel funny," I said.

He patted the trunk of the big oak in front of the barn with one hand and with his other powerful arm urged my trembling little body to hold onto the trunk of the tree.

"Here, my little Cotton Top, hold to the tree until the feeling comes back into your legs. They went to sleep while you had them stretched amongst the gear. It will only take a minute or so."

I held onto the tree and soon my legs felt normal again, although my bottom was sore from the mule's bony back.

"I'm fine now, Daddy," I said.

"Good, honey bunch! You are my little helper."

He gently patted my shoulder much as he did the rump of the mules. We were his obedient servants; feeling useful to him was our joy and our important mission.

I watched him lift the gear off the tired mules and saw them stretching and then lying down in the cool grass, rolling back and forth joyfully. I could feel the relief they must have felt. Soon they thrust their legs skyward a few times, and then they jumped up and ran down the hill to the stream at the wash place, where we did our weekly laundry. They gulped the fresh running water loudly and greedily. I remembered how graceful the lake had looked near the big hole Daddy had been digging. I was sure John and Jean would have loved to drink that clear water, as glassy as a mirror reflecting the clouds and trees.

In a short while, the mules ambled back up the hill to the barn, where each entered his own stable and began eating the dry grains off the corncobs that Daddy and I had shucked into the crib while the mules had been having their fill of water. Next, we climbed the ladder into the barn loft and I held the lantern for Daddy as he took a pitchfork and shuffled hay down a square hole. The opening in the loft floor was positioned so that the hay fell directly into the troughs, where the mules had already devoured the corn.

My sister Colleen had used a piece of chalk to write the names of the mules on their doors. I was amazed by the fact that Jean and John could read their names. They never failed to go into the correct stall.

I felt a twinge of guilt as I looked at that chalk printing, though. I had come by the chalk myself. My parents had taken Colleen and me to see the small schoolhouse we would attend in a couple of years or so, an upgrade of the one-room school where my mother had gone. When no one was looking, I had fingered the piece of beautiful white chalk in the tray under the blackboard, slipping it into my apron pocket. A few days later, I had asked Colleen to print the names of the mules on their doors. I was glad she did not ask me how I came to own a piece of chalk. I am now confessing, these many years later, my first dishonest act.

The cracking of the mules' chewing made my mouth water. I was as hungry as they were. I had eaten my scrambled egg sandwich hours and hours earlier.

As Daddy and I walked up the slope from the barn, the warm flickering glow of the kerosene lamp greeted us from the kitchen window. Our two dogs, Lead and Maude, having welcomed us at the barn, were now walking in step with us to the house, and my Great-Grandpa Eli joined us. The busy sounds of Mommy, Grandma and Colleen halted temporarily when they heard us coming. Then their happy conversation spilled out eagerly, as they shared the events of the day with us, frequently

34

interrupting each other. Finally we gathered around the supper table, with Grandma and Mommy and Great-Grandpa on one side, in three cane-bottomed chairs, and Daddy and Colleen on a long wooden bench on the opposite side, with me tucked in between them. Mommy and Grandma always sat on the side of the table near the stove so they could easily get up and fill the vegetable bowls that we rapidly emptied.

Mommy placed the huge cake of corn pone in the center of the table, where we could all reach it and break off chunks. (Corn pone is corn bread baked in a cast iron frying pan.) Next to the pone was a big bowl of shelled Great Northern beans. To the right of my Grandma stood two large earthenware pitchers of milk, one fresh (we called it sweet milk) and the other buttermilk. The milk pitchers had white sugar sacks tied around their tops, which looked like fancy women's hats. I thought they looked important and commanding of attention. Drops of water were slowly gliding down the sides of the pitchers. The room was warm, but the milk was as cool as the water in the spring house where the pitchers had sat since the morning milking. My Great-Grandpa ate his corn pone slowly, as he talked with my Daddy about what he'd tried to do in the fields that day while Daddy had been gone. Sometimes he would wink at me.

My bottom was becoming more uncomfortable the longer I sat on that hard wooden bench. I didn't want to complain, though, because I had just been privileged to have a play day with Daddy. So I just kept shifting away from the soreness and slowly sinking from exhaustion, until my head lay on the crook of Daddy's arm as he rested it on the table. I knew Colleen was stiff and irritated with me for having had a fun day while she had had to do all the chores that we usually shared. I knew too, though, that she had not actually wanted to go up to the top of Burnt Mountain, because she thought riding the mules was tomboyish. She often called me "Silly Lily" when I rode the mountain trails with Daddy.

Grandma startled us by exclaiming as she stared at me, "Arthur, the child looks terrible tired and wore out."

Mommy reached across the table and felt my forehead.

"She ain't hot," she said.

I thought how glad I was she had touched my forehead and not my bottom.

Colleen scornfully put in, "Well, I don't know why she should be so tired. She got to go somewhere and lie on a quilt and play all day while I've been home working."

A few minutes later, I squirmed from my seat in the center of the bench, being careful not to bump my sister and draw more attention to myself. Walking like a stiff little dummy, I made my way into the other room, where our beds, with sheets turned down, were waiting. My space in the center of the bed I shared with Grandma and Colleen looked inviting, and I crawled right in.

The chatter, including my sister's sharp comments, vanished. My family's conversation may have continued, but I could not hear it, since I was slipping again into the castle I had built that morning. I could just see its rocky walls and its mossy furnishings. I could just imagine the real glass in its big windows. Its kitchen would be wide enough for a family of twenty, and yet people would only eat in a pretty room with a long oak table, like I'd seen on one of our newspaper walls.

My family did not know about this castle, but I knew. Only temporarily had I allowed reality to interrupt my daydreams. Sleep brought that castle to life.

Chapter 3

March Flowers

One mid-January afternoon, when I was four years old, I was sitting on my Grandma's lap before the fire. My Great-Grandpa had been lying sick in bed for days. I wished he would open his eyes and smile at me, call me Cotton Top, but he kept his eyes closed most of the time, and he could barely move from his bed, which was in the corner behind us.

It was a fiercely windy and freezing day. I heard the wooden latch of the front door lift, and I saw Mommy, bundled in an extra coat, coming in with the wind and wrestling to get the door shut again. She held a heavy log under one arm.

"Honey," she asked, "could you stand here and open and close the door fast as I come in and out with these logs? I want to be sure to keep Grandpa warm through the night."

I moved swiftly from my cozy place in Grandma's lap to help Mommy with the fire logs. As she went outside again, I did as she asked. I waited by the door, and opened it for her, as soon as I heard her on the porch. The icy wind was so powerful it almost forced the door from my hands as I let Mommy back inside, hugging another ice covered log. With effort, I shut the door as she brought the log inside. When she started to walk back outside, I could see a sheet of ice covering the entire porch. This time, Mommy's feet slid and she fell, sitting down hard on the porch ice. I rushed to help her up and her hand felt as cold as an icicle as she grabbed mine to lift herself. She walked carefully off the porch to fetch one more bundle of logs.

When she came inside again, she brushed the snow off her coat as she said, "Well, it's a good thing that was my last load to bring in, 'cause I wouldn't want to slide out on my bottom again."

She took the small sage broom and swept the melting ice down the cracks between the floorboards.

The logs popped and crackled as the red-hot coals instantly melted the ice from the fresh logs. I again sat on my Grandma's inviting lap as we listened to the deep, hollow struggles for breath coming from Great-Grandpa Eli. I snuggled even deeper into Grandma's soft belly as she pulled up the corners of her apron and enfolded me in a baby bunting way.

"Is Grandpa going to die?" I asked.

"He is old and sick and Jesus may be ready to take him to heaven. Honey, don't let it worry you."

Her voice was reassuring. After a moment, though, she quickly turned me so that I could look into her face.

"Tell me, Odean, what do you remember about my Pap?" I felt urgency in her voice and in her earnest expression.

Not quite understanding what she meant, I said, "Lots of things."

I stared down at the side of the hearth where my Great-Grandpa's worn, crooked boots were sitting with the tongues pushed inside toward the toes of his shoes. Those boots had not been touched in some time. I realized how much I had missed following behind him as he tended his chores.

"Tell me some special things you've seen him do or you've done with him?" Grandma prompted me. "I know he is often taking you and your sister places with him when he goes to the fields or store, and sometimes he lets you sit behind him straddling the mule on the bag of corn when he goes to the mill."

38

I stretched my mind to remember, and said, "I can remember five things."

"Five!" Grandma said. "That's good! Let's hear the first one."

She held up one finger.

"Well, I remember hearing him tell a story about his Pa whipping him with a tree limb after they'd walked around the edges of the farm together. He was just little then, like me."

Grandma laughed softly. "Oh yes, they called that limb-whipping. They used to think that was a sure way of teaching a child to remember where the corners of the land lines were. You know, we didn't used to have any government people to keep those records then."

I later learned that my Great-Great-Grandpa, Eli's dad, was the last parent to use such a reminder. My Great-Grandpa did not use that method when he transferred the property to Grandma, nor did Grandma as she passed it down to Mommy, nor did Mommy use it when she passed it down to us. Now that my daughter and son-in-law own the old home place there, I rather imagine my grandson Brady would tell his parents just to keep the damn property rather than asking him to endure the ritual!

"So you remember about the limb-whipping. Good, good!!" Grandma said, as she held a second finger up, encouraging me to tell her another memory.

"I remember when he spanked Colleen a little with a corn shuck. She was mixing the big corn ears with the nubbins. It scared me because I was mixing them too, and when he spanked Colleen, I thought I'd be next."

Grandma shook her head a little as she smiled. She held up a third finger.

I continued, "Lots of times he talked about his watermelon patch and how, in the summers, the neighbors loved it when he would take the melons off the vines and let them take some home. He told me that sometimes they would sit down with him at the top of the field under the shade of the big oak and laugh as they ate them."

As I said this, I realized that Great-Grandpa's breathing seemed to be coming easier. His groans had been replaced with long, peaceful breaths. It made me feel good thinking that he might be asleep. I had already learned how sleep could ease troubled thoughts.

I heard Colleen's voice coming from the woodpile outside.

"Mommy, the sun is coming out from behind the clouds," she was saying. "Maybe it will melt the ice that's got the wood stuck together."

I looked at Grandma, who had flipped up a fourth finger.

"Last summer," I said quickly, "Great-Grandpa took me and Colleen to his watermelon patch and he thumped a big melon. Then he pulled it from the vine, and he gave us each a half melon. He let me pull out huge chunks with my hand and eat it. It was so good!"

She held up a fifth finger as I rushed to add, "I remember one time he smashed his thumb hammering a nail and said a bad word, 'Damn!'"

Grandma frowned as she glanced at Great-Grandpa's form under the covers. I was afraid she was going to scold him, but she didn't. I didn't guess he would have heard her if she had, because I couldn't be sure he was hearing anything now.

A sound came from Great-Grandpa that was a little like a cough, ending in a long moan.

"I gotta go now," my Grandma said. "I think Pap needs me."

She gently spilt me from her lap to my feet and I slid into her warm place in the rocker.

As she rushed to Grandpa's bed to help him get up to use his crudely crafted potty-chair, she spoke over her shoulder, "Tell all of these stories over to me tomorrow morning, Odean."

I sat there going over and over in my mind the five stories until I knew I would never forget them. The whipping by Great-Grandpa's Pa, Colleen's corn shuck spanking, the neighbors eating watermelon under the tree, Colleen and me at the watermelon patch, and Great-Grandpa saying the bad word. Then I remembered another watermelon story, and reminded myself to add it to my list for Grandma.

It went like this:

One day, I sat in a circle around a large red watermelon. I watched my Great-Grandpa Eli slice it into quarters, because there were four big people to eat it, including Great-Grandpa and two teenage Kennemur brothers.

Johnny -- the older of the two Kennemurs -- asked my Great-Grandpa, "Uncle Dock, do you remember how, when my brother and I was little, I would slip in here to your watermelon patch and steal your watermelons?"

"Yes, little thicf," Great-Grandpa said affectionately, "and do you remember how I caught you?"

The two brothers began shaking with delightful giggles, and Great-Grandpa fully joined in with their merriment.

They enjoyed reliving that memory as I listened. As he talked and laughed with them, Great-Grandpa kept his arthritic crooked fingers busy reaching to my mouth while I simultaneously opened it up to receive pieces of the heart of his quarter of the melon.

The fact that the Kennemurs' older brother Willis had murdered Great-Grandpa's only son Arthur, twenty years earlier, was a fact unknown to me at that time, and from all appearances around our intimate circle, it was a fact forgiven and forgotten, or more significantly, no grudge was held by Great-Grandpa toward the Kennemur family. Years later, after I discovered the tragic story of Uncle Arthur's murder, I realized that on that day, it had been my privilege to witness the ultimate lesson in forgiveness, a precious gift from my Great-Grandpa Lawing.

By early the next morning, after my cozy day with Grandma, the weather had grown warmer. I saw daylight peeking through the cracks in a space of the wall where newspapers had gotten torn off. Everyone was up, getting breakfast and doing morning chores outside.

Daddy came inside and in a lowered voice said, "This is one of them strange kinds of winters. Every few weeks we have an awful cold spell and almost overnight it passes. Like now, outside unloading the logs from the wagon, I had to take my coat off, it was too warm. Yesterday when I went out to the woods to chop some logs, it was so cold I put Mr. Lawing's coat over mine."

When Daddy said Mr. Lawing, I knew he meant my Great-Grandpa. My Great-Grandpa's whole name was Mr. Eli Whitney Lawing – he had been named for the inventor of the cotton gin – but most people, including Daddy, usually just called him Dock. Daddy was showing extra respect by calling him Mr. Lawing now.

Daddy's lips trembled and his voice broke as he cried a little. He glanced over to the corner, where my Great-Grandpa still lay quietly, and added, "I miss me and him working together."

After blowing his nose and rinsing his hands in the pan of water, he began to eat a bit off his biscuit.

After breakfast, Grandma and I sat before the fire together, shelling dried corn. This was the day Daddy would pour the grains into the meal sack and ride to a neighbor's water mill to grind the grains for our bread. When Daddy came to the porch on John, Mommy helped Colleen and me hoist the sack of grain onto John's back, behind Daddy on the saddle.

"This day is so good and warm," Mommy said, as we walked back to the kitchen. "It seems like spring! Oh, how I love this kind of day!"

"Mamie!" Great-Grandpa called from his bed in the big room.

"Oh my God, Mamie, that's the first time Pap has spoke in days!" Grandma looked as if she couldn't believe she had really heard his voice. Grandma, Mommy, and I tangled over each other, scrambling to reach him.

We found Great-Grandpa sitting on the side of his bed, looking like he had before he'd gotten so sick. His eyes were alert and there was a slight smile on his face as he rubbed his fingers through his thin hair. With a little help from Grandma to steady him, he walked the few steps to the fireplace.

Mommy and Grandma called for Colleen to come inside. "It's a miracle!" they kept saying. I had often heard my family talking about praying for a miracle, even as they acknowledged that a miracle might not happen. This time it appeared we had a true miracle right in our own house.

Soon, Grandpa said he wanted to put his boots on and go outside. Mommy and Grandma helped him get into his boots and warm clothes.

"I want me and Cotton Top to go outside together and see if we can see some March flowers peeping out of the ground," said Grandpa. "Looks like a quick thaw."

Mommy and Grandma quickly turned to me, both of them nervously fumbling to get me into my coat and cap. Once outside, I felt very important as my Great-Grandpa took my hand. From the front porch, I could hear Grandma say to Mommy, "There goes the oldest and the youngest members of our family. What a pair!"

As we walked, Grandpa suddenly stopped, pulled his right hand from his pocket, and pointed his finger toward the ground.

"Look, I see little green shoots of March flowers." He looked down at me in a way that indicated he thought he might need to explain himself. "I hear tell that a new name has been invented for our March flowers. When you go to school, Cotton Top, your teacher may call them daffodils."

I looked down at the green spears starting to come out of the soggy ground to one side of the path. It made me feel good to see Grandpa's boots looking so alive as his feet pressed them into the mud.

"It's the first sign of spring when March flowers peep up through the frosty ground, Odean. I know that is a fact, child, because I have seen many springtimes come and go."

Perhaps I didn't fully understand the significance of his words, but I did feel good as I looked up into his care-worn, deeply wrinkled face and twinkling blue Irish eyes.

Soon our little adventure ended and we returned along the pathway marked by March flowers. Grandma and Mommy met us at the porch with hugs and happy comments of thankfulness, while Daddy and Colleen stood by enjoying what appeared to be signs of Great-Grandpa's recovery.

Winter returned, though, and two weeks later, on the second day of February, Great-Grandpa went to sleep and did not wake up. The night after his death, I sat in a corner by the fireplace, not allowing anyone to know how petrified I felt. Wedged into the narrow space behind the bed, I watched neighbors bring a homemade coffin into our house. Since Mommy had brought fresh laundry from the clothesline, I was able to bunch it up in front of me, so no one could see me while I watched the neighbors place Great-Grandpa in that rough box. He had been bathed and dressed in a blue-checkered shirt and clean faded overalls. I could hear Mommy and Grandma crying loudly. I was afraid that since Colleen was outside crying also, they would surely call for me and I would have to come out from my hiding place.

I heard two neighbors speaking. Mr. Less said to the younger neighbor Mr. Kelly, "Here Lester, let me have that flour sack so I can run it under his chin and tie it on the top of his head."

"Why do you do that?" Mr. Kelly asked.

"That is to hold his mouth together. The same as we do to the eyes. We place quarters on the eyes so they will be closed when people look at the body."

It seemed like the older neighbor was teaching the younger man how to do all this. Neighbors helped each other in times like these.

Mr. Kelly asked another neighbor, "Jim, did you go by the preacher's house and get the quarters that he keeps for weighting down the eyelids?"

People who lived around us were too poor to have even a few extra coins, so the preacher kept some for just that purpose.

My family held a wake for three days, according to custom, and neighbors came with food. We lived just the same as before, except that now we all slept in the kitchen room while the neighbors, two at a time, sat up with Grandpa's body in the fireplace room. Sometimes I could see him as I passed by, and other times a sheet was draped over his casket.

As neighbors and relatives dropped by, Grandma and Mommy kept repeating the events of my Great-Grandpa's last weeks. There were no telephones, and neighbors were usually too busy or the weather was too rainy and cold for many visits, so there had not been much communication with those who lived more than a mile away. It seemed my Mommy and Grandma repeated the same sad words endlessly. I liked the part about my walk with Grandpa, though. That was the brightest spot in their stories.

"Just two weeks before he died," my Mommy would say, "one morning he surprised us all by wanting to get up and go outside with the baby. (In our mountains, if you happened to be the youngest child in a family, usually during those growing years, you would be referred to as the baby.) He wanted to show her the March flowers coming up."

Grandma would add, "And that was the last time he set foot on God's earth."

From the sound of their words, I felt that I had been a part of something important. I felt proud too as I heard the neighbors talking about how Dock had been such a good friend to them, and how he had never left the bedside of a sick friend. They told stories about how, whenever a neighbor died, Dock would stay up the three nights with the body.

That last virtue, however, was one I could not understand. Why did a corpse need someone to sit by him, since he was already dead? It would only be much later when I would discover the connection of a wake to the three days between Christ's death and His Resurrection. All I knew was that my Great-Grandpa couldn't walk outside with me anymore, or point to the green shoots that were now even taller than when he'd enjoyed them two weeks earlier.

I started to wonder, during those days, about sickness and death. I believe that it was in those painful, baffling days after my Great-Grandpa died that I started to search for the spiritual meaning underneath the physicality that I saw and felt. Grandpa was just a body now, but somehow I still felt him to be in the house, and in the world.

Before we left our farm on the rainy morning of his burial, Grandma and Mommy kept crying and saying goodbye to Grandpa, kissing him as he lay in that box. Once the box was put into a neighbor's wagon, and all of us started the journey to the cemetery, Daddy was also crying as he guided the mules hitched to our own wagon.

In summers now, when my daughter and I visit Georgia, we usually spend some quiet time in the cemetery where my Great-Grandpa was buried, next to the little wooden Baptist church established before the Civil War. We read the dates on tombstones erected long after his death.

When I was a young child, this cemetery contained only rocks at the head and feet of graves, with very few clear inscriptions. A larger rock would sit at the head of a grown-up's grave, and smaller rocks would mark graves for children. Often you could see attempted letter carvings on the larger stones, but the names were usually illegible. My family later erected my Great-Grandpa's tombstone, which reads that he was born in 1861, during the first year of the Civil War, and died February 2nd, 1932. The newer cement stone at his wife's grave indicates that she died at age nineteen from complications after the birth of their son Arthur (my Great Uncle Arthur). Arthur survived his birth, but on the other side of her grave a stone commemorates another child: "Infant son of Cindy and Eli Lawing."

Knowing I was Eli Lawing's great-grandchild has influenced me to walk proudly all my years since, especially when difficulties in my life have forced me to overcome some major heartbreak. At such times, I take courage from the life of my Great-Grandpa, a man who endured so much hardship and always bounced back smiling, right up to his last winter. The stories of the love and helpfulness he showed to family and neighbors have greatly inspired me to try to reach his example. Always when I remember him, I feel the same joy I felt on that special day when he chose me, his little Cotton Top, to hold his hand and share his thoughts as he took his last steps on "God's earth."

Chapter 4

Our House with Funny Windows

The house where I was born and lived for most of my childhood was such a special house that it still stands in my memory as my favorite. It was a weathered, two-room, unpainted shack in a small grassy valley surrounded by tall mountains. Because we had no electricity, our toilet was an outhouse about a hundred feet away, so that the smell would not be so strong when we ate our meals.

Miraculously, this tiny house had withstood about a hundred years of tornado winds, flooding rains, and accidental cooking and heating fires. It had been in the valley since before the Civil War, proudly and defiantly serving as home to six generations of my mother's family. Colleen and I, together with our brother Gene, born when I was nine, were the last members of the Lawings to be enfolded and nourished within its walls.

Many times during my childhood, winds would lift hand-carved boards from the roof, so we started replacing the boards with twelve-foot long sheets of tin. Sometimes, though, in spite of our best efforts, tornado winds would again pass through and pry off the sheets of tin, flinging them high up into the air, where they would swirl around and about before crashing into the limbs of trees a few miles away.

The fireplace could be just as insecure. Frequently, large, uneven rocks from the mud-dabbed chimney would fall into the hot coals and ashes below. Mommy and Grandma often told us to sit at a good distance from the fire, to stay safe.

One stormy night when I was about six years old, I kept listening to the winds howling outside. Often a single restless gust would spin off its wild community of winds and come clear down the chimney, sending out hot ashes and filling my nose with a generous portion. The balance of the hot ashes would go under our beds, luckily after losing the heat, so that no fire started inside.

Grandma, Colleen and I were alone that blustery night, waiting for Mommy and Daddy to come home. They had been to the other side of Yonder Mountain, because Daddy had heard of a man who had a workhorse for sale. That winter, our dear friend John, our mule, had died, and Daddy needed to buy a workhorse or mule to replace him before planting time in the spring.

Colleen was sitting properly in a cane-bottomed straight-back chair, while I sat on the rock hearth warming my butt and looking up into my Grandma's eyes peering over the top of her tiny round glasses. A rock tumbled down the chimney and landed a couple of feet from my back, startling me so that I jumped up just as Grandma whisked me onto her apron-covered lap, so I could sink down as she cradled me. Holding me safely there between her knees, she hugged me to her warm breast as she gazed at the hearth. I cozily watched the colorful flickering flames mirrored in her glasses, which inched down her nose.

Soon, however, I could see the water building up in her eyes and tears starting to stream slowly down her cheeks.

Hugging her more tightly, I asked, "What's the matter, Grandma?"

"That rock that just came down is one of the rocks my poor Pa mud-dabbed on the top of the chimney, just before he died."

In the language of the mountain folk, "poor" was an affectionate term used to address someone, much as the word "dear" is used now. As I hugged my Grandma, I remembered how my Great-Grandpa had died on the same bed in which he had been born, and how I had been born on the same bed and in our same cherished two-room house.

That particular storm was significant to our house because, in a roundabout way, it brought two glass "eyes" to the dark wall on the right side of the chimney. As the three of us sat by the fire that winter evening, my parents were skidding down Yonder Mountain dirt road in their well-worn 1927 Model T Ford, when Daddy lost control of the car. As they told us later, it slid off the road and turned over three times before lodging at the base of an oak tree halfway down the steep hundred-foot cliff. They managed to crawl out of the wrecked car, and then, holding onto each other's hand and using their free hands to grasp small bushes, they climbed back up to the road and walked the remaining five miles to our house, in the cold and rainy dark.

I can still see my Mommy and Daddy coming in the door, bloody and muddy, with torn clothes dripping with water. They talked to Grandma while she struggled to shut the door behind them, against the powerful wind. I do not remember much of the conversation, since my sister and I were too busy hugging them to pay attention. Colleen and I laughed and giggled as we listened to Mommy and Daddy describe their pure joy at being alive, and having been able to rescue themselves from the wreck.

A few weeks later my parents salvaged parts of the automobile. They took Jean, the only mule we owned now, hitched her to a sled, and dragged the rescued pieces into our yard. Carefully and with much effort, they installed the car's doors with windows into the wall on the right side of the fireplace. Placed side by side in the wall, the doors gave the house a pair of bright, shining double windows. As my parents cut and sawed the boards to fit around the doors, neighbors came by and talked about the miracle of my parents' survival and how unusual it was that the windows had not broken in the crash.

One neighbor remarked, "God was not ready to take y'all because He knows you are needed here to work and raise your young'uns."

Once the windows were in place, Colleen and I, along with our friends, had great fun turning the small cranks to open and close them. We would happily stand beside the windows for a good amount of time, and take turns rolling them up and down.

When I got older, I confess, I went through a period of feeling embarrassed by those windows. I wished that my parents could somehow manage to get money enough so that we could have real windows for our house.

About that time, some "fancy folk" from Atlanta were passing by and stopped to "visit a spell." They were looking for some pure corn moonshine liquor, which our community was known to produce. The illegal liquor made in our area was considered to be "morally clean" – that is, with no poisonous residue from being put into rusty tins or such.

After inquiring about the availability of such liquor, our visitors lingered a while and looked with awe at the windows. They even took pictures of them, a special action that suggested how unusual those windows were, because in those days cameras were very scarce and it was unusual to see someone snapping a picture. The city folk marveled at the ingenuity my Mom and Dad had shown in putting together such "unique" windows. Their affirmation of my parents' worth soothed my early teenage sensibilities.

A bonus for me, from this visit, was that I now had a new, very pretty-sounding word to add to my list of beautiful words. I had a passion for keeping a list, adding to it regularly. My new word was "unique," and for a time, I constantly spoke of most everything as being more unique or very unique or extremely unique, which greatly annoyed Colleen. I don't think she knew that my expression of different degrees of uniqueness was incorrect grammar, but the sound of me saying unique over and over again was just plain irritating.

A couple of years later, we moved about a mile down the same dirt road to a better house. My first little house with its two bright window-eyes remained for many more years, alone and quiet for the first time in its history. It continued to be battered by thunderstorms, and a lightning strike sliced off a piece of plank, setting a small fire that burned or blackened several of its gray, termite-ridden boards. Hot summers, cold winters, and invasions by rats, snakes, and buzzing insects caused the frail structure to collapse over the car door windows, which by then had become rusted and broken.

Years after the "fancy folk" admired the car windows, my daughter Jeriann and I came back to Georgia from our home in New York to see my parents. One Sunday in August during our visit, my parents' church Ebenezer had a "Homecoming Service," a day set aside when families got together to share picnic dinners and place bunches of flowers on the graves of loved ones. Our special loved one was Grandma, who had passed on about twenty years after the stormy night of the Ford's wreck, which had led to the shiny windows. As many offspring from the farm families as could possibly get there went every year to the large dinner spread on the outside tables behind the church. Jeriann went with her grandfather while I chose to stay home with Mommy, who was recovering from a cold.

After talking with my Mommy for a while, I walked out to my favorite spot on the bank of the creek for my own private communion. I preferred remembering Grandma as she still was in my heart, as I watched cattle grazing and listened to the birdsong, a much more soothing sound than shouts of "Hallelujah!" and a preacher's sermon.

About four o'clock that Homecoming day, Jeriann came bouncing from my Daddy's pick-up truck. Her feet scarcely touched the ground in her rush to me.

"Mother, please tell me about the car windows in your little old house! Gladys Miller introduced herself to me at church today. She said she was a childhood friend of yours, and some of her favorite memories of her childhood were playing with you while you and she rolled the car windows up and down."

My parents looked on beaming as I told Jeriann all about my clever parents and the best house ever, with its unusual window-eyes.

My grandma, Ethie Magnolia Lawing, taken in front of the
mud-dabbed chimney of their home in the year 1918

Three members of Mommy's family: Great-Grandpa
Lawing, my grandma (Ethie) and my mother, taken in 1918

Chapter 5

Memories of the Lawings

I learned my family history from the stories my Grandma, Mommy and Daddy told. Those stories were memories of their own or accounts handed down by other family members. Over the years, the anecdotes came up again and again at storytelling time, which was usually in the winter evenings after supper, as the family sat before the logs burning in the fireplace. The long, busy days of summer held no time for such peaceful luxury. In the winter we were not so busy with growing food for ourselves and for the animals, and we were less tired by nightfall.

After we had washed the supper dishes, we gathered before the fire. Grandma would settle into her rocker at the side of the hearth. Colleen would sit on a chair between Grandma and Mommy, and next came Daddy, sitting at the side near the window. Me, I loved to sit at my Grandma's feet with my back to the fire so I could watch everyone's eyes with the fire reflecting in them. Daddy always looked the most comfortable, since he would have taken off his shoes and placed his long bony feet on the hearth to be warmed by the heat from the coals. Because his sweaty socks would not get washed until the weekly laundry day, he would lay them over his shoes nearby to dry.

Everyone sat on straight cane-bottomed chairs, and the women's hands would be busy shelling dried beans and peas, since the fire furnished just enough light for that kind of work. Daddy did not shell peas, beans or corn because such an activity was not considered "men-folks' type work." I made it a point not to sit where Mommy or Grandma could place peas to be shelled into my lap as they did into their own and Colleen's. I also carefully ignored Colleen's stares and stiff body language, indicating her usual attitude of grown-up importance. I could tell she thought I was as useful as a hind tit on a sow's belly, as people used to say of someone who didn't do their fair share of the work.

After we had seated ourselves, Daddy raised his long body to stand up. Moving to the mantel, he took a deep breath and blew out the flame of the kerosene lamp. To put the lamp out would save oil for the next couple of hours or so.

Now story-telling could begin. Grandma's eyes danced as her tiny glass specs mirrored images of the flickering flames. Sometimes to start, one of us might request a familiar story. Tonight Colleen made the first request.

"Mommy, tell us about how handsome Uncle Arthur was?"

Oh, how Mommy beamed with that request! She arose quickly from her chair and turned her body lightly and gracefully around to stand with her back to the fire so she could face our little family circle. The flames from the logs must have been making her back toasty as mine. I got excited, seeing Mommy so happy, and I placed myself in her chair so I could see her face all aglow with precious memories about to spill out.

She began, "I love to remember how my Uncle Arthur, who lived with us, kept buying the prettiest yards of cloth whenever he came across any, for Mommy to sew me the best-looking dresses of any girl in the neighborhood. He would take me with him, sometimes on his dates with young women, in his shiny buggy pulled by his little spotted pony, named Flame. A mother of one of his girlfriends told me that her daughter was the one who had named the pony that Uncle Arthur raised."

Mommy paused and looked at Colleen. "Oh, you said you wanted me to tell about how handsome Uncle Arthur was. Well, he was the best looking young man in the neighborhood. He had a

58

full head of dark red hair and big sparkling green eyes. He was always smiling and all the older people loved him because he would go to their houses in the neighborhood and chop wood for them if they happened to be sick." Mommy smiled, remembering.

"One time he risked his life because a neighbor of ours had come home from his moonshine still, drunk as a skunk. The man was mad at his wife about something and he had run her and their three children from their home, and Uncle Arthur found them huddled in their barn freezing to death. Uncle Arthur went to his drunken friend's house, even though the woman kept protesting that her husband had a gun and Arthur might get himself killed. Uncle Arthur reasoned with the neighbor, about how his wife and children were in the barn freezing. When he had calmed the neighbor down, he went back to the barn and brought the man's family back into their home."

"Yeah, my brother was always doing something good for someone," Grandma said. "I could not have raised you, Mamie, if it had not been for him and Pa helping me feed and clothe you after your daddy left me."

My Mommy came back to her chair, and I scooted over to my Grandma's feet again.

"Ethie," Daddy said to Grandma, "listening to Mamie talk about her Uncle Arthur got me to thinking: I have forgot which one of the Kennemur brothers shot and killed him?"

"His name was Willis," Grandma said.

Colleen, who always liked to be informed, because she fancied any facts she could glean about the older family members made her appear more grown-up, asked Grandma, "Tell us again about how your brother, my Great-Uncle Arthur, got killed. I may have forgot some of how it happened."

Grandma's wrinkled face registered pain, but as soon as she began remembering her brother, her tone became animated.

"There are many sweet stories like the ones Mamie is saying today, to be told of my brother's life, but the facts on that night also need to be told to keep the record straight."

And so she began, "Much as I loved my only brother, Arthur, I must admit that making corn liquor at the head of that spring branch was not his best 'idee.'" She raised her arm and pointed in the direction of the stream flowing in the winter darkness near our house. "After getting sloppy drunk, Arthur and his best friend Willis Kennemur went to Willis' house. Arthur got to paying too much attention to Willis' wife and that made him powerful mad. He took his long hunting shotgun and shot my brother close-up, taking off half of his face."

Everything in the house became silent. Even the crackling of the logs seemed to pause a moment. As she recovered her seeming loss of balance, my Grandma's words sounded as if they were coming from the bottom of a barrel.

"Then he dropped his gun on the floor and rushed to grab brother Arthur's hand as he gasped, 'Lord help me, I've just killed my best friend.'"

After pausing a minute, Grandma continued, "Willis' wife told the sheriff that later. And she told him she ran to a neighbor's house because she thought Willis would shoot her next."

"What happened at the trial, Grandma?" Colleen asked, prompting her.

Grandma wiped a tear from her cheek as she said, "Well, during the murder trial, people who were in the courthouse said that they observed a very sad scene. Arthur's and my Daddy – your Grandpa Eli -- and Mr. Kennemur, Willis's father, would meet almost daily on the stairs of the courthouse, during the trial.

60

They would hold to the banisters while they embraced each other and cried together."

I watched the firelight from the chimney logs shimmer along the already deep creases in Mommy's face. Usually her face was expressive, yet as she listened to Grandma relate the details of her Uncle Arthur's death, her face had become a stone mask.

We all knew from previous storytelling times that if my sister had asked Mommy to tell the same story, her version would have gone something like this:

"I loved my Uncle Arthur with all my heart because he was the only father I ever knew. If someone called me a bastard, as they often did, Uncle Arthur would bust their head in. One day I seen him do that to Bent Smith after he said something ugly about me: 'Ethie's little bastard ain't much bright.' Uncle Arthur hauled off and broke his nose. Nobody could ever understand why old Willis Kennemur killed Arthur, who was his best friend. That Willis Kennemur was the meanest man who ever drawed a breath and he didn't get near enough jail time either. We all knowed he should have been hanged."

As if to substantiate her claim, she would stare straight at first one of us and then the other as she declared, "Lots of the neighbors told me that!"

Daddy would reach over to Mommy's knee and softly pat her leg.

Unlike Colleen, I wanted to hear happy stories, so after Grandma's story about Uncle Arthur, I squeezed in a stuttering comment.

"D-d-d-Daddy, tell the story about how Great-Grandpa showed us how to make a bladder ball."

I wanted to hear that story because I could dimly remember seeing my Great-Grandpa's hands as he tied a bladder ball out of a hog's bladder. For a couple of years after Great-Grandpa's death, at hog-killing time, my Mommy and Daddy and Grandma tearfully showed Colleen and me how to create a bladder ball, so that we could learn how to do it and how to play the same game with the ball that Great-Grandpa had played with his friends when he was young.

Daddy looked at me and smiled, as if he was thinking that Mommy had grown sad again about Uncle Arthur's death and he seemed in agreement that we could do with some lighter stories.

"After several big frosts every fall," Daddy said, "when we felt it was cold enough that the meat of the hog would not spoil, we'd decide on a hog-killing day. This was a special day, just as it is now, because we knew that hog would be salted down in a wooden box in the smoke house for us to have meat the entire winter and into early spring."

Colleen and I nodded, thinking of all the delicious meats our family made out of the one hog each year.

Daddy continued, "On the morning of hog killing, of course we filled a large black pot with water and built a roaring fire around the pot. It was the same pot the women did the weekly laundry in, that you children always think is such a boring day."

Daddy smiled at Colleen and me.

"Hog-killing day was different, though, because on that day the big fire around the pot meant as soon as the hog was hoisted on a scaffold, and sharp knives had made an incision all the way down the belly of the hog, the entrails of the hog would be put in a washtub and the women would cut the fat off the guts to be rendered for lard they could use in cooking."

"And what about the bladder?" I asked, eager to get to the important part of the story.

Daddy nodded and smiled. "Then the bladder of the hog would be cut out and emptied of pee pee. Your Great-Grandpa would cut a queen-of-the-meadow weed that was a hollow quill, so that he could blow air into the bladder through the quill, and that would inflate the bladder."

Daddy paused in his story to stir the chunks of the fire and add another log. He turned to me.

"You take it and finish the story, Cotton Top. . . ."

I said, "Great-Grandpa then tied the bladder so tight that the air couldn't escape, and he handed us a firm ball the size of a basketball."

I smiled, remembering how that bladder ball would give the neighbor children and us the most exciting play day of our year.

Daddy often said that he hoped his children would always keep that bladder ball tradition alive, because it had been passed down through four generations of the Lawing family. A bit sadly, I must add that the tradition ended with Colleen and me.

Now Colleen wanted to get another story in tonight, so she said, "Grandma, I heard a neighbor say that the reason we call sweet corn 'roastneers' has something to do with your Grandpa and the Civil War. Tell us about that?" This was the same story my Daddy often told as a digression inside the story of my birth. This time, Grandma was happy to be asked for her version.

She excitedly began, "During the War Between the States, my Grandpa did what many other citizens did. He joined with the Confederate soldiers and followed them for a short distance, helping them fight the Union soldiers along the way. He and his neighbors fought for a distance of perhaps a hundred miles, or as far as they felt they could make it back home, walking or on horseback."

She interrupted herself. "Wait, wait, I hear the cats jumping around in the kitchen," she said, as she hurried into the other room. "I've got to go see if they are getting into anything we eat."

Colleen had a question for Daddy. "Daddy, which side of the Civil War did *your* family fight on?"

I thought to myself, 'Someday I will be big like you, Colleen, and I'll know all that.' The truth is, I never was as much for details, since I was the dreamer in the family.

"*We* was proudly on the winning side," Daddy answered, as he playfully poked Mommy.

She squirmed a little in her chair and said nothing, but kept her gaze steady on the burning logs. I guessed her reaction of slight disapproval was not from a political point of view but more that she just didn't like the feeling of Daddy's family being on the winning side and her family on the losing side.

Grandma returned and said, "Where was I at? Oh yeah, I had just started, about the 'roastneers.'" She thought for a second and then said, "After a particularly bloody battle near Marietta, the soldiers set up camp for the night in a pine forest, near a bubbling spring a short distance from the banks of the big Chattahoochee River. There was a cornfield near the spring – Grandpa said them was the longest rows in that field, they looked to be more than a mile long. That field in the lowlands was so different from our patches here in the valleys between the mountains.

"The men took a long time, talking among themselves, reasoning about whether they should take the corn from the field for their supper. Finally they decided to take that nice green corn and roast some ears on the campfire. The Baptist preacher among them voiced strong opposition to such thievery. Ignoring his strong verbal rebukes and his certainty of their eventual burning in hell fire, they went ahead and pulled several dozen ears from the stalks of the corn. After they cooked the ears on the campfire, the hungry men helped themselves to the steamy, juicy ears, noisily chewing and sucking out the last bit of warm, sweet juice from the cobs.

"Now the preacher moved up to get his portion, but he was forcefully intercepted by Jim Lawing, my Grandpa. Grandpa pulled him from the pile of roasted corn and shoved him backwards. Staring at the hypocritical man, Grandpa yelled, 'If you are too good to steal these 'roastneers,' I sure as hell am not going to steal and give them to you!' There followed a resounding 'Amen' from all the men, and the preacher retreated hastily."

Grandma pushed her specs up on her nose a bit. "That was the first time anyone called sweet green corn 'roastneers.' I can dimly remember seeing and hearing my Grandpa tell it like this: 'So the preacher, with his tail in his crack, went back to his bed of leaves and pine needles with an empty belly but a clear conscience to pray for the whole lot of us sinners, feasting on that corn. His praying voice was loud at first but gradually faded like the flickering campfire. Thereafter, in my family, sweet corn was always called roastneers.'"

Daddy laughed, but then he looked at Mommy quizzically. I believe he was seeing that she had not quite recovered from the Uncle Arthur story. He softly patted her leg again. Sensing that the amusing stories had not eased her sadness about her uncle's tragic death, he looked up to the old clock on the mantel, and although its face was too ancient and dark to show the Roman numerals, he quickly said, "Look how late it's gettin', long past my bedtime, and the logs are turning to coals. We better get to bed or I'll have to light the lamp agin so we can find our beds."

Once I lay in bed between Grandma and Colleen, all was dark and quiet in our little house. Even though I knew I would never be in a safer place than I was at that moment, I imagined my Great Uncle Arthur with half his face blown away. I had never seen him or a photo of him, but that word picture Grandma had painted of him caused me to inch my body backward a little more into the curve of Grandma's breast with each frightened breath I took. Next to Grandma, I could feel the sure steady beat of her heart against my back and, reassured, soon I was sound asleep.

Chapter 6

Grandpa Will's Cupboard

While my childhood was filled with such stories about my mother's side of the family, the Lawings, information about Daddy's family, the Warrens, is scarce. Of the few stories that have come down, my favorite one is how our kitchen cupboard came into being.

This mission-style cupboard, having outlived five generations, still stands today in my daughter Jeriann's house in California. The boards of the cupboard are made of a sturdy unfinished oak, cut from trees in the North Georgia mountains about the time of the Civil War. In 1908 my father's father, Willis (Will) Warren, salvaged its boards from cast-off pieces of an earlier cabinet, so I feel it is safe to assume that the cupboard is in its second incarnation. Once the materials had come to Grandpa Will, his nimble hands brought into being a piece of furniture that has been cherished by our family for over a century.

The cabinet is six feet high, with four shelves in the smaller, upper part, where Jeriann now places assorted mementos open to view. The upper section of the cupboard is built on top of the wider base of the lower section, so that an ample shelf has been created in the middle, the perfect place for a large antique bowl. Jeriann likes to keep alive the memory of how five generations of our family lived contentedly and healthily by consuming bountiful portions of cooked dried beans each day. Beside the bowl sits a large antique platter, on which, years ago, my Mommy or Grandma would place the corn pone next to the bowl of "soup beans" at each noon (dinner) meal.

Along the top of the cabinet, just under a three inch wide horizontal margin, sits a smoothly carved piece of honed oak, a surprising contrast to the rough boards surrounding it. And even more surprising, a close observer might note, is how differently the corners of this smooth upper oak trim have been carved: the right top corner makes a square, while the left corner has been whittled down to create a slant.

When I was a teenager with my first job, I contributed my own touch to this cabinet by using some of my money to buy mahogany stain, and that has been the color of this cabinet ever since. The lower section, containing two wide shelves inside, has a door on small hinges and a neat little hand-carved piece of wood, which my Grandpa Will nailed onto the left side of the door to serve as a fastener. A square-headed nail holds this wooden piece in place a bit loosely (as my Daddy used to say, "In those days, there were no nails with round heads").

With usefulness and rugged grace, this kitchen cupboard began its service to our family in the autumn of Daddy's seventh year. That was a year, like many, when Grandpa Will made a little extra money peddling apples at the Farmers' Market in Atlanta. My Daddy used to tell us about his trips to the market when he was a young boy. Grandpa Will, his father, would bring a wagonload of Yates apples and sit in the bed of his wagon until he sold some and gave away a lot. That usually took a day and a night. The Yates apples were red, small, juicy, and very tasty, with tiny white dots, like freckles, sprinkled on the skin. They grew wildly and profusely in the mountains of North Georgia, bringing an abundant harvest each autumn with very little human nurturing. The Yates were not considered good for cooking, but they kept well all winter and became even tastier as the months went by if you could store them in a place where they would not freeze.

Grandpa Will would park his wagonload of apples in the market shed, among other farmers with their goods such as sweet potatoes, corn, late beans and black-eyed peas, along with sorghum syrup, pecans, pumpkins and other local products. He kept his pair of mules beside his wagon, tied by their reins to a pole with a watering trough provided by the market. Frequently, he would pull out a fistful of hay or ears of corn from a burlap tow sack, for the mules to munch on. Each day the mules fought a never-ending battle with the flies in an effort to shoo them away with their tails.

The names of those mules were Grant and Lee. In later years I would smile at this part of Daddy's story, because those names suggested something of Grandpa Warren's peaceful nature and sense of humor, gifts similar to those of his son Arthur, my Daddy.

The Atlanta Farmers' Market (actually in Decatur, an Atlanta suburb) was, and I understand still is, a complex of long, covered structures floored with cement, and containing two levels. On the lower level, cars and pick-ups drove slowly among the walking customers, who perused the goods. On the second level, waist-high for these customers, farmers sat among their baskets of colorful and enticing displays of organic vegetables and fruits.

Many of the customers told Grandpa Will that they had grown up in the mountains and remembered the Yates apples. These people usually bought a few pennies' worth. Daddy calculated, looking back later in his life, that one penny, when he was a boy, would have bought one gallon of apples. A good portion of apples, though, went for free. Daddy enjoyed remembering his Pa's generosity. He often said, "My Pa was so free-hearted that he gave most of the apples away to hungry children that dropped by his wagon."

The story of the kitchen cabinet began at this Farmers' Market. The first part of this story was frightening, yet showed another dimension of Grandpa Will's good nature.

After the market closed, Grandpa Will usually slept beside his wagon. One night, while he slept, a man smashed a rock onto his head and robbed him of the few dollars he had collected for his apples. When the police were called to the scene, they asked Grandpa to give a description of his assailant. He told them the robber was a young black man of medium height. (In telling this story, my Daddy used a different word, like most white people did when I was little, in that part of Georgia.) The two policemen then collected a number of suspicious characters, fitting that description, and asked him if he could identify one of them as the guilty party.

Grandpa said, "I can't really identify any one of them for sure. It was too dark to see well."

One of the policemen whispered to Grandpa, "Oh just pick any one of them, because we know for a fact they are all thieves."

Grandpa was adamant. "No, if I cannot be sure, I will not pick anyone."

The policeman and his partner stared at Grandpa Will in annoyance because he did not cooperate in assisting them to arrest a suspect.

Once the police left, the man who had the neighboring stall came over and introduced himself as Lawrence Andrews. He cleaned the blood off Grandpa's face and became a life-long friend. Years later, Lawrence made a point of coming to Grandpa's home in the mountains and talking about the incident that had brought them together. He seemed to enjoy telling Will's sons, Jesse and Arthur (my Daddy), how impressed he was with the character their honest daddy had exhibited that night of the robbery. I felt just as impressed and proud of my Grandpa when my Daddy told Colleen and me about this incident, years later.

This part of the story, about Grandpa Will's honesty and his new friendship with Lawrence Andrews, always brought along with it the second part, about Lawrence's life-long bonus gift, as it related to the kitchen cabinet. A few weeks after the incident, when Grandpa Will was back at the Farmers' Market with another load of Yates apples, he looked to see which stall Lawrence might be occupying, and again parked his wagon beside Lawrence so they could enjoy another twenty-four hours of companionship.

Lawrence had a blacksmith shop at his home south of Atlanta. Not being one for wasting time at the Farmers' Market, on this particular day he had brought along an old cabinet to dismantle. It was a cabinet he had found in a junk pile beside the road on his way to the Market. He was interested in salvaging three wide boards with which to make shelves at home. After Lawrence had stacked his boards into the bed of his wagon, he noticed Grandpa Will looking at the crooked nails, hinges, extra boards and rounded decorative molding Lawrence had laid in a heap on the cement behind their wagons.

"If you would like any of these scraps, you are welcome to them," Lawrence said.

"Yes, I would, if I could give you a bushel of my apples for them."

"A deal!"

Grandpa Will concocted a plan to hammer straight the crooked nails that Lawrence had extracted from the junk cabinet, and to put together a new kitchen cabinet for his wife Jane. She only had crude board shelves attached to the walls of their kitchen, on which to store her dishes and pans.

Since neither of them could read or write very well, Grandpa Will asked a customer passing by to kindly write their addresses on a scrap of paper. They exchanged the pieces of paper with their addresses and parted. Grandpa took the highway north as Lawrence headed south.

During his seventy-five mile journey home, Grandpa Will held the reins with his hands, guiding the mules as they pulled the wagon, while his mind was busy working on a plan of how he might pick up more boards to make the back and sides of the cupboard. He could already picture the finished front made from the pieces he had in his wagon. Forty miles outside Atlanta, he stopped, unhitched Grant and Lee, and fed them some corn from his bag. He cut some green grass from the banks of the highway to add to their supper, and then bedded down for the night on a quilt he had placed on soft grass beside the highway. He listened to the babble of a nearby spring as its fresh water emerged from the rocks and flowed over them. Occasionally a car would pass by, briefly interrupting the songs of the night birds, and soon he was asleep, dreaming of the surprise he would have for his wife Jane.

The day after Grandpa Will returned home, he called his children together for a meeting in the hall of the barn to discuss his plan. His teenage daughter Rosie, who had been acting as the woman of the house since before and after the birth of their brother Ira, begged to be left out of the plan.

"Pa, I have already got more to do than I possibly can," she said. Her frowning face accented her words.

Grandpa affectionately patted her on her young, yet rounded and tired shoulders, as he said, "I know, Rosie, but just make sure you don't forget and mention this to your Ma because I want it to be a surprise for her this Christmas."

"Pa, you know you don't have to worry about me keeping your secret," Rosie said, "but how are you going to keep quiet these blabbing brothers of mine?" She shook her head as she went on to the next chore awaiting her.

When telling this story, Daddy always took time out to explain how Rosie bossed his brother and him worse than his momma did.

During the two and a half months Grandpa Will worked on the cabinet in secret, he occasionally called upon Daddy and Uncle Jesse to sit on a board to hold it in place while he sawed through it with his dull hand saw.

"Mostly, Jesse and me just tried a little harder to be alert to do all our regular chores so that Pa would not have to take time to hustle us into the doing of them." Daddy would smile as he added, "We wanted to make sure he got that cupboard built."

Grandpa Will and his children were worried that Jane would discover the cabinet, especially when the neighbors would be helping them bring it inside to the kitchen side room on Christmas Eve. As it happened, though, a few days before Christmas, Jane had taken to bed with a bout of the flu. As she was still recovering, it looked as if it would be easier to make sure she had no reason to go into the side room.

(In those days and on through my childhood, most houses in our area had a slant-roofed room attached to the original structure that ran the length of the living room. My guess is that would have been the cheapest way to add extra space, since the additional room would share the strength of the foundation of the original structure. The Lawing house, where I was born, had the same kind of slant-roofed side room, and we too used that room as our kitchen, although it also contained the bed where I slept with Colleen and Grandma.)

Together Grandpa Will and his children followed carefully the plan to bring the cupboard into this kitchen area. On the morning of Christmas Eve, Aunt Rosie took no chances that her ma might peek into the kitchen side room from her bed in the other room, so she nailed an old quilt over the opening between the two rooms.

With the hammer poised to hit the nail, she turned toward her mother, who was in bed in the fireplace room, and said, "Ma, it may turn colder tonight, so I am going to nail this old quilt over the door so the cold air won't come in on you and give you a 'back-set.'"

"Thank you, Rosie. You and all my family are so good to me," Jane said, smiling.

"You are good to us all and we want you better soon," Rosie said, just before she gave the nail one last hit.

At twilight on that peaceful Christmas Eve, with the help of neighbors, Pa carefully and quietly brought the new cupboard from the barn into the kitchen room. As the neighbors hoisted it up over the steps and slid it into the room, Arthur and Jesse broke into a shuffle dance they called "The Buck dance." They felt that their dancing would drown out the noise of pushing the cabinet across the kitchen floor.

"There it stood, looking and smelling so shiny and new from the oil that had dripped on it from the handsaw," Daddy would say. He would take a deep breath with his eyes closed, as if he were, once again, breathing in the smell of it.

"My brother Jesse danced merrily around the cupboard with me, while Rosie kept telling us to 'quieten down and shut up, Ma and baby Ira are sleeping.'"

Like many of their neighbors in those times, my Grandpa Will's little farm family was again surviving another hard winter. Daddy often allowed that their Christmas celebration was a thankful prayer that they were healthy and had a new member of the family, baby Ira, to enjoy this Christmas and to make it even more special. Daddy was always careful to interject, "The joys of my childhood far outweighed the hardships."

Their Christmas supper, at twilight, would probably have been dried beans from the summer fields and gardens. These beans would have simmered for hours in a black iron pot hanging from a chain in the center of the fireplace. Adding a ham hock would have made it special for Christmas. On the hearth, corn bread would be baked to a brown, thick crust in an iron skillet. The cast iron lid would be heated separately and lifted by putting an iron poker through the ring on top. After the heated lid was placed onto the skillet, hot coals would be piled on top.

The bread's tantalizing smell must have mingled with the succulent bean aroma from the simmering pot. While these smells filled the house for hours, the family would be gathered around the fire, basking in its warmth and comfort, and enjoying the feeling that this holy night must always be felt as a special night.

On Christmas morning, Grandpa Will and his children brought Jane into the kitchen to see the beautiful, handmade kitchen cabinet. Daddy would smile broadly as he described how his mother's pale face had brightened when she first saw her new cupboard. She clapped her hands together and kissed each one of them, for their part in this great secret.

It was customary on Christmas Day for neighbors to drop in for short visits and swap stories of past Christmases. As twilight approached, Grandpa Will and Grandma Jane gave their children special presents: a slice of orange and a half stick of peppermint candy. An orange was a Christmas delicacy. Following a long tradition, Grandpa Will cut this orange into slices with "Pa's pocketknife," one slice for each member of the family. On this holiday, they all ate the orange pieces while they watched Ma squeeze a bit of juice into the mouth of baby Ira, who smacked his lips and gave out "pig-like" satisfied grunts.

Soon thereafter the family enjoyed the simple but generous country Christmas dinner. Then they rested contentedly before the fire, with wonderfully full stomachs – a great treat for this family, so used to hunger – while the burning logs disintegrated into dark, dying embers that signified bedtime.

It was during that quiet and satisfying hour that Arthur (my Daddy) made his mark. He could not resist the impulse to slip into the kitchen room to look at the beautiful cupboard once again. He pulled a straight chair to the left side of the cupboard. Then he took his barley knife and carved a slanted edge into the top left edge of the honed oak trim, leaving his handiwork for us to enjoy, years later.

My Daddy had kept the cupboard a secret for over two months. Even though Grandpa had done all the work on the cupboard and had not allowed anyone else to touch it, now my stubborn father just had to be part of it!

While grinning as he would say how guilty he felt at having marred his Pa's handiwork, we never believed for a moment that he felt guilty, especially after my daughter Jeriann said, one day when she was small, "Pop, your carving made it look a lot better." He gave a big smile at her heartfelt observation.

She actually feels the truth of that statement, even now that the cabinet sits in her own dining room.

This cupboard has had its own adventures since that Christmas so long ago. At a certain point in its life, it wound up in the crib shed on the farm to which my parents had moved. The rats started to make nests in the upper shelves and pilot snakes were sometimes seen to inhabit the lower shelves.

Later, after I had married for the first time, I was visiting with my Mommy and Daddy, helping them sell their vegetables in the Atlanta market next to an elderly man and his son, who had rented the stall next to my parents' stall. They were selling watermelons from their large farm in South Georgia.

Daddy introduced me to them. Pointing to the elderly man, he said, "Odean, this is the man who gave my Dad, your Grandpa Will, materials that he used to build our old cupboard in 1908. This is Lawrence Andrews."

Mr. Andrews shook my hand warmly.

"Glad to meet you," I said, and in that moment I resolved to myself that I would move the cupboard from the crib shed back into the kitchen, that coming weekend, out of respect for my Grandpa Will.

However, I am sorry to say that I failed to act on my guilty resolve. It would be thirty years later, when Jeriann was a teenager herself and visiting her grandparents, that she discovered the old cupboard in the crib shed, cleaned it, and moved it back into their farmhouse. Fifteen years after that, the old cupboard found itself on a rental truck being driven to California, when I moved there to live with Jeriann.

On a recent December holiday, over a hundred years after the cupboard spent its first holiday with Grandpa Will and his family, I sat near it, sipping green tea as I took another nostalgic look at its familiar features. With deep appreciation, I remembered it as the backdrop of many of my childhood activities. Now, during Hanukkah, it held the Menorah on one side of its wide shelf while a Christmas angel graced the other side, as our family celebrated our combined Hanukkah and Christmas season.

Chapter 7

A Summer Day with Grandma

My Grandma Ethie Lawing, the most loving and accepting person I have ever known, was and still is the most influential figure in my life. She loved me fiercely and unconditionally. I was different from other children around us, and I think that my parents often felt confounded about how to make me fit in. Many people thought I was not just a dreamer, but "off in the head." Grandma, however, never felt that way about me. She was my rock of comfort.

A typical summer day in my young life always had my Grandma at its center. She was in charge of us most every day in summer, since Mommy and Daddy worked as a team in the fields or else in the forest of our farm, where they gleaned pulpwood to make a little money for the essentials we could not grow on our own.

Grandma was kind, but she had no patience with laziness. She kept her eyes on Colleen and me to see that we followed the daily chores she laid out for us. Mostly, she spoke loving words to us, but if we were not keeping up to speed, her tongue could be sharp.

"Come on, girls, let's get moving and get things done," she would say. Then she would add the guilt factor. "Your Mom already got up early to do the milking, and here are the two pitchers just sitting here. You girls have got to get them into the spring branch water double quick, or else the milk won't be cool by supper."

As we rushed to stand in front of her, she handed Colleen a bowl of fresh butter and the larger pitcher, which held freshly churned buttermilk. I reached to hug the smaller pitcher, full of the morning milk, and off we went down the steep bluff to the spring branch. Years earlier, Grandma had taught us how careful we must be not to drop the pitchers and spill the supper milk, because corn bread and milk were the main parts of our evening meal. She often told us that the clay pitchers containing the milk had served three generations before us, and were irreplaceable.

"They're irreplaceable not because they're antique, but because it would cost money to buy new ones," she often added, to give us a sense of their practical value.

After we had carefully placed the open pitchers in the cold spring, with sugar sack coverings tied around their tops, we lay a large flat rock on each pitcher to keep dogs and cats from poking noses or paws into the milk.

"I'm going to stay a while here and splash in the water," I told Colleen.

I always delighted in dipping my feet in, right where the spring branch joined the larger stream. I had a fondness for that shady nook and crook in the bigger stream, because I remembered one day, the summer before, when I had sat with Great-Grandpa on the soft green moss and violets on that bank. He had taken a watermelon from his patch, which was just up the bluff and across the pasture fence, and he had placed it in the spring to cool that morning. Since he didn't have his knife with him, he had burst the watermelon on the big gray rock, and we had pulled out fistfuls of red, juicy pieces and devoured them. I was sad when I thought about us not having any of his watermelons this year, because he had gone to heaven.

Just as I started to dip one foot into the rushing, cool water, Colleen's voice broke into my daydream.

"No, no, Odean, you better not play here, cuz Grandma is expecting us back right now!"

"I will be back in a little bit."

"You'll get in trouble," Colleen said. As she started walking home, she called over her shoulder, "Remember, I told you!"

I walked into the water in my bare feet, enjoying the feel of the sand and little rocks. I thought about how this stream would go into a bigger stream, and that one would go into an even bigger one. If I could turn into a stream like this one, I could adventure far, far away and see the big ocean.

After a while Colleen interrupted my daydream, as she yelled from the top of the bluff, "Grandma said you better come back now! Daddy left a letter here and some pennies. He wants you to meet the mail and send the letter off."

Mail collecting was a kid's job. Grandma didn't have time to wait for the mailman, and I liked the idea of going to meet the mail at the big road about a quarter of a mile from our house, so I yelled back, "Coming!"

When we got back to the house, Grandma handed me the letter and the two pennies.

"Hurry, Odean! Your Daddy said to tell you to be sure and not miss the mail, because in this letter he is telling someone he's going to be late paying a bill, and he hopes, after the man gets the letter, he won't come out to collect the money."

She softly patted my shoulder and then turned it into a light, quick hug. "After the mail comes, you will come right back, won't you?"

"I will, Grandma."

Mr. James, our mailman, was such a nice old man. Sometimes he had a cookie for me. I sat a while on the bank of the road playing with rocks and sticks, until I saw his horse and buggy coming up the hill. Sometimes he would be dozing, but his horse always knew to pull over and stop when he approached a mailbox.

This time he was awake, and waved to me as he came up the hill.

"Howdy," he said.

"Howdy."

He took my letter and pennies and licked a stamp. After he placed the letter in his mail sack, he began rummaging through his lunch bucket and came up with a piece of homemade syrup candy. He handed it to me.

"Here is a piece of candy Mrs. James has put in my lunch," he said, "but I don't really want it. Would you like to have it and share it with your sister?"

"Thank you, sir." As I reached for the candy, I saw a little of it had melted on his finger and thumb. He carefully licked the sticky sweetness off.

I rushed back over the trail past the playhouse and down the other side of the hill to our house, where together Colleen and I could enjoy that succulent piece of candy before it melted entirely. I wished I could stop to tarry as I usually did, at our playhouse, among my sister's and my treasures of broken dishes and pans with holes in them. Mommy and Daddy had made us tables out of sawing logs, and kitchen cabinets out of old pieces of boards nailed to the trees. Grandma had given us one of her black and white checked gingham aprons to tie between two saplings for a curtain. We didn't feel we needed anything else, even though there was not a single toy in our make-believe house.

By the time I returned from my errand of mailing the letter, it was about time for Daddy, Mommy and the mules to come from the fields to the house for our noonday meal. Grandma was rushing to finish cooking the beans, boiled cabbage and a large cake of fresh-baked corn pone. She was trying to have it on the table by the time my parents got the mules unhitched and freed from their gears to cool off a spell.

"Odean, could you bring in another armful of wood so I can make the oven hotter so as to brown the bread?"

I rushed to the woodpile, and while wrapping my arms around sticks of stove wood, I heard Daddy call me.

"Cotton Top, would you take the knife and cut some ragweeds from below the garden fence and bring them for the mules to eat?"

I said, "O.K., Daddy," and quickly ran into the house to toss the sticks into the wood box beside the stove. Then I grabbed the long knife and headed below the garden fence to get the ragweeds.

The noontime sun was beating down relentlessly, causing animals and people to seek shade, and so it happened that as I turned the ragweeds to the side to cut them, I disturbed a pilot snake. Pilot snakes were vicious. Before I could think, my hand touched it. The snake raised the upper half of its body and commenced striking at me, but fortunately it did not bite me.

"Snake!" I screamed.

Grandma was fast coming from the kitchen, praying out loud, "Lord, please save our little girl." Colleen appeared from behind the house and rushed past Grandma. Daddy and Mommy had rushed from the barn and were flinging rocks at the head of the snake, and with excellent aim they hit its head. Immediately the snake's striking and lunging stopped, and it lay dead on the ground.

We went back to the house and enjoyed our hearty meal even more than usual, giving thanks that I had been saved. Living in the country, you had to accept things like snakes, because life did not give you time to be traumatized.

After we ate, we took our usual places for noontime rest in front of the fireplace. In late spring, the fireplace had been cleared of burned charcoal and ashes and swept clean with a bunch of broom sage bound together and tied with a string. As was our custom, at midday, Mommy spread out an old worn quilt on the floor in front of the clean fireplace. She and Daddy lay down beside each other on the quilt, with their shoes off and their eyes closed, napping before heading off to the fields for more long hours of work. As they slept, the cool breezes softly pressed down the chimney and met the smaller breezes curling up through the cracks in the floor. The result was pure ecstasy. I would always sit on the edge of the quilt reading, while Colleen sat in a straight chair patching holes in clothes. Grandma's hands were constantly busy, sewing, shelling peas or stringing beans for the evening meal or for canning.

Grandma was my parents' saving grace, in that they knew Colleen and I would be cared for and kept on task to weed the garden, feed the hogs, help her prepare supper, and draw water from the well to cook with and to wash dishes. The spring water where the milk cooled didn't taste good at all, so we fetched our drinking water from the Andy spring, a fountain of the purest and best tasting water I have ever known, forever bubbling up from the rocks. I chose the fetching of drinking water to be my daily job, because it gave me a cherished hour to be alone and dream on the two-mile pathway through the woods to the mountain spring. Many times I followed the small stream downward as it curved and rippled over the rocks in a quiet chorus of playful sounds.

Following the stream, I sometimes found arrowheads on the banks, and I would daydream about American Indian children who had lived there in years past and the stories I would write about them when I became a grownup and an author. The Andy spring always gave me the best inspiration for my writing ideas.

Twilight would bring my parents and the two dogs, Lead and Maude, down the hills from the fields. Sometimes the dogs would come down first and we could hear them as they followed the scent of a squirrel, possum or rabbit. They would speed along, one behind the other, simultaneously barking and running, until the animal they were chasing got too far away from home, or Lead and Maud lost the thrill of the chase. Frequently, upon hearing the dogs in a race, Daddy would remark, "Listen to that heavenly music." Obediently, I would listen, but I could not figure out what was heavenly about their racket.

Upon reaching the kitchen, we sat in our usual places around the table, happily talking as we relished each bite of Grandma's good supper. We were usually ready for bed at the same time the chickens were finding their choice limb of the apple tree in the yard to perch upon for the night. Grandma felt that the day ended well if she had managed to stir us to bed before Daddy had to light the lamp, because he would look so pleased that she had saved money on lamp oil.

Even though my parents were not graceful, and expressing gratitude was not easy for them, many nights, before going to bed, I would hear either Mommy or Daddy say something to Grandma, expressing appreciation for the blessing that she was, living with us. Smiling, she would lift her tiny specs off her nose, lay them on the table for the night and make her way to join Colleen and me in bed for a peaceful night of sleep.

Chapter 8

The Taxman Cometh

My first thought upon awakening one June morning was that today was a special day – today was the day my family and I would be making jelly for Mrs. Leach. She was the Coca Cola heiress whose mansion had been built over the big hole my Daddy had dug in Tate Mountain Estates a few years earlier. We sold "The Coca Cola Lady" a variety of vegetables that we grew on our farm, in addition to eggs and the fryer chickens we hatched from eggs in early spring. The dewberry jelly that my Mommy and Grandma made was Mrs. Leach's favorite.

I heard Mommy's footsteps as she entered the house and carefully closed the door behind her, clicking the wooden latch back into its socket. Our door had no screen, so even though it was summer, the door had to be quickly shut when we entered, else the dogs followed, and Grandma strictly forbade dogs inside the house. Mommy hugged short sticks of wood for the cook stove.

She glanced at me in bed and chided affectionately, "Toddy Frog, you better get up! You know how much I would like you to help me bring wood to that hungry stove."

"Mamie, hurry, help! I'm about to drop the jelly pot!" Grandma shouted from the kitchen side of the room, where she and Colleen were trying to move the jelly pot from one spot on the stove to another, to get a different simmering tempo.

Mommy rushed to help Grandma and Colleen. A minute later, I could hear them speaking calmly with each other. I could sense they were relieved and amused as they talked among themselves about how Grandma had managed to save that very important jelly. Their conversation made me feel uncomfortable about still being in bed. I began to feel a twinge of guilt and a longing to be older and more useful, like Colleen, so I could take a bigger part in helping out on this jelly day instead of keeping my mind so busy dreaming.

My Mommy and Daddy were clinging fast to the hope that we could make enough money from the jelly to pay the delinquent taxes on our farm. I had heard them talking with Grandma about how the taxman would take our home away if we could not pay the money we owed. My family had no hope of ever having money to pay the actual tax bill. Our taxes were always overdue, and the fines would keep building up. Most everyone I knew lived exactly the way we did, struggling to hold on to whatever property they owned, and fearing that the government would seize their land if they couldn't scrabble together the tax money. I figured that The Coca Cola Lady and the other rich people up in the Tate Mountain Estates could find tax money easily, but they appeared to be more like story figures than real people.

I listened to the chop-chop of Daddy's ax cutting stove wood, and to the door opening and closing as Mommy went outside again. That twinge of guilt became stronger as I thought about my family letting me sleep later than the others. It was probably because I lived in such a dream state, I was not a frequent contributor to household conversations. My family sometimes seemed to be unaware that I was even around. That was the advantage of not being heard; sometimes they forgot to look for me. Maybe I should live more like the rest of the family, I told myself as I crawled out of bed. Maybe I could help protect our house from the taxman.

I smelled coffee boiling in the black water pot, its fragrance mixing with the aroma of Mrs. Leach's favorite dewberry jelly simmering on the stove. Slipping out of bed, I went onto the porch outside the kitchen door to the wide railing where the water bucket and wash pan sat. I dipped water from the bucket with a crookneck gourd and washed my hands and face over the tin wash pan. Then I reached for the old dingy sugar sack towel that hung on a nail outside the door, being careful to find a clean and dry section of the cloth. As I lifted the wash pan of dirty water to empty it, I remembered Grandma had said yesterday that no one was tossing the dirty water far enough to reach the last dahlia in the row beside the house. With powerful energy, I flung my pan of water far out to hit the ground where the last dahlia stood. It gave me a comforting feeling that I had done at least one good thing on this day, even if I had started late. Then I took sheepish notice that the flowerbed had not even needed the water. I could see the dahlias were steeped in red muddy soil. It had rained last night! I remembered the preacher had prayed for rain at church the previous Sunday. Still, I was glad, because I knew the rain was a good sign. Mommy and Daddy had been hoping a big rain would end the summer drought.

From the porch, I saw my Mommy walking up from the barn, and I leaned with my elbows on the railing where I had washed my hands. Daddy had built the railing low so I could reach it. As she came nearer, I asked, "Mommy, will you tell me when I will be seven?"

She paused, with one foot inside the house and the other on the big flat rock that was the doorstep leading to the kitchen. She stretched inside the door to reach and lift the Lady's Birthday Almanac that hung on a rusty nail just inside.

"I'll tell you," she said, as she spread the worn pages on the wide railing beside me and bent to look at the calendar part of the almanac. As she bent over, sweat kept dripping from her nose and chin onto the page. Absorbed in the calendar, she brushed the moisture off with her sleeve. After spending a few minutes calculating the time between June and August, she came up with the answer.

"Today is June 30, 1934, and your birthday will be on August 15th, so I reckon in one month and fifteen days you will be seven."

"Thank you, Mommy." I hugged her bony body, as I often loved to do.

As Mommy headed back toward the stove woodpile, I walked into the kitchen and helped myself to a big biscuit, which I stuffed with the scrambled eggs left for me. As I ate, I thought about how glad I would be when I was seven. Time was passing slowly for me up here in the hills. I wanted to start school, and so did Colleen.. We had tried to learn to read and figure out the world from the newspapers pasted on the walls of our home. Even when I stood in a chair, though, the pictures and words I wanted to study most were almost at the ceiling, too far away for me to see clearly. How could I ever help fight off the taxman if I could not go to school?

I watched Colleen standing at the wood stove, continuously and slowly moving the fluttering newspaper fan back and forth just above the simmering jelly pan to prevent the flies from getting into the sweet jelly. Looking at the fan Colleen was using, I remembered seeing Great-Grandpa Lawing and Grandma make one just like it. Great-Grandpa took a sour wood sapling and cut it about five feet in length. Grandma then draped newspapers along the fold line and secured them to the flexible stick with a needle and thread. With scissors, she cut the newspapers in strips up to where they were sewn around the stick, making a lot of ribbon size pieces of paper dangling down. The stick could then be waved gently back and forth, with the newspaper ribbons floating, to shoo away the flies either from a very sick person lying in bed or, as Colleen was doing, from a simmering jelly pot. Great-Grandpa said it was a must to have one in the home if there were no screen doors. Most people in our neighborhood didn't have screen doors.

"Maybe if you –." I started to tell Colleen that she needed to fan faster because the flies were getting stuck on the rim of the jelly pan, but I changed my mind when I saw how cross she looked. It didn't appear to be a day when she was "walking in high cotton." I liked that expression of Grandma's. She had told me that when the season had been good in places where farmers grew cotton, and the cotton was growing tall with lots of cotton balls to harvest, then people would feel happy. Colleen looked like the cotton was pretty low.

"What a blessing that rain was last night!" Grandma happily shouted to anyone who could hear.

"You are right! It sure was a blessing," said Mommy.

Continuing to watch the flies, I could see that more and more of them were getting stuck and desperately flapping their wings, trying to get airborne again. They were now lined up in a row around the beat-up edge of the pan in such a way that I decided they looked like parachutists who had flown in from the air. Just such a picture was in the newspaper pasted on the wall behind the stove. It was of an army base where a group of parachutists were landing in the mud. Mommy came into the kitchen with the stove wood, and picked up the pitcher of morning milk that Grandma had strained through a white sugar sack to filter out cow hairs and bits of grass.

"I'll take the milk down to the stream to cool," Mommy said to Grandma. "Arthur is gone to look at the corn in the Long Patch. He hopes that big rain last night didn't beat the fodder off the stalks." By "fodder," Mommy meant the leaves of the corn stalks, which we gave to our animals as food. She added, "He's checking to see how soon he can plow."

Colleen started to take notice of the flies and silently stepped up her movement of the fan. It was then that I heard a strange sound coming from outside. I pulled the string latch of the front door upward, peeked out, and saw a model A Ford car zigzagging down the hill through the slippery red mud. I felt a little frightened. After the car turned into our yard and stopped, a man got out of the car. As I watched him unfold his body, I decided I had never seen such a long man.

He looked like trouble. Unlike Daddy and our neighbors, he had a citified look. He wore tan seersucker pants, a white long-sleeved shirt, and pointed shiny black slip-on shoes. There was no doubt about it, his clothes meant uppity, including that brown and white striped tie and the straw hat pushed so far back on his head that the front brim was standing straight up to the sky. Yes, he looked too well dressed and confident to be someone who lived around here. He might be the bailiff, who I thought lived in the courthouse on the square. I had heard Daddy talk about the bailiff coming to take things from people's houses and barns when they could not pay their bills.

Once, the funeral director had sent the bailiff to collect money for the funeral expenses of Grandma Warren, Daddy's mother. This man, now standing beside the car, looked to me like the same kind of man. I remembered the story about how, after the bailiff had come that time, Daddy had had to borrow money at the bank against his mules to pay part of the debt. The next night, though, the mules had gotten out of the pasture. They had eaten so many green corn stalks that their stomachs had swelled, until they had looked like two huge brown balloons lying in the pasture. My parents and Grandma had worried that if the mules died, no money would come in to finish paying the bailiff, and Daddy would not be able to drag logs from the mountains to the sawmill. "As good luck would have it," though, as my Grandma would say, the mules had gotten well, so that Daddy had been able to log with them and pay back his debt.

Now, this new man was starting to walk toward Mommy, who had been headed to the spring branch with the pitcher of fresh milk. Mommy turned to walk toward the man, and waited for him on a grassy patch. As I rushed outside and stood beside her, I could see that she was looking very afraid. When I reached for her, my hand touched hers, and I will never forget how cold and clammy her hand felt.

The fancy dressed man had to cross a patch of mud before he reached firmer ground, where grass and weeds grew. Georgia red clay, being glue-like when wet, sucked at his feet. Lifting one foot at a time, he tried to get rid of the mud, flailing his arms as he tried to keep his balance in the slippery ooze. His face reddened and he looked madder and madder as his pointy shoes became muddy right up to their tops.

Reaching the grassy patch, he introduced himself to Mommy as the tax collector. So here was the taxman Mommy and Daddy had been worried about. Maybe he was just like the bailiff. Removing a paper from the pocket of his shirt while snatching a pencil from behind his ear, he spoke sternly to Mommy.

In short, scolding sentences, he said, "These taxes have been overdue for a number of years. The small amount your husband has paid on them is not enough. On different trips out here, I have told y'all what would have to happen."

I felt he looked down his nose at my Mommy as he said all this. Her voice, when she spoke up, was quivering.

"I know, sir, but we just have not had hardly a cent to pay on them. Last year was such a wet summer the crops drowned out, and this summer so far it has been so dry our crops are drying up and dying because there ain't been no rain. . . . "

I was so embarrassed and saddened by Mommy having to grovel to this cold, uncaring man. As she spoke, he jerked his head up as if the air at our level stank. His long nose went skyward at

91

the same time his taut, tobacco-stained lips pushed down at the corners almost to his chin.

Scornfully he interrupted her. "Yeah, I know, ma'am, but most other people around here are a proud lot and they take care of their obligations even though they are farming in the same climate conditions as y'all are. I tell you, if you do not have some money to pay on these back taxes in five days, we will have to start foreclosure and sell your house and land. That is the way it works and the Good Lord knows I have been patient with y'all."

Such an awful man, I thought, as I stood there listening. I had heard stories about what might happen to families who could not pay their tax bills. I knew we could all be separated. Colleen and I could be put in the Georgia Baptist Orphanage and sent to different houses. We would never see each other again, and we would never see Grandma and Mommy and Daddy either, because they would be so far away. They wouldn't even know our names anymore, because that was the way it was when people became adopted. We would no longer share our little home here. All that we had could be gone. I felt sure that without us, Grandma would soon die all alone from sadness. Mommy and Daddy might be so lonely and cry so much for us that they would die too. Thinking about our situation, my throat became so tight and dry that I could not swallow. All my dreams for a better life for my family slipped into the red mud and vanished.

The man wrote on a piece of paper as he continued to speak slowly and loudly, repeating himself.

"Ma'am, tell your husband that if I don't have some money paid on these back taxes in five days, I will be forced to foreclose and sell the house and land for the debt!"

Grandma and Colleen, who were now standing behind us, listened in silence to Mommy's trembling, soft voice.

"Sir, we will have some money by the day after tomorrow, because we have, right now, a pot of jelly on the stove. We are selling it to The Coca Cola Lady, who lives on top of yonder mountain." She pointed toward the mountain in back of our house.

The taxman seemed unconvinced and uncaring as he bid us a cold "Good day," and cranked his noisy motor.

It started to rain lightly again, but the taxman rolled down his window and shouted, "I will ask the elders of my church to pray for y'all because it is my Christian duty and I am done with trying to get the money from you people . . ."

His voice trailed off. He seemed to imply that we were just a no-good family that God did not find very useful. His last words were a yelling quote from the Bible, "The Lord helps those that help themselves."

I wondered to myself, what more could my family do? They worked almost every waking hour. Maybe Daddy could have made more corn liquor, but then the law could have caught him and put him in jail. The taxman just didn't know or care how hard they tried.

We stood huddled together as we watched him, slowly and with effort, spin his tires through the deep gullies filled with soft red mud. Maybe the rain had not been such a good sign after all.

I held my breath while listening to his engine screech as it struggled to free the car from the mud. Whatever happiness I still had about the rain was cancelled out by the real possibility that this man would not be able to get his car unstuck and would have to stay with us until the rain stopped. Although it was midday, the dark storm approaching had made the chickens hop up to their individual bedroom limbs in the apple trees, thinking it was twilight. A flash of lightning was followed by a blast of thunder, and a cloudburst of rain poured down, with large hail the size of pullet eggs. What would we do if that man could not get out?

"Run! Quick! The porch!" Grandma yelled as she rushed to the house for shelter.

Shaking the rain off, we stood close together on the narrow porch. The hail was hitting the tin roof so hard that if the taxman still had his motor on, we couldn't hear it, but we could see his car, still stuck in the ruts on the hill.

Soaking wet, Daddy came onto the porch, back from the cornfield.

"Who was in that car?" he said, with a worried look on his face.

Looking up the hill, I felt glad to see the taxman's car begin to move out of the mud and onto the wet road. I watched the tail-light make one last zigzag as it slid over the hilltop and out of sight.

"Oh good, he's gone!" I blurted out, but I was ignored, since all ears were listening to Mommy carefully laying out the facts about the taxman for Daddy. In order to help Daddy, who was always inclined to think on the bad side, Mommy braced herself as she spoke calmly.

"Arthur, that was the tax collector, and he said we have five more days to get money to pay on the tax."

Mommy made the five days sound like a long, comfortable block of time.

"Mamie, we're going to lose our home." Daddy's words sounded very weak, as if he had no breath coming out of his throat.

Lose our home! It was true then – I was going to an orphanage!

Continuing her stream of encouraging words, Mommy declared, "No, no, Arthur, we will have jelly money tomorrow! With the money from Mrs. Leach, we'll be able to pay enough on the tax bill to buy a lot more time. And look how it's raining now. The fields will be alright. It will work out just fine."

We all went back inside the house. Colleen and I left the grownups still talking in the fireplace room, as we referred to the biggest room, and we walked together into the kitchen.

Before I placed myself on the stool at the stove, I said to Colleen, "Let me shoo flies for a while. You've been doing it all day."

Colleen smiled. "Alright, Odean, and I will read to you higher up on the walls tomorrow."

I knew she would, because she never lied to me. Colleen and I carefully pulled the jelly pan to one side of the stove. Then she added two more sticks of wood to the coals. The fire started burning again. Together we placed the jelly pan back on the stove to simmer a while longer.

I began to shoo flies briskly, moving that newspaper fan with a vigor far beyond my ordinary dreamy movements. I was filled with a passion that only being on a mission can evoke. I was going to help save our home. Tomorrow we would bring the dewberry jelly up to Mrs. Leach, and then we would have jelly money.

Chapter 9

Mrs. Leach and the Sundial

The weekly trips I made with my parents to Mrs. Leach's summer home on top of the mountain were among my happiest times. It was always a special thrill for me when we arrived at The Coca Cola Lady's estate and Daddy turned off the old truck's noisy, steaming motor. As soon as I stepped onto the lawn in my bare feet, and smelled the heavenly fragrance of her gardens in that rich and quiet atmosphere, I began daydreaming. My parents would let me stay outside to play in a pretty spot while they unloaded the goods and got paid for them. Sometimes it would take Mrs. Leach half an hour or more to come hand them the money.

Luckily for me, the waiting spot my parents had chosen contained a large square brick pillar, four feet in height, with a sundial on top. I would lean on the sundial, caressing the gold letters printed above the Roman numerals on the clock face. The message read, "My face marks the sunny hours. What can you say of yours?"

Often, as I enjoyed the sundial, I daydreamed about adding just such a beautiful object to my own imaginary mansion, the dream version of my mansions made out of sticks and moss. The house I pictured, in my future, already had a nice little red barn in the back for our milk cows Cream and Dolly. It was Dolly whom I loved dearly, since I had raised her from a calf. I had planned a green pasture for her and Cream, so they would have good food. I thought my sundial should go in the middle of their pasture. A child's eye view of heaven!

The real sundial stood about halfway between the back of Mrs. Leach's big house and the complex of smaller houses she had for her domestic help. A fence enclosed the servants' area, made of thin, white, vertical boards about five feet high, with a half-inch of space between them. I often pictured how Grandma would love to have that neat picket fence around our vegetable garden, instead of the rough patched one that closed it off from dogs, chickens and possibly a run-away cow. Our garden fence had been haggled together from rotting pieces of boards, and in some spaces Daddy had placed old chicken wire, which he had found in the Leaches' garbage pile. There was no trash pick-up service in those days, so when our neighbors or my family passed near her garbage heap, we often found valuable items. What the Leaches thought of as junk was a tangled mess of treasures to us.

A few weeks before my seventh birthday, the same summer of the taxman's visit, I got up the courage to peek through this neat white fence. I could see two black men sitting and resting outside one house. I had seen these two men many times at Mrs. Leach's; just that morning they had unloaded the vegetables and chickens from our truck. Their dark blue overalls were new, as usual, a fact that always surprised me, because my Daddy's were so faded and patched. About twice a month, Mommy washed Daddy's overalls, but he immediately made them dirty again, as he was constantly in the fields.

I wished Mommy and Daddy could come and sit a spell and rest, like these men, before going back to work on our farm. As I continued to peek through the fence, I was surprised to see four black children playing – although my family would not have said "black" in the early 1930's in Appalachia, but "Negro." One boy and girl looked about a year older than I was, although they might have been six, like me. I had often been told that I was smaller than most children my age. I was definitely thinner than they were, but I bet I was stronger and could do more work. Playing with them were three more children of three or four years old. The little boy wore a red and white striped short sleeve shirt and dark blue pants. The two little girls were dressed alike in light blue dresses with white ruffles, and had large white ribbons in their hair. Looking at those ribbons, I touched my own thin hair, which came about to my chin, and wondered how I might look with a big ribbon on my head. I had never owned a ribbon.

The little girls' shoes were pretty and white. They looked "bran' spank'n new" – that's what we always said when we opened a delightful package of new shoes from Sears Roebuck. Such a delivery came about once every two years for us, however. Most of the summer, Colleen and I went barefoot.

The little boy started to trip on his shoestrings, which had come untied, and an old lady rushed to him and took him on her lap to tie them. The old lady was so much like my Grandma in her actions that I really wanted to climb across the fence and play with those children. I so much wanted to get to know them.

I figured the grown-ups were grandparents looking after the children while their parents worked on the estate. These grandparents sat in soft cushioned seats of white wicker furniture, near flower gardens wrapped round with what looked like whole lengths of chicken wire, as they read and watched the children at play. I watched one grandma, who was about the same size and age as my own Grandma, smile at the children just as my Grandma smiled at me.

The children were having so much fun playing with huge toys the likes of which I had never seen, even in the Sears and Roebuck Catalog. The older girl was pushing a baby carriage in which a doll sat, so big and fully clothed that at first I thought it was a real baby, until she lifted it up into her arms. The older boy was doing something inside a fancy playhouse, maybe pretending to cook. I wouldn't dare hope for a fancy playhouse like that, but I did start to try and figure out how Daddy might make a roof between the trees, where Colleen and I had our playhouse on the hill. I figured that would be nice, because our playtime happened most often when it was rainy and too wet to work in the fields.

What struck me most was the fact that those children and their grandparents had the richest, darkest skin I had ever seen. It looked so smooth and different from the sunburned, peeling, or freckled skin of my friends and me. I felt sure that, to get to live in such comfort, they must be the most privileged people on earth. Maybe the older folk sat in the sun all day, talking together. That was different from my parents and my Grandma, who never paused until evening. Work seemed more like a never-ending battle, because in my family the chores were constant and necessary.

I would realize as I grew older, of course, that those black grandparents had most likely had a life filled with chores and hardship, and that their grandchildren – comfortable and lucky though they appeared to my child's eyes – did not necessarily face a life of simple ease and inherited privilege.

In any case, I thought those children might want to play with me, but I could tell that their grandparents forbade them even to talk to me. The girl who was about my age, with long black curls like Shirley Temple's, pointed her finger in my direction a few times. She looked as if she was saying something about me to her grandma, and the older lady would shake her head, no.

Years later I still wonder why we could not play together. I do not remember talking to my Mommy and Daddy about this situation. I am not sure if my parents were prejudiced, or if the black servants considered us to be poor white trash. Or maybe the servants knew that no good could come of mixing the races in such a prejudiced area. I will never know for sure.

Thirty years later, living in New York and closely following Martin Luther King's crusade, I was reminded that in the same summers when I was standing barefoot at the sundial or peeking through the white picket fence, dreaming of a glorious life of plenty for my family, Martin Luther King was probably going barefoot on the same red Georgia clay some miles to the south. While he may have already been dreaming of freedom and an equal chance for a better life for a whole race of people, I was dreaming fervently for freedom from poverty for only one family, and that family was mine.

Soon I became aware of mysterious food smells coming from the houses of Mrs. Leach's domestic help. The fragrances made my mouth water and brought pangs of hunger to my belly. Oh, how I would have loved to taste that food! I kept sniffing the air, trying to identify what was cooking. It was like no food I had ever smelled before. The daily scent of corn bread baking at my own house was more common and plain. Even my Grandma's good cooking – pork frying, cabbage boiling, beans simmering – could not compare with this. Fond as I was of the appetizing smells of rabbit stewing or chicken frying, those too were totally different from the tantalizing scents teasing my nose now.

Many years later I identified that aroma to have been, of all things, a tomato spaghetti sauce, a scent unfamiliar to us in the Appalachia of my childhood. When I was a child, I never saw anyone cook ripe tomatoes, although sometimes we had the luxury of fried green tomatoes. The ripe tomatoes were sliced raw and eaten with green beans and corn pone, or sometimes with sweet cake, if we happened to have money to buy sugar.

One memorable day that August, The Coca Cola Lady hired my parents to work in the afternoon, clearing briers and underbrush on both sides of one of her driveways. As Mommy and Daddy cut and piled small limbs in heaps, I dragged the wood to an area several yards away to be burned later.

Mommy said, as she cut some briers, "I hear tell the servants have a kind of white candy that they put on sticks for each child to hold, and then they let the candy cook over a fire at night, and it turns brown."

"What kind of candy?" I asked.

"I don't know. I've never been here at nights."

As we continued working quietly, I kept thinking of how much fun it would be to cook candy over a fire in this big back yard. Later I learned that candy was called marshmallows.

Soon I looked up to see Mrs. Leach walking toward us from her house. I liked to have her come by because she smelled so good, and her short brown and gray hair was clean and fluffy, so neat that she looked like a picture on our newspaper walls. I so loved my Mommy's long, light brown hair, though, especially when she had washed it recently. Mommy usually plaited her hair into one braid, and then wrapped the shiny braid around her head. Today, however, small pieces of sticks and leaves had fallen into her curled-up braid as she worked. I pictured her hair as clean as Mrs. Leach's.

Mrs. Leach was wearing a light blue skirt and a white blouse, which I knew Mommy would look so pretty in. Mommy had the sweetest blue eyes that could either smile or quietly insist that what she was saying was what had to be. Her face was care-worn and weary, but it was still beautiful. I thought the dainty white shoes on Mrs. Leach's feet would look so fine covering Mommy's toes, which now peeked from holes in her old work shoes. I often pictured Mommy in Mrs. Leach's nice clothes, because I knew that someday, when I was a grown-up, I would earn lots of money, and then I would see my Mommy dressed every day like Mrs. Leach. Everything in the life of my family would be better, when I could help with my own earnings.

Mrs. Leach motioned for Mommy, Daddy and me to come and sit with her at a table nearby.

"Come, I have cookies and milk," she said.

Before we sat down, we expressed our thanks to her in a kind of chorus, with the three of us speaking at the same time. In our home we never said grace like some people did. Daddy would sometimes say, "Saying grace out loud is done to show off, and more often it's done by hypocrites."

After our expressions of thanks, Mrs. Leach surprised us by sitting down with us. It was not unusual for her to send a servant with refreshments, and sometimes she might bring them herself, but to have her sit with us was a surprise! She spent a few minutes talking about how good the jelly was and how she wanted us to bring her twice as much next Friday. She was nervously stroking and wringing her hands with her soft looking fingers, each fingernail tipped with bright red paint. She seemed to want to say something she wasn't quite sure how to say.

After a pause she spoke.

"Mr. Warren, you may tell me that what I am about to say is none of my business, and I respect that, but I have to say something. I worry that you are working your little girl here much too hard."

She reached to pat my shoulder.

Both Mommy and I looked quickly at Daddy. We knew that Daddy had a hot temper. Hearing those words, he might get really mad.

But Daddy remained calm as he answered, "Ma'am, I know it is hard for you to understand this, but our kind of people have to work hard for everything we get. It was like that with me, and my parents, and their parents before them, and I know it will be the same for our children too. So the best we can do is to raise our

102

kids to be honest, God-fearing and hard-working people like we are."

Bending low, he reached to touch my back softly, saying, "Odean is the child that worries us the most. She is always dreaming crazy dreams, like one day when we were here, she said she was going to have a big rock mansion like this for us to live in some day, and she can't seem to get it out of her head. We don't want her to get disappointed and hurt."

He rose up straight again and turned back to Mrs. Leach, a tiny indulgent smile flickering and vanishing across his mouth.

A similar fleeting smile now brushed across Mrs. Leach's face as she gently answered, "Odean is a marvelous little girl."

At that moment one of her servants came to tell Mrs. Leach that she had a phone call, and she left.

In the moment after she departed, Daddy looked straight into my eyes. I could see tears were about to rise into his own eyes. He was biting his lip, trying to stave them off. My heart went out to him and it beat with even stronger determination to make money and change my family's lives. They would never have to worry about the tax money again, or the corn getting ruined from hail or drought, or the mules becoming sick and dying. I felt sad that I had to keep being a child and could only dream and wish for all the good things I wanted for them, like new clothes and sundials. What if Grandma, Mommy or Daddy died before I could get grown and go away and make money? Feeling sadder with each passing second, I thought about how hard they worked, and how frightening it was when they got sick and there was no money to pay a doctor.

I felt painfully doubtful, though, too. I had not known anyone who had gone out into the world from our neighborhood and been successful. The words that Daddy had just spoken to

Mrs. Leach tore at my heart. *It was like that with me, and my parents, and their parents before them, and I know it will be the same for our children too.*

I thought to myself, if Daddy doesn't have any idea that I could get rich, then how could I be so sure myself that I could do it? Maybe I just had to take things like they had always been. Going over in my mind the words on the sundial – "My face marks the sunny hours. What can you say of yours?" – I felt sick in the pit of my stomach. We must be people who were not meant to be happy, and to see and feel the good of "the sunny hours." Maybe those were just pretty words that had no meaning for our kind of people. The preacher's words might be the real truth. As he always said, "Be good and work hard and life will be good in the hereafter." I had never liked that idea, however. I didn't want to wait for the "hereafter," whatever that meant. I wanted a good life like Mrs. Leach's, filled with flowers and green lawns and a big house.

After our cookies and milk, we got back to work on Mrs. Leach's driveway. I continued to drag the piles of brush until I saw the sun almost touching the trees on the far side of the lake. In the morning the brush I dragged had felt bouncy as I had happily pulled it along, but now it had become so heavy that I heaved and trudged to haul its weight along behind me.

After my parents had burned the brush, it was time for Daddy to crank the truck again so we could head down the mountain. At first, the motor refused to start, as if often did, even when Daddy pressed the gas pedal on the floorboard. He took the steel crank that lay in the back of the truck, pushed the crank into a small hole in the front, just under the radiator, and laboriously turned it over and over until the motor started. Once the engine coughed, he swiftly flung the crank into the back, jumped into his seat, and pushed and patted his foot rapidly on the gas pedal until the motor stopped blasting loud popping noises and began to move.

As we headed back down the mountain toward home, I could see that Mommy and Daddy were tired. They seemed to be enjoying a peaceful silence as one does after a day of hard work. Since we were coasting to save gas, I didn't have to exert much effort to hold the gearshift in place. One of us kids always straddled and held the long gearshift with our hands so that the bumpy roads didn't jostle it out of gear. When we coasted, I could hold the gearshift more lightly as I let my mind float back into my imaginary mansion. I could see my Mommy, Daddy, Grandma and Colleen in that mansion surrounded by green pastures, contented cows, and me leaning on my very own sundial. I felt the solid brick of it pressing against my belly.

It must have been on another day that August, around my seventh birthday, that Mrs. Leach approached Mommy and Daddy once again, this time with the bold suggestion that she would love to adopt and educate their "bright little girl Odean, who exudes enthusiasm."

Afterward, at home, my parents talked to Grandma about Mrs. Leach's suggestion, laughing as they described her offer.

Mommy said to Grandma, "What made her think that we would let her have our little girl? Arthur answered her in no uncertain terms. 'We take care of our own,' he told her. He spoke harshly and he didn't thank her either."

Grandma, when hearing about Mrs. Leach's suggestion, began to cry. At that time, I didn't understand why she cried. Years later, in thinking back on the incident, I came to the conclusion that she realized how, with Mrs. Leach, I would have had a chance to get a good education and have a fancy life style, and she felt sad that she, along with my parents, could not let me go.

That night after we went to bed, I hugged her bigger than usual to make her feel better, because I heard her still softly weeping. I was happy that Mrs. Leach wanted me, although I didn't understand much about adoption. I was especially proud that my parents and Grandma wanted to keep me, and now I was going to make them proud of me by being a big success, without Mrs. Leach's help.

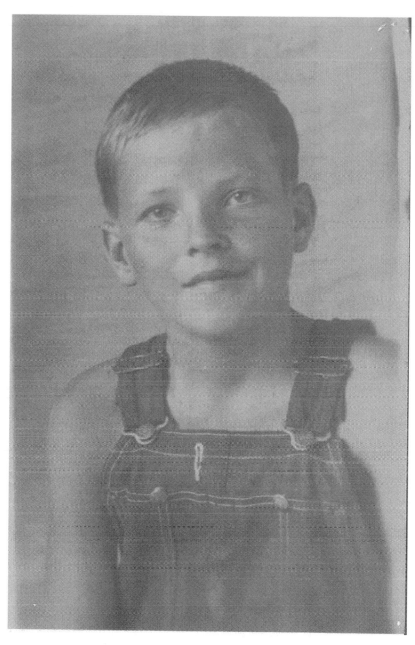

My brother, William Eugene Warren,

when he was about 8 years old

Chapter 10

The Birth of Gene, Our Little Prince

One day in the middle of summer, a few months before my baby brother Gene arrived, Colleen and I were hoeing corn in the "mountain field patch." Both of us had started school two years earlier, and we were looking forward to third grade. I was almost nine, and Colleen was almost eleven.

"Colleen, why is Mommy getting so fat?" I asked. This question had been on my mind for a few weeks by then, and I had a feeling Colleen might know the answer.

For the most part, we had been silent that morning while we worked, except for the cling-clang of our hoes hitting small rocks as we chopped the weeds from around the corn plants. This was the "laying by stage," that is, the last time we would hoe the corn that summer. The stalks were about eight to ten inches tall, on their way to becoming ten to twelve feet and yielding two large ears per stalk, if we made sure to chop the hungry weeds down before they sucked up all the nutrients and moisture from the soil around the corn.

As soon as I asked the question about Mommy, Colleen stopped chopping, dug her hoe into the soil, and with her foot moved a rock onto the dirt covering the hoe, allowing the wooden handle to stand up straight and give her support as she leaned on it. She then turned to face me, wiping sweat off her face with her dirty hand.

"Odean, that's something I've been thinking I should tell you for a long time, but you are so young I thought it best to wait.

108

When we get to the end of these rows, we can sit in the shade and I'll tell you."

She glanced at me, as I kept chopping in my row a few steps behind her. I knew she expected me to say, oh, no, no, tell me now, but much as I wanted to say that, I restrained myself.

Colleen did not wait, however, until we hoed to the edge of the field. After a minute or two of our hoeing, she said slowly, "This is something I have known for years."

I wanted to say I knew better than to believe that, because she always told me everything as soon as she heard any news that would place her in a more informed position, like a grown-up. I let her remark pass, though, because I wasn't interested in any quibbling. I just wanted to hear what she had to tell me about Mommy.

"Mommy is going to have a baby, and I know you don't know where babies come from, do you?"

Not wanting to appear dimwitted in the presence of all her gleaned facts of the grown-up world, I said, "I've heard the doctor brings them in his bag."

As I said this, I thought about how I had actually heard a number of different stories from girls in the neighborhood. Ruth said her mother had told her that she'd looked under a cabbage leaf and found baby Ruth there on the ground. Some other girls said that God brought us to our parents, but that sounded about as unbelievable as the cabbage leaf story. God was so far away in the sky, I couldn't figure out how He could find our parents' tiny two-room shack way down here, where there were only narrow dirt roads. The songs in church told how the streets where God lives were paved in pure gold.

Speaking again now and full of her eleven-year-old sense of importance, Colleen said, "Babies come from the mommy's belly and the daddy puts it there to grow and be born."

She continued with all the shocking details until I became ill and felt like vomiting. I could not believe all this could be true, about our Mommy and Daddy, and I decided to try to forget the whole thing.

In any case, William Eugene -- named after Eugene Talmadge, the governor of Georgia -- was born in October of 1936, in the midst of the busy hay-stacking time. The farmers in our neighborhood worked long hours to get the cut hay off the ground and onto stacks before heavy rains came and rotted it. Without Mommy being able to work side by side with Daddy, pitching hay onto the stacks as she usually did, Daddy was having to work extra hard that year.

My parents told us later that Gene's birth had been much easier on Mommy than mine had been. Whenever Daddy retold the story of my birth, in fact, after Gene had joined the family, I always did a dry swallow when he got to the part about my Mommy's pain. I felt sorry that I had not been as easy on Mommy as Gene had been.

Because I knew I could get a satisfying answer from Grandma, I once asked, "Grandma, did I really hurt Mommy more than Gene did when we came into the world?"

"Well, I don't know," Grandma said honestly, "because both times I was in the kitchen cooking for all the neighbors gathered around."

"I didn't mean to hurt Mommy."

She hugged me and said, "Of course not, honey bunch. Maybe it felt good staying in Mommy's stomach and you were stubborn and didn't want to come out. Stubborn is good. I'm stubborn."

During all the years that have passed since then, the many times I have been told that I was stubborn, I have always answered, "I am stubborn because my Grandma said stubborn is good, especially if you are standing up for what you believe is right."

About mid-afternoon, when Mommy began having severe labor pains, Daddy emptied his truck of hay, and he came home to pick Colleen and me up. We jumped into the back of his truck, with our school clothes for the next day hanging over one arm. With the other arm, we held onto the sides of the truck, our feet planted firmly on the floor of the truck bed so we would not be bounced around. As Daddy started the loud motor, I could smell the bits and pieces of fragrant, fresh alfalfa above the gas fumes from the exhaust. (Sometimes these days as I work at Whole Foods, when I am measuring a cup of dried alfalfa for a customer, I smile, because this is the same scent of those bits of hay left in Daddy's truck after he had unloaded it in the barn loft.)

Soon Daddy dropped us off at Jane and Henry Wilson's home. They were our nearest neighbors, and it was always a thrill for us to spend a night with them, because they pampered us with many store-bought goodies. Since they had no children, they usually had a little extra cash on hand, whereas when my parents got some cash it would have to be spent on Colleen's and my shoes and school clothes.

On his way back home, Daddy picked up Mrs. Cantrell, a woman well known for her successful bringing of babies into the world. He also picked up a couple of our close neighbor women to spend the night and help Mommy give birth.

Early the next morning, Daddy came to Mr. and Mrs. Wilson's home to give us the news. Mrs. Wilson had already fed us a big breakfast of sausage, eggs and biscuits. She welcomed

Daddy in, and invited him to sit on a chair in the kitchen by the chimney. Soon Mr. Wilson rushed inside from the barn. As Mr. Wilson opened the door to come in, I saw that everything outside was covered in a heavy frost -- the first frost of the season.

Daddy called to Colleen and me, and we came over to sit on the floor in front of him, with our backs warming by the chimney fire. Mr. and Mrs. Wilson joined us, completing a cozy circle around the fire.

Daddy said, "I have good news. A baby brother for you girls has come to our house last night."

Mr. and Mrs. Wilson began exclaiming how wonderful that was.

Colleen, following the example of the grown-ups, said, "I'm glad about having a little brother."

I remained silent, and I didn't feel any better when Daddy pulled me off the floor and into his lap. Evidently, it had become apparent to Daddy that he needed to bargain with me.

"I tell you what, girls, if you decide you don't want that little brother when you come back from school this evening, you come down to the hay field and tell me you don't want him and I will take him back."

With that promise from Daddy, I felt better. Colleen and I hugged Daddy goodbye, and thanked the Wilsons, as we rushed outside to catch the school bus. Colleen was the star of the show in our little bus, which was built like a little house, with canvas walls, on the bed of an old pick-up truck, as she told everyone that we had a little brother. Two kids who didn't have a younger sibling got all excited along with her, but the three kids who had a number of brothers and sisters didn't seem excited at all.

Once we had bounced along the three miles of rutted roads to Oakland Elementary School and begun our lessons, I felt an urge to go up to our teacher Miss Mary and tell her that we had a little brother.

"Oh, that's wonderful, Odean. I am so happy for you!" Miss Mary said. "He will be like a little doll that you and Colleen now have to play with!"

Her remarks made me feel a whole lot better, especially when some students seemed to be a little unhappy that they didn't have a little brother to play with, like a doll.

When the bus driver brought us home, we rushed into the house, and sure enough, there was a little doll wrapped in a bundle lying on Mommy's chest.

Excitedly jumping up and down, I said to Colleen, "Come on, let's go to the hay field and tell Daddy we want to keep our little brother."

Mommy, Grandma and a neighbor looked at each other, smiling, and I figured they must approve of our decision.

As soon as we found Daddy pitching hay, I rushed to tell him. Colleen didn't say anything, which puzzled me then. It took a few years for me to realize that she had understood Daddy's promise as a joke.

I was dead serious, though, as I looked up into Daddy's face and said, "Daddy, we want to keep our little brother!"

He hunkered down and hugged me beside the haystack, and took pains to explain how much fun it would be to have that "little guy" around.

"He will make us all so happy, especially your Grandma."

Oops, Daddy had almost gone too far with that remark, because I felt a rock had hit my stomach. I wasn't yet sure I wanted "the baby" on my Grandma's lap all that much.

Gene was about a month old before I could kiss him, since I couldn't totally forget about that place he had come from. After a couple of months, though, I happily buried my face in his little belly, and between my kisses and his wiggles and giggles, the blunt information about sex and birth that Colleen had put in place in my mind had become just a hint in my memory.

Our two-room shack began to overflow with joy and a new kind of happiness, which made our daily battle to survive more light-hearted and hopeful. Although he was so little now, Gene offered us the promise of a young male to carry on the name of our Daddy. The heritage of a male to carry on the name was just as important in our mountain community as it was in the most purebred aristocratic families the world over.

I remember many funny incidents about Gene, like the time when he was three years old and dropped Grandma's butter dish, which crashed to bits on the kitchen floor. She rushed to the kitchen, where she had been stringing beans in the "big room."

"Oh child," she moaned, "you have broke my butter dish that belonged to my Grandmother."

"Ah, Grandma, it was old enough," he wisely answered.

Another day, Colleen and I were running with him down the little dirt road, me grasping one arm and Colleen the other, as we swung him back and forth like a swing between two moving posts.

"Don't! Don't do this!" he cried. "You might fall down and hurt my pretty knees."

Now, of course, these many years later, when we are visiting, I often inquire about his pretty knees!

Actually, until Gene was about four, and I was thirteen, Colleen and I did in fact treat him like a little plaything. Halfway into his fourth year, however, he developed a severe illness that lasted many months. None of us could get him to eat and he became very thin. Through some of our friends we kept hearing troublesome rumors that their parents were expecting Gene to die. Although Grandma kept saying she knew God was looking after our little brother and would make him well again, Daddy and Mommy looked sadder and sadder with each passing day.

After a few months, thank heavens the crisis passed. We never knew any name for his illness, but the blessing of him returning to perfect health was a source of great rejoicing. As he became strong again, I felt that our joy shook the rafters of our house and echoed among the tall Georgia pines on the mountains nearby.

In August of his sixth year, Gene started school. He was shy, and we could barely get him to come to the old shed to wait for the bus with us.

"I don't want to go to school," he would yell on many occasions, and Colleen would use all her strength of persuasion, holding the collar of Gene's jacket in her fist, until our faithful bus driver Hoover Kincaid would appear and order Gene to get on board and come to school.

One recent summer, when Jeriann, Brady and I were on our yearly visit to Georgia, I commented to Gene about the decision his sisters had had to make, after his birth.

"Gene, aren't you glad Colleen and I told Daddy in the hay field that we had decided to keep our little brother?"

Sitting around Mommy and Daddy's old dining table, Gene, happily grinning, glanced at Edith, his wife of fifty years, sitting beside him. Then he proudly looked at his daughter and son, with their own beautiful children.

Gene reached over to pat my shoulder.

"Odean, you're mighty right, I am."

Chapter 11

The Sharp Ax

It was a hot, humid summer morning around my tenth year, and I was hungry. The day began, as it had all week, with corn bread crumbled in a pan of gravy, and no milk, eggs or biscuits. Because there was no milk for the gravy, Grandma had mixed a little lard into the water for flavor, along with the only egg remaining from the ones our hens had laid. Mommy said she hoped that somehow we could find a way to get a bag of flour, so we could make a batch of biscuits. We were also hungry for some milk to drink with the biscuits, but we knew milk would be hard to come by. Our cows Cream and Dolly were both dry and awaiting the birth of their calves in two weeks.

About seven months earlier, a neighbor's bull had jumped over his broken pasture fence and then had delighted in soaring across our equally dilapidated fence, managing to get both our cows pregnant in the same day. That unfortunate incident had upset Daddy's usual plan of spacing the breeding of the cows so that only one would go dry at a time. The previous day, Nancy, another neighbor, to whom Mommy had loaned a pitcher of milk a few months earlier, had promised to bring us a gallon of her cow's milk that was staying cool in her spring branch. She had said she would bring the milk to keep cold in our spring branch early that morning, but she still hadn't come.

Mommy so wanted a little milk that she had already sent me on two trips to check and see if Nancy had delivered the fresh gallon yet, but each time I got in sight of the spring, it still contained no cloth-covered pitcher. That pitcher of milk, if used sparingly, would almost fill six glasses, so that each of us could have the feeling of a full stomach once again. The second time I went down the hill to the spring branch, I felt weak from hunger and wondered if I would be able to tote the pitcher of milk back should Nancy have left it. But I need not have worried about whether I could tote it or not, because it was still not there.

I was glad, though, that it was Nancy who had promised to leave the milk in the branch, because I was frightened to see her husband Luther. Just a month before, he had done something to me in the back of Daddy's pick-up, as we headed home from church, and I could not erase it from my mind. Each time someone in my family mentioned Luther or Nancy, I felt sick.

My family and many of our neighbors had just attended a four-hour church service.

"Arthur!" Luther had yelled across the churchyard as Daddy, Mommy and I were starting to get into the cab of our truck to go home. "How about me and Nancy hitching a ride with you'ns back home? The ride we come with had to go on to Jasper to buy some fertilizer."

"Sure thing," Daddy said.

"Nancy can't ride on the floorboard in the back of a pick-up, is the only thing. The jolting kills her back, and I was thinking this young girl Odean here won't mind lettin' her have her seat in the cab."

Mommy, standing beside Nancy, said, "Oh sure, Odean would love to let Nancy have her seat in the cab. She says she likes to ride in the back anyway, because she likes the wind in her face." Mommy turned to me. "Right, Odean?"

"Sure," I said. I really didn't want to ride back there with Luther, but knowing how my family liked to accommodate neighbors, I wanted to be like them, so I agreed.

I asked Daddy if he would let the hind gate down so that I could swing my feet off toward the ground. I figured that Luther, like most grown-ups, would ride sitting on the floorboard and resting his back against the cab. I was wrong about that, though, because he came and sat beside me with his legs swinging down the same as mine.

Daddy started the motor and we were off. About a mile down the mountain, Luther moved over closer to me and flung his arm around my back.

"Honey, I'm afraid you gonna slide off. I better hold onto your shoulders."

Before I could answer, Luther took his big, dirty right hand and cupped it around my right breast, grasping tightly. I tried to squirm out from under his arm. I was too young to have real breasts yet, and his touch felt the same physically as when he had touched my shoulders, but there did well up within me a nauseating disgust, different from when he had touched my arm and shoulder.

"If your Daddy could see how you were about to get jolted off the truck, he would want me to hold you down."

Since my parents and Nancy were in the cab facing the forward direction, they could not see us in the back without turning square around. The more I squirmed, the tighter his grasp became.

As if an angel was protecting me, a fast moving car came from around the curve and started coming closer and closer. Seeing the car, Luther let go of his grasp and I rushed up to stand against the cab and hold to it, so that if he should touch me again, I could beat on the cab window and get my parents' attention.

I was glad at least, on this hot summer morning, that Luther would most likely not be coming around today. Yet in addition to

118

being extra hungry, I was as tired as the rest of my family, because we had been woken up about nine o'clock the night before, when a noisy car without a muffler had paused near our house without turning off the motor. Our four mutt hounds – Lead, Maude, Jeff and Jethro – had begun a chorus of angry barking, becoming louder and louder as the departing car sped off. That had been unusual, because they were faithful watchdogs, who only barked fiercely when something was going on outside that was not good for our family.

Speaking loudly, perhaps thinking Colleen and I were still asleep, Daddy had said into the darkness, "Some damn son-of-a-bitch has let out a gang a dogs here on us."

Sure enough, in the morning light we had discovered half-grown pups on our property, madly racing from under our house to the barn and back again as they searched for food. Their constant barking disturbed the chickens, roosting in the usually peaceful limbs of the two apple trees in our yard. We felt sorry for the dogs because they were starving, but we had nothing to feed them. We scarcely had enough to feed our own animals, or ourselves.

The practice of dropping off dogs on an unsuspecting neighbor's property was quite a common occurrence in our community, whenever someone had more dogs than they could feed. Dogs were often a problem in our area of Appalachia. There was no such thing as neutering at that time, as far as we knew. When female dogs were in heat, conscientious citizens would lock them up in a stable until about three weeks went by and they were past their breeding time. Dogs would generally roam loose, and during the weeks of a female dog being in heat, male dogs came from miles away to hang around the stable of the female. Clearly such precautions did not always succeed, and people wound up with more pups than they could feed. Rabies was so common in those days that Mommy and Daddy always warned us to steer clear of strange dogs, and Grandma would be constantly warning us to run from any dog we did not know, especially if it was foaming at the mouth. One of Grandma's friends had gone mad from being bitten by a rabid dog.

Luckily, the big pups had not bothered me on my trips to the spring, in search of Nancy's pitcher of milk. On my third trip back from the spring, however, as I reached the top of the hill, still without any milk, Mommy shouted, "Odean, Colleen, come! Help me and your Grandma keep these baby chicks inside the fence, the pups are killing them! Lord help us!"

I could see those new pups shoving their noses in under the wire fence penning in the chicks' small area of the yard. Grandma was on her knees, trying to hold the wire fence to the ground as the pups pawed her, scratching her hands in their effort to get under the fence and grab some more of the fluffy chicks. Her hands were bloody as she held on, while Mommy rushed to pick up more rocks to barricade the fence, and little Gene sat nearby and cried. Quickly Colleen and I joined Mommy and Grandma as we worked together furiously, laying the rocks one on top of another. But unless the rocks were large enough, the desperately hungry dogs would push them aside as they snatched up another chick in their jaws. Working silently and swiftly, choosing the biggest rocks we could, we succeeded in building a wall around the fence that would keep the dogs out.

Now, dripping with sweat, the four of us stood in silent frustration. Mommy picked up Gene, to calm him, and Grandma sighed.

"Those dogs got half of the chicks we were growing to sell Mrs. Leach as fat fryers," Grandma said. "Mamie, we are depending on that money to buy all our supplies for the winter months." She counted off each item on her fingers, "Flour, meal, salt, and coffee."

Mommy's face flinched with pain as she bounced Gene up and down on her hip. She said, "Maybe we will have enough summer months left to hatch and fatten another bunch. We'll get by somehow."

I reached for my Grandma's bloody hands and held them in my own. Those beautiful hands that worked so hard every single day, from the time the sun rose in the sky until well after it set in the evening. Those hands that moved constantly, cutting cornbread or scrubbing pans, mending holes or sweeping floors. I looked up to her face and saw tears of discouragement almost forming in her eyes. My heart broke, knowing I was powerless to help her.

As we shared a sack towel to wipe our faces, our attention turned in the direction of a one-horse wagon lumbering down the hill and stopping in our yard. It was our neighbors, Nancy and Luther, bringing the milk straight to us. Hugging the pitcher, the new pups barking and running in circles around her, Nancy came walking toward the house. Luther stood by the wagon, and I tried not to look at him. I stood close to Mommy and Grandma. Mommy had placed Gene on the grass, where he was sucking on his fingers.

As Mommy reached for the pitcher, she said, "Thank you, Nancy. I was sorry to have to ask for some of your milk, but we haven't had a sip in the house in a week."

I saw Luther approaching where we were standing in the yard. I felt frightened, just being near him. I remembered that when I had told Mommy what Luther had done to me, she had said, "Child, don't ever tell that to your Daddy or he will murder Luther!" Since that day, Mommy and I had kept stone quiet, even with each other, else Daddy might hear about what Luther had done and become a murderer.

Luther was standing next to me now. The deep wrinkles in his face held a perpetual sun-induced smirk, and now he was looking at me, stretching that grin, causing his snuff-dabbed lips to curl up while uncovering more of his rotten snaggle-teeth. Holding an ax in his left hand, he held out his right arm, ready to lay it on my shoulder, hunkering over to reach down to me. I jerked away, but in so doing I tripped on a loose rock that sent me down against Luther's chest. The smell of his sweaty body triggered that frightening memory of the back of Daddy's pick-up. Regaining my balance, I placed myself as close to Mommy as I could.

"I got to thinking that if I brought Nancy over here with the milk," Luther said, "it would be a good chance to get this tough little girl here to turn Arthur's grindstone while I sharpen my dull axes. How about it, hon?"

He looked at me for agreement as he paused to spit, aiming for the red clay dirt at our feet, although most of the spittle just dripped from his lower lip to the bib of his overalls.

I gave him a fleeting glance, not able to speak, but nodding affirmatively, feeling powerless to say anything else. I let my eyes look at the grass a few feet away, and when I looked up, I saw that my Mommy had picked Gene up and walked with him over to the garden, to start hoeing again.

Smiling at me, Luther said, "I seen you turning and turning that grindstone for your Daddy yesterday when I come by from squirrel hunting."

Luther had been caught in an unexpected rain shower the day before, and had gotten dripping wet. He had stopped to talk with Daddy before heading home. Tied to his overalls had been two dead squirrels, hanging by their hind feet as they dripped a mixture of rain and blood from their wet fur. In disgust I had watched the little dripping pools expanding on the ground.

"Dang it, Nancy," Luther said now, "why didn't you holler at me yesterday and tell me to stop letting all them juicy squirrel dumplins slide down my throat? We coulda had some left to bring Arthur and Mamie."

Nancy didn't answer, since she had walked over to the garden where Mommy was hoeing weeds. Grandma and Colleen had gone back to work picking bugs off the bean vines with their right hands and dropping them into the tin cans of kerosene they held in their left. That was the only bug prevention available to us.

I heard Nancy ask my Grandma, "Miss Effie, have you got any of that thar kerosene oil that I could borry?" Sometimes our neighbors gave Grandma's name Ethie this familiar flavor, changing the more formal "th" to "f."

"If you've got a tin can I could pour you some from mine and Colleen's cans."

"Luther has got some tin cans in the bed of the wagon," Nancy said, and as she started walking over to it, a couple of the hungry pups followed at her heels.

"Hey, kid," Luther said to me, "go see if thar is any used water left in the hand wash pan. I could use it to pour under this cement wheel so we can start grinding the axes."

I walked nervously to the hand-washing shelf on the kitchen porch and saw the hand wash pan half full of dirty water. I knew I was supposed to toss the used water on the ground at the roots of the dahlias, but I supposed Mommy wouldn't care if I used the water this morning for Luther's axes, without asking her, so I picked up the basin and turned back in the direction of the grindstone and Luther, the new pups following me and poking my legs with their noses.

Glancing over my shoulder at Mommy as I carefully carried the water, I saw that she had paused a minute from hoeing beans. She was leaning gently on her hoe handle, and she was looking irritated. At first I thought she was annoyed at me for wasting the water she had saved for the flowers she loved so much. Then I realized she might be wishing there was some way she could get Luther gone so that he wouldn't keep me working so hard turning the grindstone in that broiling sun. Or maybe she was thinking about what had happened with Luther. I wondered if she would be able to protect me if something happened again. I decided, though, that Mommy had sufficient cause to look irritated today, considering all the trouble she had had with the dogs getting the baby chicks and Nancy taking so long to bring the milk and now asking to take the last bit of kerosene Mommy had. I felt so sad for her that I wanted to cry, but there was no time for crying.

"Hurry, Odean, time's a wastin'," Luther said as I walked slowly toward the grindstone with the basin of water. He was frowning as he began fiercely flinging his arm in my direction, motioning me to get to work on his axes.

"Coming," I said.

I poured the water into the receptacle so that the cement grindstone could pass through the water as it moved, making the stone wet to better sharpen the ax as I turned the wheel around and around.

"Let's you and me get a move on, kid, and get these axes sharpened, 'cause look at that sun —'fore we know it, its goin' to be gettin' late."

When I didn't say anything, Luther added, "Odean, you ain't much of a talker. Or has the cat got your tongue?" He snickered. "I jes' been lookin' at your little bony arms. Dem bones ain't no bigger than the iron handle of the grindstone, but they're just as powerful!"

124

He snortled out a laugh that sent liquid from both his nose and mouth spraying straight down into my upturned face. With my right hand still keeping my momentum, turning the wheel, I reached my nose with my left hand to wipe his spit off the end of it, but my nose was so wet from sweat, I only managed to make a bigger and more watery wad of his chewing tobacco go deeper into my nostrils.

Daddy was now approaching us with Jean, his mule, pulling a sled with a plow on top of it. They were on their way to a field. He stopped Jean and tied the rein to a limb of the pussy willow tree.

"Hu'lo Luther."

To which Luther responded, "Howdy."

Noticing me turning the grindstone, Daddy asked Luther, "Where's Robert? He usually comes with you to turn the stone." Robert was Luther's son.

"You know ole man Mulkey sold his timber. So when the sawmill owner moved his machine and crew to the property, he hired Robert to be 'slab toter.'" A slab toter carried away the less desirable early cuts of wood near the bark.

"That's good Robert got a job," Daddy said.

"He's goin' on fourteen years, it's time he quit school and started working. He finished seventh grade this past spring and that's enough schooling for anybody. I say any more education than that ruins a young person. It makes them uppity."

Another nasty spit came out as Luther threw his head back in a self-satisfied way, as if he thought he had done a good job educating Robert.

Daddy started to reach for Jean's rein. I panicked because I realized that as soon as Daddy left I would have to be alone with Luther again.

I bolted into the house and hid behind the tall headboard of my bed. Immediately, Daddy came after me and shoved the door open, stomping his feet on the floor as he rushed in. I knew he was really mad as he stood towering over me.

"What's the meaning of this, Odean?" he said loudly.

"I don't want to sharpen Luther's axes," I said, starting to cry.

Looking into Daddy's red, angry face, I became very frightened. I had never seen him look like that before, and I never would again, during all the years thereafter.

"Look here, young lady. Get yourself out there NOW, and help our neighbor. You have been raised to help a neighbor in any way you can, like you see all the rest of the family doing, the same as you see the neighbors helping us. Get yourself back to helping Luther. Get into your head right now, this lesson that I am trying to teach you: no one in this family is going to get above their raisin'."

I couldn't think what to say. I thought Daddy would remember his kindness and his care for me, but instead he raised his voice even louder.

"All your life you have gone around pretending you was some fancy person pictured on the walls. I let you get by with it, but now that babyish dreaming is over. You are big enough to help out and I aim to see that you have learned this lesson I am teaching you right now! If I ever see you treat a neighbor or anybody like that again, I will pull that bee bush up by its roots and wear it out on your butt. You hear me?"

Now I felt scared for my life, because I thought Daddy had gone crazy. He had never beat on us with tree limbs, the way some other parents in the area whipped their children, but I feared he might do that now. I followed him out and with trembling hands I started turning the wheel as Luther moved in near me and placed his ax on the moving stone wheel.

Daddy untied Jean's reins and looked over at me for a moment, with a sad expression on his face. Then he and the mule turned to follow the well-worn trail on their way to the field on the other side of the mountain.

After one of Luther's axes was sharp, he leaned it up against the oak tree, and handed me the other one.

Thinking back on that horrible day when Luther had touched me in the truck made me shake harder and harder now, as I turned the wheel. Suddenly I heard Mommy call out, "Look, Odean, Luther, the dogs have tore down the fence again!"

I quickly looked at the big head of a greedy pup, who had a crying baby chick clamped between its teeth. Watching that dog destroy my Grandma's hard work made something snap in me. I *was* going to stop that dog. I would protect my Grandma. I would protect my family, and somehow I would protect myself. I did the only thing in my power to do. I grabbed the newly sharpened ax Luther had leaned against the oak tree, and with a flash of uncontrolled speed, I lifted it and brought it straight down through the head of that dog, slicing it in the center. The brains and blood spilled out on the ground as the dog's rigid stance gave way and it crumbled to the ground. Another dog lunged to snatch the chick from the fallen dog's mouth.

"God damn it, child! I ain't never seen nothin' like that!" Luther shouted, as he reached to retrieve the ax from my limp hand.

Mommy, Grandma, and Colleen rushed to gather around. They stared me as if they were in shock.

"Oh, Lord, child. What's happened to you?" Grandma said.

Mommy spoke just above a whisper. "Why did you do that?"

"I could not murder an animal like that," Colleen said smugly.

I broke into a run straight up the playhouse hill. Once on top of the hill, I lay in the pine needles feeling myself in such a rage inside that I cried like I had never cried before.

After I had spent all my tears, I saw Grandma, tired and slow, coming toward me with shoulders stooped. She placed her arm around me and said, "Come, let's go back to the house now."

We slowly walked back to the house. Luther and Nancy were gone. Mommy was not there; maybe she had taken the dead dog away. Colleen was quietly working, making a stronger fence around the baby chicks, as Gene slept on a big cloth nearby.

Daddy had that same sad expression on his face as he'd had earlier, when he and the mule had left for the field. I remembered what I had heard him say so often: "I could never kill an animal except for food for my family."

I felt like an outcast, not good enough to live with my family. I wished I could die or run away.

Later that night, lying on my stomach in bed between Colleen, who was now fast asleep, and Grandma, I gingerly let my arm encircle Grandma's neck. She rolled toward me, her warm breath gently rustling the hair on top of my head. As always, she tenderly comforted me. She was the only one, I felt, who accepted, understood, and loved me despite my transgressions.

128

She softly patted my shoulder before moving her tired arm to her other side, as she whispered, "We better go to sleep now, so we won't be too tired tomorrow. Remember, we have some milk now, and I'll make you a good breakfast in the morning."

I lay awake a while in the darkness, feeling better, but still worried about what the preachers spoke of as the "big Gray-haired Man" in heaven who sits in judgment of us. I was wondering what that heavenly judge thought of me now.

My family moved on past that devastating day, and my relationship with my Daddy went back to normal. I was again his Cotton Top, and a good helper. Soon our cows gave birth and started to have milk again, and we saved the rest of the chicks for fat fryers we sold to Mrs. Leach.

As I grew a little older, I realized that Daddy had not intended to frighten me when he shouted at me to help Luther; he had just been trying to teach me an important lesson about neighborliness. I came to realize too that if Daddy had known about Luther's behavior, he would have understood. Mommy and I never did tell him, though.

Forty-five years later, the day Mommy passed on, Daddy and I were sitting beside her hospital bed, listening for any words that she might speak, and watching for any expression on her pale face or movement of her still body, when suddenly she became rigid with contortions. Her voice, which had been silent for days, screamed loud and clear, "Luther, Luther, go away! Go away!"

Chapter 12

Reading *Gone with the Wind* to Mommy

The spring and summer when I was twelve years old, going on thirteen, stand out in my memory because they contained the unfolding of a happy time with my mother, a time like none I had ever had with her.

In the late spring of 1940, my teacher Mr. Shepard came over to my desk and said, "Odean, over the past year I have observed how much you love to read, so I have been thinking that you might like to borrow my copy of *Gone with the Wind* for the summer."

The movie of *Gone with the Wind* had been Atlanta's first big premiere, winning much show business coverage the winter before. I had been keenly interested in the newspaper articles about this premiere, filling the pages of the newspapers Mrs. Leach had given us, and I had heard people talking about the book, which had become a bestseller as soon as it was published.

As I quickly followed him toward his desk, my skinny body bumped into a couple of other students' chairs.

I said, "Oh, Mr. Shepard, I would be so thrilled to have that book for the summer."

He smiled with the tender expression he brought to class every day. "Here it is," he said, holding a hardback book as big and important-looking as the black Bible that sat on top of Grandma's sewing machine. I had not read from our Bible, however. My Mommy and Daddy only opened it on rare occasions, to record important dates on the white inside cover, such as family births, marriages, and deaths.

I was delighted beyond words when Mr. Shepard handed me *Gone with the Wind*. Looking at the title page, I was even more delighted to realize that the author Margaret Mitchell, who lived right in Atlanta, had autographed the book for him. It was the first time I had ever seen an autographed book.

Sitting at my desk again, I moved into a familiar dream state, in which I envisioned myself as a famous writer. I began to see a line of people holding my own book, waiting for my signature. Most likely my book wouldn't have a thousand pages, like Margaret Mitchell's. But it didn't have to be that long, I figured.

At that moment the school bell rang, signaling the closing of the school day. The Principal would tug on the rope that attached to an actual bell high up in the loft above the ceiling. My classmates speedily rushed out of the classroom.

I thanked Mr. Shepard again and ran to our old school bus, hugging *Gone with the Wind* to my chest. I squeezed into a spot between two neighbor girls, on one of the three benches Hoover Kincaid, our bus driver, had installed when he built the bus. The canvas sides were rolled up part way, because it was a clear, sunny day, and I felt that I was in heaven as I held the book on my lap. As the bus reached our narrow dirt road – more like a wide pathway – I stood up ahead of time, ready to dash out. Once I jumped to the ground, followed by Colleen, I practically danced the quarter mile distance up and down the hill to our house.

Grandma greeted me with her sweet smile, as I handed the book to her.

She said, "I do declare that is the biggest book I have ever seen. It must have in it every word in the English language."

"I know, and I am going to read every one of them this summer. Where's Mommy?"

"They're planting corn in the Long Patch," she said. "I've just made some half-moon pies. Do you want one?" Half-moon pies were small pastries you could hold in your hand, made of biscuit dough folded and crimped with a fork around delicious and fragrant sliced apples.

"Sure, I do. Thank you, Grandma."

I grabbed a warm pie and raced off to show my new book treasure to Mommy. I ran nearly all the way to the Long Patch, through the pasture and past the apple tree where our cows Cream and Dolly were resting in the shade.

My heart overflowed with love when I saw Mommy in her old shoddy shoes, as she trudged along the furrow carefully dropping grains of corn into the furrow's center. Daddy was guiding Jean the mule along another row, as Jean slowly drew a double-foot plow, which pulled the soft soil down from the sides of each furrow to cover the corn seed.

As soon as I showed Mommy Mr. Shepard's copy of *Gone With the Wind*, she was delighted with my good luck.

She reached for it, but then quickly drew back her hand, saying, "Oh no, I won't touch it with these old dirty, rough hands."

I could not wait to share the book with her.

I had loved words before I even understood what they were. Our house had always been filled with them, to my delight, because they covered the newspapers pasted on the walls to keep out the cold wind.

I had not had access to many books before I started school. My family owned three books. In addition to our Bible, we owned a book my Daddy called "A Fifth Grade History of the United States." Occasionally, when he had time, he allowed me to look at this book while he kept a watchful eye on my impatient little fingers as I rushed to see more pictures and begged him to read about them. Having not had much schooling, he was limited in supplying me words to go with the pictures.

My Grandma owned a "Blue Back Speller," which I had not been permitted to touch at all when I was little. With great fascination, however, I had listened as she spelled the words out slowly by syllables and proudly exhibited her ability to pronounce them. In fact, she liked to pronounce that big word "syllabification," and carefully taught it to me. I think it might have been the only grand-sounding word that she knew. As a child, I was a bit sad that I never could find a chance to use that word.

My favorite few minutes of each day, though, had been spent with my beloved companion, the wallpaper. I was so grateful to Mrs. Leach for giving us the newspapers for our walls. Grandma told my parents how often I would touch the pictures and print, and gaze at them as if they held the secret to the world. Even before I could read, I knew that a wealth of information lay in these magical papers, if only I could find the key.

Apparently I asked my Grandma hundreds of times, "What does the black marks say?"

Grandma would say, "That child ain't gonna have no eyes when she grows up, she's making herself blind."

Sometimes I was lucky enough to have a family member read to me. As I listened, the wall would simply cease to be there. I was often told, later, that as I got a faraway look in my eyes, my Mommy or Grandma would be able to tiptoe out of the room and go back to their chores, leaving me wrapped up in whatever story they had read. No walls could hold my boundless spirit as I metamorphosed into fabulous characters living in grand places. Often I talked to Shirley Temple or Little Orphan Annie, from the "funny papers," who were on the walls closest to the bed I shared with Colleen and Grandma. I asked them about their lives, and it didn't bother me that they couldn't answer me, although it must have been a problem for Colleen, who would disturb me by yelling, "Mommy, come here and make Odean stop talking to the pictures!"

Mommy would then give me a chore to do. Often she would send me crawling under the floor to the nest where one of the hens laid an egg each day. Collecting the eggs under the floor was my job, because I was the only member of the family at that point small enough to reach into such a cramped space.

Each morning, though, I liked to stay cozy in bed, and as soon as Colleen got up, I would roll over to her warm space near the wall to talk with all the characters closest to the pillow. Then I would stand on the bed to communicate with Amelia Earhart, and fantasize about flying in that plane with her. As I grew a little older, I felt confident enough to imagine myself speaking with as much authority as Eleanor Roosevelt. I had little knowledge of what she was speaking about when I looked at her photographs. I just knew that she was an important person, and pretending to be her made me feel important too.

One day I was disappointed to awaken and find that Mommy had replaced the pictures of Little Orphan Annie and Shirley Temple with Dick Tracy.

She responded to my yelling disapproval, explaining, "Shirley and Annie have become smudged and dirty from your hands, Odean, and also from your constant breathing and spewing bits of spit as you talked to them through their pictures."

Once I was in school, my teachers started to let me borrow books to bring home. I would read those books from cover to cover many times before returning them, and I read entire books to my family.

Even my chores couldn't stand in the way of my reading. During summers when the well dried up, and we had to fetch our drinking water from the spring, I pleaded or bargained to be the one to walk along the trail to get the water. Carefully, I would place a book in the empty bucket when no one was looking, and I would read as I walked the half-mile to the spring. Sometimes I stopped to read more comfortably, sitting on the protruding root of the big oak that stood beside the pathway. Often I tarried so long on those trips that my mother felt it necessary to take Colleen from her chores and have her come look for me.

During my fourth grade year, as Mommy did her daily chores, I read to her from the stack of newspapers Mrs. Leach had given us. During the winter the newspapers lay stacked in the corner of our front room (named the front room because it faced the road by our house). Grandma gave strict orders that no one should use the papers for kindling fires, because she and Mommy were trying to find time to paper over the faded newspapers on the walls. She looked at me indulgently and teased me.

"Odean," she said, "I know *you* won't burn the papers. In fact, if the house got caught on fire I'd bet you would grab them papers before you helped your Grandma get out of the burning house."

"No Grandma, I would lead you out with my other hand," I said.

I think Mommy's intense interest in my reading came out of the fact that she struggled to read, and her ancestors could not read at all. Few occasions arose in our daily life when anyone needed to read, and most parents felt that "book learning" didn't teach their children what was really necessary in life: to work hard and survive. Sitting down with a book was often considered to be a lazy way to get out of work. But my Mommy, Daddy, and Grandma had a strong drive to make sure we could read well.

They believed in the value of knowledge. Mommy especially took great pride in keeping Colleen and me in comparatively regular attendance at school, as we got older, while most of the neighbor children dropped out as soon as they reached the age of ten or twelve and became strong enough to do manual labor.

On the day I brought *Gone with the Wind* home from Mr. Shepard's classroom, I showed Mommy some of the pages, as we stood on the edge of the Long Patch, and she and I started to talk about how we would find time to read it.

Daddy continued to plow awhile. Soon he and the mule approached from the other end of the field and caught up with the row of seeds Mommy had just planted. Daddy leaned on the plow and looked inquisitively at the big book. He smiled when I told him I was going to read every word of the book aloud to Mommy that summer.

I added, "Maybe it will rain and rain all summer so that we can stay in the house and read."

I looked up into Daddy's face with a big grin, so he would know I was teasing.

He smiled back and said, "Now I'm getting worried that the Good Lord will hear and answer your sweet little prayer and give us a rainy summer, while He pays no attention to my demands for lots of sunshiny days so I can make a good crop this year."

Mommy, ignoring our banter, continued to spell out her plan for finding good blocks of time to read.

"I believe we can get lots of hours of reading on wash days, Odean. You could sit on the battling bench and read while I wash the clothes."

The battling bench was a tree stump where we placed especially dirty clothes, which had been soaked first in homemade lye soap to loosen the ground-in dirt. Once the wet clothes lay on the stump, we took a large paddle and pounded on them. After the pounding, we washed the clothes in washtubs sitting on other blocks of wood, before carrying them to the stream. The rinse tub sat at a special spot right in the stream, and just below higher rocks, so that a downward rushing flow of water could rinse the clothes naturally.

The battling bench was the remains of a huge oak that Great-Grandpa Lawing and Daddy had sawed with the crosscut saw. I had a memory of seeing them saw it as they laughed together. That had been perhaps some months before Great-Grandpa Lawing had died. I had watched them carefully measure the large block of the tree to a table-top height so that Mommy could be comfortable when she would stand to do her washing.

Mommy said now, "Arthur, I've been thinking we should help your mother with her wash, since she's so sick. You could ride Jean over the mountain and bring back a bag of your mother's dirty clothes, and then take the clean laundry back the next morning before going to the field. Your mother would love having more time with you."

Daddy agreed that would be a good idea, as he started Jean moving the two-foot plow again.

Mommy, realizing that she needed to keep ahead of Daddy and the covering plow, started walking up the field, dropping grains into the next furrow. If a grain happened to land on the side of the furrow, she took her right foot and with the toe of her shoe, which had a huge hole in it, she flipped the grain into the furrow without missing her tempo of drop, drop, drop. She and I talked as I kept step with her, still holding the big book close to my chest.

"That will be two full days a week of doing the washing," Mommy said, "which means that for the next six weeks until school is out for the summer, you would have to miss school one day a week to help me. The other washing day we could keep on Saturdays, the same day as we have been doing it."

She carefully guarded her words, since she did not want to promise me more leisure to read than I would actually have.

"Oh, that'll be fine with Mr. Shepard," I said, "because I've been making good grades all year. All the teachers know that most of us have to miss a lot of days in springtime, when it's planting time."

The next day after school, Mommy and Grandma placed me among the newspapers spread out on the floor. For several years now, knowing how much I loved to read the walls, they had let me select the pictures and news stories I liked best. Once I had chosen the pages, we could paper the walls freshly.

Of course, on that spring day I especially chose the pages featuring news about Clark Gable and Vivian Leigh, stars of *Gone with the Wind*, taken when they had been in Atlanta for the premiere of the movie at Loew's Grand Theatre in December of 1939. I especially liked the copies of *The Atlanta Journal* and *The Atlanta Constitution,* because they had large pictures and dozens of current events stories.

These newspapers given to us by Mrs. Leach, together with a large battery-operated radio Daddy had acquired during the previous year by trading a gallon of corn liquor to a man in Atlanta, gave us access to the outside world. I realized, as I chose the newspaper pages, that I was learning so many new things about people, historical figures, and the world outside our valley that I no longer fit in. I wanted to know more about how other people lived, who didn't have to work so hard to scratch out a living as my parents and our neighbors did.

While I selected the sheets of newspaper, I stared at Mr. Shepard's book, which I had placed on the sewing machine table, near the dust-covered Bible. I was eager to get to reading it to Mommy. Proudly, I kept thinking that no one in my class had ever read a nearly one-thousand-page book.

During the following two months, Mommy and I had two wash days a week. Before Mommy and I could start our scrubbing and reading each of those days, I had to start a fire to heat the water. I searched for kindling and dragged fallen limbs and resin-rich pine knots from decaying pines, and soon had the big black pot boiling in its spot outdoors near the stream. Then I would take a bucket and dip it into the pot, so that I could fill the washtubs with the hot water. It had been only about a year since Mommy and Grandma had decided that I was big enough to handle the dipping of the bucket into boiling water, as Colleen had been doing for several years. It felt good to be so grownup.

I would sit then with my book on the large block of the battling bench, where Mommy's washtub also sat. As she listened, she would constantly press and move her hands among the folds of the soaking dirty clothes. We did not own a washboard like the ones the slaves used in doing the laundry of Scarlett's family. Reading the description of how helpful the tin washboards were, I wished Mommy had one to help her get out the dirt.

As Mommy did the laundry, passing neighbors often stopped and talked "for a spell," temporarily interrupting the flow of our reading and scrubbing. Some neighbors appeared to be a little surprised and curious about how we were teamed-up to wash and read together. Most children at my age of twelve stood side by side with their mothers as they scrubbed the wash together. My Mommy enjoyed our approach, though, often saying, "Odean, we are a good scrubbing and reading team."

One older neighbor commented to Mommy about how her wash-stump table was "holding up."

He said, "I remember helping your Grandpa and Arthur roll that big block of oak across from the other side of the road from where they had sawed it."

Mommy lifted her hands from the tub, shook the water off and reached to push her long braided light brown hair back. She looked as if she might cry.

"Phillip, that wash stump was the last thing Grandpa helped make for me before he died, and that was years ago," she said. "I still miss him."

Phillip had been a close friend of Great-Grandpa. For a moment I saw tears come to his eyes as well.

"Mamie, I remember how close your family were. Over the years, as I often passed here, I always saw them speaking kindly to each other and laughing together."

"I appreciate you speaking that way about my Grandpa, Phillip, because Odean here cannot remember him too well."

Phillip looked at me, then patted my shoulder and said, "Young lady, you can always be proud of your Great-Grandpa. His father and my father's father were friends dating back to the Trail of Tears, when the Government passed laws for the Indians to live in reservations. Our families were close neighbors and friends even then, and that was before the Civil War. In that war Mamie's Grandfather fought on the side of the Confederacy, while my Grandpa fought on the Union side. After the war, I never heard of them ever mentioning any differences of opinions about that war."

As if realizing that they had gotten way too serious, Mommy began to scrub more briskly. Phillip immediately slapped his right hand to his face where that tear kept standing in the corner of his eye.

Then as he wiped his tear-wet fingers on the sides of his overalls, he looked up again at Mommy and changed the subject by asking, "Is Arthur getting his early crops in the ground in this nice dry weather?"

It was a serene springtime that year, with few ravaging winds or boisterous thunderstorms. March flowers, violets, and wildflowers were profuse in the mild and sunny weather. I was so happy reading, and I frequently glanced at Mommy's smiling face as she listened to descriptions of the opulent life style of Scarlett and other characters who had lived so close by, just two counties to the southeast of where we lived, yet in a totally different world from Mommy's people, who had shared that time in history. I am sure that, to her, the greatest fascination with the book was how close geographically her family had been to Scarlett's, and yet how different their lives had been. If possible, she was enjoying hearing me read more than I was thrilled to be reading.

To Mommy and me, *Gone with the Wind* was of even keener interest than most books, because it was "no made-up story." She knew this to be a fact, because her Great-Grandfather had been right there fighting on the same side of the Civil War with Scarlett and her family. During the months of hoopla in the Atlanta newspapers about the movie premiere and the book, the word "fiction" had not stuck into our heads.

Often Mommy would make such a comment as, "I have never been to Forsythe County where Scarlett and her family lived, but I did hear tell that there are huge farms over there. I never heard, though, that the people was so rich."

Thinking about the situation of slavery on plantations like Tara, Mommy would say, "My Grandpa never knew he was fighting to keep people in slavery. I bet a lot of people were like him and didn't know what the war was about. Maybe since they couldn't read, they were just following what they had heard." As she patted my shoulder, she would add, "I am so thankful that my children can read."

Once in a while she would interrupt the story by saying something like, "I wish my Great-Grandpa and Great-Grandma could hear you read this book."

In the middle of the summer, Mommy announced surprising news during supper one night.

"Children, I want to tell you something," she said to the three of us. "You are going to have a little brother or sister in four months. That's why I have been getting fat."

Gene, who was three years old then, looked fairly nonchalant as he ate his beans, but I was startled. I hadn't noticed any change in Mommy during our weeks of reading *Gone with the Wind.*

Colleen, though, piped up. "I have been knowing about it a long time."

Some hours later, our excitement about the new baby was put on hold. That night, Mommy commenced screaming, crying out that she had pain in her jaw and on the side of her head. We all dashed about trying to help her, but we could do very little.

By the following morning, Mommy claimed to feel much better, and our household appeared to return to normal.

About a week later, Mommy and I reached page two hundred and twenty-six, the end of Part Two. As I started to place the piece of newspaper – our bookmark – between the pages, Mommy raised her hand, dripping with water.

Pointing to the book, she said, "Honey, just read the first sentence or two so that we know how Part Three begins."

I held the bookmark between my fingers as I read the first sentence.

"'*May of 1864 came – A hot dry May that wilted the flowers in the buds – and the Yankees under General Sherman were in Georgia again, above Dalton, one hundred miles northwest of Atlanta. . . .*'"

Daddy was nearing the wash place with Jean, on their way to another garden patch. The mule was pulling the slide (a large wooden sled), which was hauling a plow.

When he stopped to let Jean drink from the stream, Mommy called, "Arthur, how far are we from Dalton?"

"It's just on the other side of Chatsworth Mountain, probably about fifty miles from here," he called back to us as he moved on. He was grinning, like he was happy to furnish us that bit of information.

I placed our bookmark at Chapter 17 and closed the book, with no idea that I would not open it again for over a month. That night Mommy was stricken with horrible pain in her ear and her whole head. We discovered then that her jaw and her head had continued to hurt all week, but, as was her habit, she had hardly spoken of her difficulty. She had spent a lifetime ignoring pain, believing that if she gave it no thought, it would go away.

A month of sadness and helplessness paralyzed us that summer, as Mommy suffered. We knew we did not have a penny to pay the doctor.

Mommy prayed aloud many times a day, "Jesus, Jesus, please give me just one hour of peace so that I can talk to my children and then please take me out of this awful pain."

I remember days when I ran through the trees crying and cursing God. When Grandma saw me running wildly and lashing the trees with my fists, she would chase me down and hug me saying, "Honey, please don't cuss God."

At the end of what seemed an eternity, and with the encouragement of Grandma and the neighbors who sat up with us many nights, Daddy finally realized that it was necessary for Mommy to see the doctor. Her pain had only increased, and she could not endure the misery any longer. Taking the chance that the doctor would see her, in spite of the debt my family already owed him, Daddy and Grandma made her as comfortable as possible in the cab of the old pick-up truck and took her to town.

The doctor did kindly take her in without payment, and after examining her told us that she had a severe case of mastoiditis, an infection of the mastoid bone, which had started as an ear infection. He gave her strong medicine for the infection and the pain so that she could sleep, and over a period of several weeks she did get well again.

Mommy's face began to have color again, and she started to smile more often. Her pregnancy seemed to be going well, and she enjoyed every day she spent with her family. We responded to her love and joy in full measure.

On my thirteenth birthday in August, Mr. Shepard came by and told us we could keep his book for one more year. I was supremely happy to have more months to finish the story. Since Mommy's illness, I had helped more with the scrubbing and read fewer pages.

Much as she was glad to be with all of us again, I was quite sure in the following weeks, before the baby came, that her happiest hours were those spent listening to *Gone with the Wind*. Since she had never quite understood me and could not communicate with me in the same way she could with Colleen, I remember those reading hours as some of my dearest times with her.

Unfortunately, Baby James came early and only lived one short day. He was buried in a small coffin in the cemetery near Ellijay, where my family still goes each August to lay flowers on his grave.

When, after many months, we finished the last page, I reached to hug Mommy. We held each other in a long embrace and cried together a few minutes. I felt, within my heart, that I would never read the book again or see the movie. I wanted to carry with me forevermore the image of Mommy bending over the tub, listening as I read. I wanted to remember the echo of the bird songs and the smell of gentle smoke escaping from the fire underneath the black pot. I wanted to keep always imprinted in my mind and heart the sound of the stream as it gently troubled the water in the rinse tub so as to loosen the dirt and send it further downstream with the lye soapsuds. At that time, I felt I must always cherish the memory of *Gone with the Wind* in just that way.

In the late 1950's, however, I did finally watch the movie, when my husband Jerry and I joined friends in their plush apartment at the Ritz Carlton for a private showing. I enjoyed the movie thoroughly, yet I felt no more comfortable settled in a velvet-cushioned chair than I had felt sitting on that battling stump and reading while Mommy washed the dirty clothes. Mommy and I often spoke about the joy of that special time, when the story of Scarlett O'Hara and Rhett Butler mingled with the light sifting through the trees as we scrubbed and read together.

Chapter 13

The Great Change

One wintry, rainy Monday morning, about a year later – on December 8th, 1941 – Colleen and I waited as usual for Hoover Kincaid's old school bus, in the small abandoned house that served as our bus shed. Its chimney had finally given up on the effort to stand taller than the roof, and had let its rocks sink and fall away, until the chimney stood at only half the house's height. A walnut tree dropped walnuts onto the sunken, rusty tin roof. I always had goose bumps in that ruined house, because of all the stories I'd heard about ghosts, especially from the neighbor girl Lurlene, who loved to tell her grandmother's old tales.

An especially sharp bang on the roof, as keen as a rifle shot, caused me almost to jump free of my chill-bumped skin. Colleen reached over and hugged me as a grown-up might. That tender warm hug was comforting, since it didn't contain any of her usual cautioning grown-up attitude.

"Lurlene says this house is hainted," I said. No one ever used the word "haunted" around there. "She says people passing this house after dark have seen white sheets covered with blood, going across the road right here."

"Oh, that bang was only a walnut falling off the tree from way up high," Colleen said.

"Lurlene says the haints started living here the night Willis Kennemur shot the head off of Grandma's brother Arthur, because this is where Willis lived."

Colleen just shrugged and tossed her head. "Everybody around here knows this old house has ghosts living in it, but I'm not afraid and you shouldn't be either." Colleen said this with just a touch of her "know-it-all" tone.

When we had been very young, Lurlene had felt important telling that story loud and clear, about the ghosts in Willis Kennemur's house, but as we grew older, her tone of voice had become softer and more sympathetic. I sensed that she had learned to appreciate my Grandma even more, and to feel more deeply "Miss Effie's" loss of her brother Arthur.

Not wanting to think another troubling thought about the old house, I changed the subject.

"I really liked that tenderloin we had with Grandma's biscuits this morning, didn't you?"

"Yeah, it's been good since hog-killing day last month, but Grandma said we've cooked almost all of it, so we'll be starting on the shoulder, and that meat is much fatter and tougher."

"I like the shoulder meat, too."

Colleen was silent a few seconds as if she were thinking. Then she said, with a smile, "Like Daddy always says, you are just like Mommy, always looking on the bright side of things. I'm like Daddy, I look at what needs to be done and fix it."

As the bus came in sight around the curve, we rushed out of the little house. The rain was now beginning to pour down, and I could see Hoover Kincaid biting his lower lip and fast turning the steering wheel as he worked to keep the bus from skidding into the ditch. Just before he got it stopped to let us enter through the rear door, its right wheels spewed cold, squishy mud right in front of us, and one big blob landed squarely on my nose. With frozen red fingers, I pushed my right hand inside my coat pocket, pulled out a piece of thin, white cloth, and wiped my nose as I moved toward the door. Grandma had slipped that piece of cloth into my hand. As was still her custom each morning as we started for school,

Grandma had chosen clean cloths from her rag bag to give to Colleen and me. The size of the cloth she gave to each of us depended on the amount of coughing, sneezing or sniffling she had heard the previous night.

"Colleen, I'm going to the outhouse to try and clean some mud from my shoes before I come on inside."

I went on down to the school outhouse to clean my shoes with pages from the Sears and Roebuck catalog that were used for toilet paper. Soon I went up the hill and around the school building, hoping to enter the auditorium from the outside. To my surprise, I realized that the auditorium had become crowded. It was filling up quickly, with teachers leading students to chairs in rows. As I came inside, I saw Colleen sitting down with our class. I started to walk toward her through the cold room.

As I came down the aisle, I paused beside a friend.

"Bonnie, why is everyone in the auditorium? It's not Friday," I whispered to her.

She whispered back, "I don't know. Our teacher Miss Martin and the other teachers were very quiet and I saw them talking to each other. She only told us that Mr. Worley had an announcement."

After The Lord's Prayer and The Pledge of Allegiance, the principal, Mr. Worley, slowly walked to the podium. He was a stern man who wore thick gold-rimmed glasses, which he kept pushing back up his nose. His upper back was formed in a large hump, accentuated by his forward-bending shoulders, and all of us prepared ourselves to hear his deep voice ring out, as always, like the "voice of doom."

That morning, in fact, I thought his words had an even more ominous sound than usual as they hung in space a few seconds in the high-ceilinged room before falling down to our ears.

By now we were feeling a little warmer, as the comforting smell and heat of oak logs burning in the heater had started to spread over the big room. Mr. Worley's simple words painted a picture of what might happen because of the events of the day before: December 7, 1941.

He began, "Yesterday, President Roosevelt declared war between the United States of America and Japan, a country across the waters that is ruled by a terrible dictator."

For a considerable length of time, he continued speaking in this childlike vocabulary in an effort to help us understand the gravity of the situation. With rapt attention, every student was seriously trying to understand, but we just could not clearly comprehend the facts inside Mr. Worley's strange speech. The immediate reality for most of the children was the hunger in their bellies and the drone of a faraway airplane that occasionally soared in the sky. War seemed as distant to us as God and the devil.

As we discovered, it had been just the day before, when it had been announced on radio that the United States had declared war in response to the bombing of Pearl Harbor. People in Ellijay, many miles of dirt road from us, had heard this fact on the radio, and news had spread quickly through the other towns and villages. My family, like a few others in our rural section of the county, owned battery-operated radios, but since the batteries had a short life, they were used sparingly. December 7th having been a Sunday, no one had had their radios turned on, because it was expected that we go to church, pay a visit to an ailing neighbor, or both. So families in our remote area had heard no news of the momentous event until Monday morning in school, and then it was the children who heard it first. Because we were so young, we didn't understand what this news would mean to our parents.

When the school bus brought us home in the late afternoon, we rushed to tell Mommy, Daddy and Grandma about the War.

They immediately pulled the straight cane-bottomed chairs to circle the fireplace. Daddy took a fresh log from the wood box to the left of the fireplace, and pitched it on the simmering coals. On cold winter evenings my family always started up a bigger fire to warm the house as soon as the school bus brought Colleen and me home, but usually everyone continued with their chores, inside and outside, until supper. On that day, however, the chores could wait. Gene climbed into Grandma's lap, his eyes open wide as he sensed how momentous this evening gathering was.

The rushing red, orange and greenish flames fiercely devoured the bark on the logs as Mommy, Daddy, and Grandma chimed in and at times interrupted each other as they urgently asked Colleen and me for more information.

After we had told them all we knew, Daddy slowly said, "I was one year too young to go to the First World War. In this one, they will most likely take me."

With that remark, the seriousness of the situation instantly became clearer to me. The thought of my own Daddy having to be gone from us for a long time, fighting and maybe killing people in a war and possibly getting killed himself, was incomprehensible to me. What I did understand was this: without Daddy we would lose our farm.

Usually each night, snuggled next to Grandma's plump, warm body, I fell asleep as soon as my head touched the pillow, but that night it was a long time before the fearful thoughts crawled from my mind. Colleen had gone to a neighbor's house for the night, so she was spared all the war talk that continued in our house even once we had all gone to bed. No one in our neighborhood ever thought of sparing the children worrisome subjects of conversation. Sex was the only subject that never entered the discussion, within groups of grownups and children.

Any news of who might be pregnant or any details about the process of the birthing of a baby were also kept very hush-hush.

As our family's bed-to-bed conversation started to ebb away, Grandma became restless and kept turning in bed. Finally, she spoke tearfully, as if to herself.

"In the war that commenced in 1917, a young neighbor man got shot in the head and it made him shell-shocked and kind of crazy for the rest of his life. His condition brought back memories of how my brother Arthur got shot in the head and died. I wonder how the good Lord can let such things happen to the young."

"Ethie, don't talk like that! It's a sin to question God's work," Daddy said sternly from his and Mommy's bed in the darkness.

"I know," said Grandma. She seemed startled, as if she had lost control of her thoughts and they had come out as words.

Now, additional awful feelings began to make me shake. I was so afraid for Grandma because Daddy had said she had sinned, and I knew the preachers said God caused bad things to happen to us if we sinned. I felt myself becoming angry at God, and mad at all the people who had ever hurt Grandma and made her cry.

I reached and hugged her and she hugged me back as she whispered in my ear, "Let's be still and try to get some sleep."

In an effort to help me go to sleep, Grandma became motionless, and I couldn't hear or feel her breathing. Now I feared she might have become so upset thinking all those sad thoughts that she had had a heart attack and died. Gently, I placed my hand just over her mouth and was happy to feel her warm breath touch my fingers.

Soon weariness overcame me and I dozed off, only to be awakened after a horrible nightmare brought images of forms wearing bloody sheets swarming over our bed, just like the ghosts at Willis Kennemur's abandoned house. For quite some time, I tried to calm myself by listening to Grandma's peaceful breathing. Slowly I thrilled with the sweet feeling that Daddy, Mommy and little Gene were safe, and Colleen was safe with a neighbor. I knew that, as I lay in bed, walnuts were hitting the tin roof of that little ruined house at our bus stop, but the fear I had felt in the morning was now far, far away.

As I cuddled closer to Grandma, I fully realized that life should be gratefully cherished in each moment when it is happening, because I knew that Great Uncle Arthur had also once breathed warm breaths inside these walls.

That glimpse of wisdom has not always held its brilliance, but I have remained grateful whenever I am able to leave the world of outside confusion and quietly realize the profound truth I felt that night long ago.

The declaration of War marked the beginning of great change not only for our family but also for our community. For better and sometimes worse, our lives, along with millions of others', took on a different form of existence and perspective. Listening to my family and the neighbors talk, I gathered that the close-knit ties they had for so long cherished were quickly to be torn asunder. Many boys and young men would be drafted and sent to foreign countries, where they would be exposed to the larger world, which most of them had not even known existed. Sadly, many would never come home again. It was a turbulent upheaval to a little mountain community, which had existed relatively unchanged for more than a century, almost like a lost tribe cut off from mainstream life. Never would it be the same again.

In the months and years that followed, my family had dozens of conversations with people in our neighborhood about particular neighbors whose grown sons had been drafted. Often we heard about young men who had been missing or killed in action. I became familiar with words that had not previously been in any of our vocabularies.

The war years brought many changes in our community, but the one I most dreaded did not happen. Daddy did not get drafted. During the three and a half years of American involvement in the War, however, Daddy kept a thought in the back of his mind, that he might be drafted. He expressed this worry occasionally, but as it turned out, the age limit for the draft, including the final call, was for men one year younger than he was. In the years afterward, whenever the subject of the War came up, Daddy would say, "I was one year too young to be drafted in World War I, and in World War II, I was one year too old."

Not being able to do anything about what was happening overseas, I busied myself as much as possible, studying in school and dreaming of a better future, as I had done all my young life. Luckily, I was about to discover a kindred spirit, who loved books as much as I did. His house would become for me a new window into the best aspects of the world, envisioned by writers like Emerson and Thoreau. As the world went through tumult and upheaval, I would find peace in the volumes on his freshly constructed shelves.

Chapter 14

Early Transition from Girl to Young Woman

In my early teenage years, my family enjoyed a promising time. Colleen and I, having passed the defining age of twelve, now were considered to be young women. The fact that my parents and Grandma had raised us to be healthy and industrious young grown-ups was a great joy and comfort to them. Just how grown-up I would have to become, however, would soon be evident.

Appalachia was certainly not a place to grow up with a plan for continuing education; most of my friends had already dropped out of school. Children my age were already parenting their younger siblings, and some young people just a couple of years older than I were starting to get married and have their own children. Colleen and I often helped take care of Gene, in addition to doing our other chores at home, before and after school and on the weekends, yet we felt lucky because our education could continue. The Warren girls, as people often referred to us, were a rarity, because our parents wanted us to finish high school.

One of my best friends, Dorine, who had been in the same grade with me although she was two years older, had married her cousin at the age of fourteen. She had dropped out of school, and I missed seeing her in my classes and on the bus.

Surprisingly, I caught a glimpse of Dorine one early spring, when our class went on a field trip to learn about the herbs that grew in the mountains of our area. While we explored the woods, around noon, a cloudburst dumped blinding rain on us. When one of the students noticed a sawmill shack, we rushed there for shelter. As the man who lived in the shack opened the door to let us inside, I recognized him as Dorine's husband. His long brown beard and hair had grown longer, however, and his overalls were filthy. One strap was unfastened and dangling down. His shirtsleeve was torn at the shoulder, revealing a tattoo of an exotic woman.

For a second I was thrilled, thinking that I would see my childhood friend again, even though I understood that her circumstances were dreary. Once inside, I saw Dorine working hard, spooning out soup beans. Three large pones of corn bread had been placed along the naked, rough boards that lay across two barrels, serving as a makeshift table. The entire crew of the sawmill were wolfing down the dinner she had prepared. She was very big with a baby inside her belly.

"IIi, Dorine," I shouted above the thunder and the massive waves of rain pounding the tin roof. Water was spilling onto the table and floor from the leaky ceiling above, and some of the men had left their plates to help Dorine find buckets to put under the leaks. Dorine didn't answer me then, because she was so busy taking care of the leaks and the dinner, but later we did talk a bit.

She spoke almost in a whisper. "I wish I was still in school like you are, but this is the way it is for me now."

I wanted to hug her, and I reached my arm around her shoulder, but she froze and did not respond. I ignored her cool response, noticing her husband's glare at us. It was clear that he didn't like her talking to her old friends who were still in school.

"I married Jim because Mommy found us in bed together, and she told me I had better marry him and soon, because, she said, 'If he don't marry you, you will never get married because no nice man would marry a woman that's not a virgin, and especially if she has got a bastard – and that's what it looks like you may get.'"

I later heard that Dorine's baby didn't live long after he was born. So many babies died, in those conditions. Not long after that, the sawmill finished cutting the trees on that mountain and the operation moved to another area. Dorine and her husband moved too, to the new mill, and I never saw her again.

The following spring, when I was in seventh grade, my own life and the life of my family took a difficult turn, because of my Daddy's health.

I could not have imagined what was in front of me, on the day before I discovered Daddy's condition. I was hoeing alone in the Hollow Patch, a small, fertile piece of level land that was blessed to be in between two mountains. This patch received the rich compost of decaying leaves, which washed into it from the spring rains. It was late afternoon and the garden patch was shaded, since the sun had gone down behind the mountain to the west. I especially liked to work alone there in the silence, interrupted only by sounds of birds and the movement of small animals living nearby. A dove was calling peacefully while a squirrel raced past, almost colliding with a more deliberate traveler – a turtle. I spoke to the frightened turtle, by my bare feet, although it had already withdrawn its head, along with other body parts, into its protective shell.

"Don't worry, little friend, the squirrel won't harm you. He's only scampering like that because of two-legged predators that seek his species with a loud gun."

"Hello, Odean."

This greeting came in a dear familiar voice from behind the underbrush. It was Miss Mary, who had been my first grade teacher. She was walking the trail coming from her house to ours, a distance of a mile. A visit from her was always a pleasant surprise.

"Hello, Miss Mary," I said. She was really Mrs. Mary Jones, married to a well-liked man, Andrew, but it was customary for young children to address women as Miss, followed by their first name.

She rushed to hug me – not a casual hug and peck on the cheek, but a heartfelt embrace from her heart to mine. As she let me go, she gave me a warm pat on my shoulder. I always felt so good in her presence.

"Odean, I'm going to miss you now that you're a big girl, leaving us and going all the way to high school next year."

High school started in eighth grade back then. I had started first grade at the age of nine, and I'd been going to the same school, Oakland Elementary, from first through seventh grades, much closer to my family's house than the high school, twelve miles away.

Miss Mary added, "I cannot imagine a school year now without being able to glance up and see you with a book in a quiet corner or on a root of an oak tree. It's been such a long time since I had you in first grade."

"I'll miss you too, Miss Mary," I started to say, as she excitedly interrupted me.

"I'm on my way to ask Mamie if you might come and spend the night with me tonight, Odean, since Andrew is in South Georgia visiting his family."

"Great! I'll keep hoeing until you come back. I hope Mommy lets me."

It was always so much fun to spend the night with Miss Mary. For years I had been doing that every few months. Miss

Mary and her husband Andrew owned lots of books, and they always let me read undisturbed for hours. Although Andrew had not been able to go to high school, he could read pretty well. They owned rich bottomland on the banks of Turkey Creek, which assured them of much better crops and more money than our rocky mountainside property could produce. They did not have children, and Miss Mary often told me that I was the daughter she had never had. She had even made a nightgown for me, made out of new flannel cloth, white with a pattern of small blue roses, which she kept at her house for my sleepovers. I loved her dearly.

Soon she and Mommy came back to the field.

Mommy said, "Odean, as soon as you have breakfast with Mary tomorrow, be sure and hurry on home, because you and Colleen should go straight to the mountain field and hoe the corn. Your Daddy plowed the center of those rows today and they must be hoed early tomorrow before it rains."

Mommy's face looked careworn and worried, but that was how she often looked that spring, and I didn't think too deeply about it.

After a happy night with Miss Mary, I skipped along on my way home, busy remembering the characters I had visited in the books at her house.

I knew I should hurry to get home before the rain came that day. A heavy rain would make the soil muddy, and we'd have to wait a week before we could walk in the field without marring it. Letting the weeds grow another week would mean they would grow so tall, Colleen and I wouldn't be able to separate them from the corn.

Still, I sat a few moments on the bank of the dirt road. Feeling joyous and looking skyward, I breathed in the sweet perfume of the blue, pink, red and orange honeysuckle just over

158

my head. The honeybees were buzzing as they gathered nectar. I smiled, as I knew Daddy would soon be following the bees to their home in a hollow tree nearby, so that he could take their delicious honey in good conscience, knowing they would soon be making more honey as they hovered over the corn silks of his sweet corn. The bees generously made us gallons of honey in the comb, which we ate all summer with Grandma's hot buttered biscuits. As with all her cooking, those biscuits had a reputation for being the best in our neighborhood. With those thoughts, I soon became even more refreshed and eager to join Colleen in the mountain field.

As I neared our barn, I saw Colleen coming from the crib shed carrying our hoes. I greeted her happily, but she responded in a more subdued manner as she handed me my hoe. A habit of greeting each member of our family had been chiseled into our psyche by Daddy's often-expressed belief: "All family members must greet each other every morning upon awakening."

Colleen and I started walking together up the steep trail to the hillside field.

"You know, Daddy isn't plowing corn today because he's home in bed with the flu."

I was stunned, as I quickly tried to absorb this new and frightening information.

"Oh, I didn't know!"

"He didn't sleep much last night, Mommy said. Mommy and Grandma and I have been noticing that Daddy hasn't been looking well for over a month, but I guess you're always dreaming, so you don't notice much of what's going on."

With that remark, we dropped into silence as we climbed the rocky hill.

Leaving the dense, shady woods, we came out into the brilliant hot sun at the edge of the field and commenced to chop the weeds with our hoes. As I thought about Colleen's somewhat inflated grown-up remarks, guilt started to overwhelm me. She was right. I had not been noticing how Daddy had been looking lately. Thinking back over the early spring, I remembered that he had been coughing even when he had been turning the ground in March, and now it was almost May, and he was still coughing. He spoke always in a tired voice. I felt very uncomfortable for not having listened more closely when my Mommy and Grandma had been talking in low voices. They must have been speaking about Daddy not being well.

I vowed to take notice of the needs of my family from now on. No more losing myself in dreaming, and picturing Mommy and Grandma all dressed up in Mrs. Leach-type clothes. No more imagining Daddy driving a shiny new pick-up truck like the servants of Mrs. Leach. I chopped more vigorously after concluding that I was finished with that kind of child's play, since now I was no longer a child.

It certainly proved to be a good time for me to shape up to our reality, because Daddy became weaker and weaker during the following eight months, even after it looked as if he had gotten through the flu.

All that spring and summer, each Sunday, friends and neighbors stopped at our house on their way to church. They offered a ride to any members of my family who could go to church, and they offered to stay with Daddy, if we would all like to go, but I much preferred staying home while Mommy, Grandma, Colleen and Gene went to church. At every service, I knew, the congregation would be making loud, emotion-filled prayers to God on behalf of my Daddy. My Aunt Rosie was a leader of the fervent church's prayer group, who exerted powerful effort to reach God for His help in restoring Arthur back to health.

Everyone in the community was especially surprised and worried about the deteriorating condition of that strong man, Arthur, whom they had known as a fearless trainer of wild young horses and mules. They appreciated the fact that he was a gritty, stubborn farmer who worked desperately hard to feed and clothe a family of six.

Neighbors often dropped in, asking to help us, but it so disturbed Daddy to have people do his work for him that he kept saying, in a trembling voice, "I'll be out of this bed and doing that myself in a few days." It was almost impossible for a rugged Appalachian man to give in to physical weakness.

Mommy found it too hard to contradict Daddy by letting friends do more than chop stove wood. One day she said to us, "Since your Daddy can't get out of the house, he won't see when neighbors cut our stove wood. If we move the wood pile to the other side of the barn, he won't even hear the ax."

A dear neighbor and his son, my friend Glen, helped us move the axes and chopping block one morning, before I caught the school bus with Colleen. I watched Glen, his overalls greasy and dirty as he helped. He smiled shyly, with his head bent. I felt he was thinking like me, about how much we missed seeing each other and talking about books on the bus as we went back and forth to and from school. He worked now at the sawmill and the family farm. No more school for him, but I felt sure that he read, from cover to cover, the monthly *Market Bulletin*, *The Farm Journal*, and the local weekly paper, *The Times Courier*.

"Glen, I miss you at school," I said.

A sad look came across his face and then his head tilted even lower. He stared at his shoddy shoes as he turned to leave for a long day of work.

After he had walked several yards, though, he turned back and smiled slightly as he waved. Then he disappeared among the trees, walking hurriedly along the trail to the sawmill.

During all those summer months, Daddy never saw a doctor, because we had no money for that kind of care. Neighbors brought herbs from the mountains, such as wild cherry bark and rats vein root. They brought mayflower from the mountain soil and yellow root from the creek bank. Yellow root was a liver tonic the American Indians had used. Considering that Daddy's color was so yellow, many neighbors believed he had a liver problem. As Daddy tried each new remedy, he would smile and say, "This one will do the trick; this one will cure me."

Over the summer Daddy gradually became so depressed that he no longer talked very much. He would just sit in Grandma's rocker and stare out the car door windows by the fireplace, day after day. Grandma cooked and coaxed him to take nourishment, but he refused even the dishes he used to delight most in eating, or else he would have only a few small mouthfuls of the good-smelling chicken soup, tomato gravy, and baked sweet bread with milk.

Grandma was so determined to find something Daddy would eat that one day she combed the house, trying to find a few pennies to buy a can of salmon so that she could prepare his most favorite dish – creamed salmon. Having no luck scraping up pennies, she tossed her apron onto the back of a chair and hitched a ride with a neighbor to the country store, about three miles away. She bravely went up to Mr. Jones, the proprietor of the store, and asked him if he would mind adding a can of salmon to our long bill, which had increased as we had bought bare necessities like flour, lard, and baking powder on credit.

Upon returning home, Grandma exited the neighbor's truck and broke into a happy little trot. As she came into the house, hugging the small brown paper bag close to her heart, she was smiling as if she were holding a great treasure. With her free hand, she motioned me to come closer, and I rushed to her.

"Odean, get a basket of dry wood chips so we can get a quick fire in the stove. I have a can of Double Q salmon that your Daddy loves."

Grandma cooked up the dish in a great flurry. Unfortunately, though, Daddy took only one bite of the biscuits and creamed salmon. He swallowed hard and then looked up into her anxious but smiling face. He smiled briefly, but then he turned away and closed his eyes.

"Thank you, Ethie. I want you, Mamie and the children to enjoy eating all this good food. . . . " His voice trailed off.

That summer, Mommy, Colleen and I kept searching for any opportunity we could find to make a little money. It was hard for us to make ends meet, with Daddy so sick. Most everyone within walking distance had enough children to take care of all their chores, though, and even if they didn't they were like us, just trying to find enough money to get by from day to day.

Uncle Berry, Aunt Rosie's husband (known to us as Uncle Berry), hired Colleen and me to work a couple of days to hoe a field of his corn. Before sunrise, eager to make some money, we excitedly hoisted our garden hoes over our shoulders and walked the trail across the mountain down to their farm in a valley. Uncle Berry met us at the edge of the field with a pitcher of drinking water.

"I'll ring the cowbell that hangs on the porch when Rosie gets dinner ready at about twelve o'clock," he called over his shoulder as he left the field.

We talked very little as we busily chopped weeds and dug up crab grass roots from around the corn. As we made our way for hours down one row and back up another, our hoes made steady thumps as they chopped into the soil. Often the sharp clang of steel striking small rocks contrasted with birds singing and crows steadily "kwakking." The hot sun bore down on us unmercifully, until finally we heard the welcome sound of the cowbell. Hot and sweaty, we rushed to the house.

Aunt Rosie gave us a dinner much more sumptuous than our meals had been lately. She served a large bowl of green beans – picked fresh from her garden – with a hunk of tender fat back meat, which we could spoon out with our helpings of beans. She also served a platter of fried Irish potatoes, a lettuce salad with new green onions, a jar of tomatoes preserved from her garden the year before, a large pone of corn bread, and sweet muffins made from the cast iron muffin pan that her mother (my Grandma Warren) had given to both her daughter (Aunt Rosie) and her son (my Daddy). Colleen and I looked at each other and smiled, because we knew Rosie put herself in charge of that pan, and whenever my Mommy would borrow it, Aunt Rosie never let more than two days go by without walking across the mountain to get it back. I remember Mommy looking up from bending over the wash tub where she was scrubbing clothes, seeing Rosie coming down the trail and saying to Colleen and me, "There comes your Aunt Rosie after the muffin pan."

(If truth be told, after Aunt Rosie died and I was grown, I slipped into Uncle Berry's house one day when he was in the field and stole that muffin pan off the nail behind Aunt Rosie's stove, where it had gathered dust, and brought it to my Mommy. Mommy and Daddy laughed when they saw me walk in with it and knew I was as stubborn as Aunt Rosie. That muffin pan now hangs in my daughter's kitchen in California, where it still makes wonderful muffins.)

Colleen and I enjoyed the muffins, with delicious butter and honey on them, and Aunt Rosie gave us second helpings of the beans, the potatoes, the salad, the corn bread and the tomatoes. Each of us had a big, cold glass of milk to top it off. We hungrily consumed this generous lunch, until Uncle Berry, sitting on the bench beside me, said, "I'm awful afeared that you'ens Daddy is going to die."

Hearing that, I almost choked, and I could see Colleen's body flinch as she sat in a chair beside Aunt Rosie on the opposite side of the table.

Aunt Rosie commenced praying, "Lord, please have mercy on my dear brother Arthur, and don't let him die. He's needed here to raise his children."

Her shouting and screaming became so loud they caused the dogs outside to start barking. Her large body began heaving and jumping as she rose from her chair and then lunged into pacing the floor while she flung her arms outward and upward, a form of erratic behavior typical of some in her religion who exerted great effort to reach and be heard by God. She and my Daddy were members of Ebenezer Baptist Church, although Daddy was a more subdued member, partly because he knew, and Rosie often reminded him, that "anyone who made that foul corn liquor were in danger of hell fire." A remark to which I remember him retorting, "Well Rosie, our Pa, Will, made pure corn liquor on that little copper still that he gave me and I don't think that good-hearted man, our Pa, is now burning to a crisp in hell, do you?"

I never heard her respond to Daddy's humorous question. At such moments, she would sit staring at the floor, probably praying for the souls of both him and their goodhearted Pa.

With a loud cracking noise, the aged wooden floor and walls of Aunt Rosie's house now creaked and protested in their joints and weak foundation. Dishes and glasses shook on tables as

165

they clattered against each other. Colleen and I stopped eating and tried to avoid looking at her as we began helping Uncle Berry clear the table.

"Now, now, you girls leave the table as it is and go on back to your hoeing. Rosie will quieten down in a few minutes," he assured us.

We still hung around for about ten more minutes. Aunt Rosie did become calm and seemed to doze in her rocker as cool breezes softly ruffled her graying hair and the skirt of her navy gingham dress. Once Uncle Berry began washing the dishes, Colleen and I headed back to the field to resume our weeding for the rest of the day.

When the sun had slid down the other side of the mountain, Uncle Berry came across the field toward us. As he came nearer, I could see that he had a dollar bill between two fingers of his cupped hand.

As soon as he reached us, he said, "I think it's fair, since your Aunt Rosie cooked you girls a big dinner, that I pay you, Colleen, a dollar, and I'll give Odean a fifty cent piece because she is so small."

I was surprised by that. The way I figured it, I had chopped as many licks with my hoe as Colleen had. To tell the truth, I had seen her pause and lean on her hoe handle a few times while I had kept steadily chopping on. I just stood quietly beside Colleen, though, and watched as he gave her the dollar, and then rummaged inside his overall pocket. When he pulled out the round piece of money, he rubbed it slowly between the palms of his hands. Worried that he might not give even the coin to me, I reached out my hand and he reluctantly placed it in my open palm. We thanked him and continued hoeing to finish the rows we were working on. By then it was twilight, and we trudged wearily the mile back home.

As we started walking, Colleen said, "With my dollar and your fifty cents, we can buy a whole fifty-pound sack of flour, and that will make Mommy and Grandma so happy."

"I'm happy, too," I said, trying to say the words happily, because I did not want Colleen to know how disappointed I felt that I had got only half as much money as she had.

I changed the subject. "We will still need to do some of our chores when we get home."

"Yeah, I was just thinking about that. I know that Mommy and Grandma can't get it all done."

"I hope Mommy can manage to get both cows milked before dark," I said, "since the pilots sneak into the barn when it gets dark sometimes."

I was remembering the scary night, a couple of years earlier, when Mommy had been late getting the milking done and a pilot snake had struck at her. Luckily, it had just hit her skirt as it zigzagged out into the hall and then outside. These snakes would make their way inside the stables at night, waiting to eat stray grains of corn from nubbins the cow would drop from her mouth while being milked. The pilots would lie camouflaged in a corner of the stable, blending perfectly with the cow manure mixed with bits of hay.

"I hope so too," said Colleen, "but most likely Mommy will have to light the lantern to milk the cows, and you and I are going to have to feed the hogs."

"Well, I know for sure, it's too dark to crawl under the floor where that red hen lays her egg every day, so the chicken snake will probably eat her egg tonight," I declared.

In mid-August, Colleen asked me to go with her to the playhouse hill, where we used to play among the tree stumps with our broken dishes. It was an unusual request, because we had not had time to relax there even a few moments, as we had done when we were younger.

Colleen started to speak, but choked up with tears for a few seconds. Then she tried again.

"Odean, today I overheard Mommy and Grandma talking so sadly and this is what I heard Mommy say: 'With their daddy so sick, there is no way that we can possibly send the girls back to school this coming September.'"

The heartbreak I felt at that moment is impossible to put into words. I knew that should this happen, it would be the end of all my childhood dreams of getting a high school education and going out into the world to find a good job, so that I could help my family have a better life.

No more words passed between us as we embraced each other, with tears flowing from our eyes. We were two young sisters whose personalities and goals were totally different, but at this moment, we were one, as we experienced the hardest blow of all – the damper being clamped down on our lives, because we both knew that we might no longer be able to go beyond where we were.

Soon Colleen, the more practical thinker, dried her eyes and said, "We had better get back to helping Mommy and Grandma pick more green beans for canning tomorrow."

"I'll be right on down to help with the beans. I just want to sit and think about what all this means to us."

"Don't worry too much." Colleen spoke in a comforting tone. "There's nothing that we can do about it."

I sat there on the stump a while after Colleen left. My heart went out to Daddy, who was lying in bed, so very sick. I remembered the many years when I had seen him work all day plowing the fields and then, under cover of darkness, slip off to the mountainside, where he had the shiny little copper still that his daddy had soldered together for his own use many years earlier. Daddy had worked so hard to help our family survive. He had run the risk of "running-off" a batch of moonshine liquor whenever our need for food or clothing or late tax money had gotten overwhelming. The government revenue officers in their skinny black automobiles, a dreaded sight to me, combed the mountains weekly, trying to locate and destroy any bootlegging materials, and Daddy had been courageous in his efforts to make us the necessary money to get by, even if it was against the law.

Sitting on the stump, I remembered worrying, when I was little, about Daddy getting caught by the government officers and maybe being put in the chain gang and having to wear the kind of clothes the prisoners wore. Each spring, throughout my childhood, I had seen the prisoners scrape our dirt roads after the winter rains had washed ruts in them. Their uniforms had big horizontal white and black stripes. I had worried that if the law caught my Daddy for his occasional batches of moonshine, he would have to live as those prisoners did, working with mattocks and hammers, being watched by a guard always holding a shotgun ready to fire at him should he try to run away.

In the past these frightened thoughts hadn't lasted long. When Daddy had handed me a quarter of a dollar to buy a notebook and pencil I needed for school, my anxieties would be eased. Holding that piece of money in my hand, I had felt happy. Sometimes I could even hope for a penny left over from my necessary purchases, with which I could buy a succulent red-striped peppermint candy stick.

All that was over, now that Daddy was so sick. Not only would I have no candy sticks or school supplies from Daddy's courageous and untiring efforts, but I would not be able to go back to school at all. I would no longer have my cherished refuge in a classroom, where I could study, learn, and read about people who had become educated and whose lives could be so fulfilling.

Realizing I had lingered too long, I got up from the stump and rushed down the hill to our house. Approaching the yard, I heard Daddy struggling, trying to make his voice come out strong and angry.

"What do you mean, the girls will have to quit school? No! No! No!"

As I came closer, I could not quite hear Mommy's words, but it sounded if she was gently persuading Daddy to calm down, in her patient, love-filled way.

Two weeks later, we did commence high school after all, because Daddy could not be convinced otherwise. Mommy and Grandma told us, however, much as they hoped we could continue, we must keep ourselves prepared, because it might not be possible for us to go to school the entire year.

Mommy had asked us to be careful speaking to anyone about our situation, since it would be so upsetting to Daddy should word get back to him. I could not help talking with Miss Mary, though, about the possibility that I might not be able to complete my education, and once, at a church gathering, I told Mr. Shepard too. Both Miss Mary and Mr. Shepard were sympathetic and urged me to try not to think about leaving school, because they believed there would be a way for me to continue.

"Odean, don't worry," Mr. Shepard said. "You love school so much. I know there will be a way."

Miss Mary agreed. "Please promise me, Odean, that you will continue to speak to either Lee [Mr. Shepard] or me about how you feel and how your family is doing." He heartily agreed, adding, "Henry Wadsworth Longfellow wrote a poem that seems to be speaking about you, and I quote,

'The love of learning, the sequestered nooks, and all the sweet serenity of books.'"

Their caring helped me to concentrate more steadily on the thrill of learning, amidst the worry.

My sister Colleen and I, at a neighbor's home. I was 16 and she was 18 years old.

Chapter 15

Mr. Hagan Returns to Appalachia

One bright late August afternoon, the school bus stopped at our mailbox, and Hoover Kincaid let Colleen, Gene and me out as usual. This makeshift bus constructed on top of his Dodge pick-up truck still took us the three miles to and from the elementary school; the big yellow county school bus picked us up at the elementary school and brought us to the high school, which was nine more miles away. As Colleen and I waved goodbye to our friends and started walking up the road to our house with Gene, we met a long, brown, shiny new car, slowly coming down the hill. My heart dropped from fear that something had happened to Daddy while we had been at school. The only people who drove a nice car like that were doctors or revenue officers. Oh, how I hoped it was not a doctor on an emergency call.

We rushed up the hill and down the other side, and practically tumbled over our feet getting into the house. Daddy was sitting in the front room, near the windows, looking very sick but luckily not worse.

"Here are my two little girls," he said, raising an extremely thin hand to beckon us, and I rushed to hug his frail body as Colleen asked Mommy, "Who was that man we met in the big brown car?"

"Oh, that was a man from Birmingham, Alabama. His name is Hillyard Hagan. He used to live near here when he was a child, and he's bought the Anderson farm that joins our land lines. He told us he had such a longing to come back here to these mountains, and that he and his wife are going to retire and live here. They're going to build a broiler chicken farm on their property."

Mommy's words caught my total attention. I had to stop and try to figure out how anyone who had had the good fortune to get away from this place to live and make money in a big city would ever want to come back.

After supper that night, we had what you might call a family conference, although we never thought of our family talks as such. Grandma was drying the dishes and putting them away, as Colleen and I did our homework at the "eating table," and Gene had been put to bed. Mommy was in the other room, coaxing Daddy to take some warm grits with milk that Grandma had prepared. He was still desperately ill and weak.

Grandma was the first to speak her thoughts. "Now, children, let's not mention a word to the neighbors about what that man said about coming back and building a broiler farm here."

"Why?" Colleen asked.

Mommy called out from the other room. "Yes, children, your Grandma is right about not talking to the neighbors, and Arthur is agreeing."

She was speaking for Daddy, because she knew his voice wasn't strong enough to carry his words all the way to the kitchen.

"Well," Grandma said, "we don't know that man and he might have just been talking."

There was no more response from the other room except the sharp clang of the "slop-jar" as Mommy placed the metal container in a bottomless chair that Daddy used when he needed to relieve himself during the night. Mommy was getting Daddy ready for bed.

Grandma started to sweep the kitchen floor, and Colleen had resumed her homework, but I sat with my eyes closed, making doodle marks with my pencil while my mind was busy fervently denying their assumption that Mr. Hagan might be "just blowing hot air." Somehow I knew that Mr. Hagan was telling the truth. I felt deep inside that his presence in our life was going to be much more real than my fantasies about the people on our newspaper walls. I could tell by the way Mommy and Grandma talked about Mr. Hagan that he was a good man, and I trusted that somehow he could help us. Maybe he could even help Daddy get better again. I had never known anyone as rich as Mr. Hagan must be, who chose to live so close to us. He must be a very special kind of person, I thought, and I couldn't wait to meet him. I wondered if he would bring books to his new house, like the ones filling the shelves of Miss Mary and Andrew's living room. Maybe he would let me borrow one, the way Mr. Shepard had let Mommy and me borrow *Gone with the Wind.*

Grandma interrupted my thoughts as she took off her apron and hung it on its peg.

"Now, let's blow out the lamp," she said, "because we have only a few more hours of light in the lamp oil we now have, and Lord knows when we will have money to buy more."

On a Monday morning, three weeks later, it was necessary for one of us to stay home from school and help with canning. I agreed that I should be the one to stay, since on that particular day Colleen had a test to take.

"Girls," Mommy said that morning, "I know it's hard for you to hear this, but I am afraid there will be many days like this when you will have to miss school to help Grandma and me."

Her voice quivered and tears welled up in her eyes. Simultaneously, Colleen and I rushed to hug her thin body. (Writing this, tears are welling up in my eyes, but my heart feels good remembering that we reached out to Mommy with hugs at that moment.)

It was bean-canning day on that particular Monday. As usual on canning days, we worked for hours. First we picked the beans from the vines in the garden. Then we carefully drew the strings off the green beans and broke the beans into one-inch pieces, which we washed. Next, with our fingers, we packed as many beans into the half-gallon glass jars as possible. I pressed hard to pack them tightly, until my fingers were first sore and then numb.

Now came the process of carefully pouring boiling water onto the beans inside the jars and sealing them. We then placed eight jars into a huge pot of boiling water to cook. The wood stove would already be burning sticks of wood so that the pot would come to a boil again. Every twenty minutes Grandma, Mommy, or I would add fresh sticks to the fire in the stove so that the pot kept a steady boil. I knew that if the beans cooked thoroughly, and the jars sealed properly, we could be sure of having delicious green beans with our milk and bread for eight dinners of the coming winter.

That morning of canning took place under the tin roof of our little side room kitchen. The September air was filled not only with steam from the big pot, but with heavy humidity. Not one leaf outside the window moved in a breeze. The thermometer nailed to the shady side of the house registered ninety-six degrees, even though it was early autumn.

After I did the first twenty-minute check and placed more wood in the stove, I decided to ask Grandma if I could take a brief rest. Our morning canning had gone well, and now we had about an hour until we started another canning in the afternoon.

"Grandma, might I take a walk to the mailbox while I am resting a little?" I asked.

"Sure," she answered from where she sat on the porch, stringing beans for the next batch. She looked at me and smiled as she reached for the cloth she had taken earlier from the rag bag, and wiped the sweat from her forehead.

"I'll be back for the next twenty-minute check of the fire," I said, as I bounced down the steps leading off the porch, jumping over the space where the missing middle step should be.

Nothing ever gave me more renewed energy than going over the hill to the mailbox at the main road. Even though we ordered only a few things like cloth to make each of us a dress once or twice a year, the companies kept sending us the catalogs, and it was fun to look at the colorful pictures and dream about the possibility of buying something more. About once every couple of months Mrs. Leach would send a box of luscious candy. We were strictly cautioned not to "brag" about those goodies to our neighbors' children, who were not so lucky to receive them. In January and February we received Hastings' seed catalog from Atlanta, along with a couple lesser-known publications. If Daddy happened to go to the mailbox and bring home seed catalogs in early spring, he would call to Mommy, "Look, Mamie, what came in the mail! Your sure sign that spring is here." That was their little private joke – when the spring seed catalogs came she always declared, "Spring is here!" even though it would be mid-January.

When I pulled down the door of the mailbox that day, I could see that Mr. James, the mailman, had left a three-cent stamped letter, which meant it was not a local letter, requiring only two cents. My eyes flashed to the return address in the corner and I held my breath a few seconds when I read the big, bold, hand-written words: *G. H. Hagan, Birmingham, Alabama.* Mr. Hagan had written! Maybe he would really move here from Birmingham. I swiftly turned toward home, grasping the letter in my hand, and I skipped all the way back, instead of walking with my usual leisurely, dreamy stride.

From the top of the hill, I could see Mommy sitting on the porch next to Daddy. She was fanning him with the pasteboard fan advertising The Logan Funeral Home in Ellijay. I had never liked that fan, and I felt uneasy for a moment seeing it in Mommy's hand. Almost everyone in the church congregation at summer revival meetings would be busy waving those fans in front of their red, sweaty faces. I did not like being reminded now of funerals and of all the times I had heard the congregation yelling to be heard by a far-off God "way up yonder in heaven." I wanted my Daddy to stay on earth. That thought made me stub my toe on a rock as I rushed down the hill, but I felt so buoyant about Mr. Hagan, our possible new neighbor, that I recovered my balance quickly.

I passed Grandma, busy now turning the handle of the well in our front yard in order to pull up a bucket of water with the heavy rope. I briefly waved the letter in front of Grandma and barely missed her nose.

"Mr. Hagan," I breathed out before the next short pant could surface from my throat. She smiled, and I felt her smile meant she was happy for me that Mr. Hagan was not just a passerby that we might not ever see again.

"Mommy, look, Mr. Hagan!"

I handed the letter to her and she quickly opened it.

"Arthur," Mommy said, after she had read the letter, "Mr. Hagan is returning the first weekend of October. He's bringing the blueprints for six broiler chicken houses to build on his farm and he wants you to recommend local carpenters to work for him."

For the first time in months, I saw a brief flicker of hope pass over Daddy's face. It made me feel I was seeing a rainbow after a storm.

The first Saturday in October of that year was a glorious, balmy Indian summer day. Some trees in our yard were brilliant with orange, yellow, and bright red-purple leaves. However, a few trees were stubbornly refusing to give up their green summer garments. The scenic mountains surrounding our house would soon be at their peak in the changing of colors. With confidence, they appeared to be quietly waiting, daring all artists who thought they might emulate their magnificence on canvas.

October was a busy time for us, as we tried to keep preserving as much of our winter food as possible before the frosts killed the vegetables. Working all day and into the night, if we could afford the lamp oil for light, Colleen and I managed to do as much work after school and on weekends as we might ordinarily accomplish working a week of full days. This year, the special joy of still being able to be in school lightened our hearts, so that we felt more accepting of the heavier workload.

On that warm, busy Saturday, Grandma, Colleen, and I were peeling and slicing apples and placing them on the tin roof of the shed to dry them so we could preserve them for winter. We had spread some of Mrs. Leach's old newspapers on the tin to protect the slices from absorbing the rust. We were sitting on chairs under the shade trees in the yard as we prepared the apples, and Gene was munching an apple as he played with sticks.

In the winter, Grandma would be able to make her delicious half-moon pies, stuffed with these sweet apples, for our after school treats. My mouth watered as I peeled the apples, just thinking of how delicious those pies would smell and taste when we would come home from school each day.

I was the first to see Mr. Hagan's big brown Buick slowly coming down the hill. I thought it looked even fancier and shinier than it had a few weeks earlier. As he parked, we stopped our apple peeling in the yard and walked toward him. After parking on the red clay we had swept earlier in the morning, he climbed out of his car and gave each of us a direct and friendly smile as we introduced ourselves. He was a tall man with warm brown eyes that sparkled as the smile lingered on his face. I thought he looked much younger than my Mommy and Daddy, but it's possible that he looked younger because he had had a life less filled with hunger and constant physical labor. I would guess that in fact he might have been about fifty years old, or more. He wore a fancy brown suit and tan shirt, with a green and white striped tie, and his shoes were shiny. All in all, he looked more like the guests I had seen at Mrs. Leach's home than like any of our neighbors. He acknowledged each of our introductions, paying close attention to each of our names, even Gene's.

"Please come in," Grandma said, as she motioned Mr. Hagan toward the three steps leading to our narrow porch. I felt glad that our neighbor Mr. Reece had repaired the steps a couple of days earlier, replacing the missing middle board with a better one, although I wondered what Mr. Hagan would think of the older two boards with their rotting edges. Mommy led the way to the door of the main room, where Daddy sat in his rocking chair. As Mr. Hagan entered the room, Grandma, Colleen and I followed close behind. Mommy motioned to him to take a seat in the cane-bottomed rocking chair she had placed close to Daddy, and she took a spot just behind Daddy's rocker. As she stood there, she wrung her hands nervously.

"Mr. Warren, I hear that you have been ailing this summer?" Mr. Hagan said, as he moved the chair nearer to Daddy.

Daddy spoke weakly. "Yes, I have not been well for many months. How long have I been sick, Mamie?"

As if to save Mommy the bother of answering, Mr. Hagan turned his face from Daddy up toward her, saying, "Too long, right, Mrs. Warren?"

She smiled and said, "Yes, much too long."

Grandma, Colleen, and I seated ourselves on the bed and chairs nearby. I looked at Mommy's face and saw how Mr. Hagan's kind deferral to her had brought a healthy color into her face, which had aged years over the summer. Although she had rarely put it into words, Mommy had been gripped with fear that Daddy had cancer of the liver, because he had experienced the same symptoms his mother had suffered for several months before dying a year earlier.

"Mr. Warren, I'm looking forward to you being well soon," said Mr. Hagan, as he opened a manila folder, "so I can hire you to find some good local carpenters for me. I want you to see the plans I have had drawn up."

He showed Daddy a drawing of his property, with a curving line for the creek. "I'm building the chicken coops in this level area alongside the creek bank," he said, tapping on the paper. "Is that a good place?"

Daddy studied the plan. After a minute he nodded and said, "That is a very good place to build them, I would think."

Mr. Hagan's eyes suddenly went to the double car door windows. "I can hardly believe my eyes. What an excellent idea! Who installed those windows?"

He arose from his chair and took a few steps toward the windows to see more closely how they had been installed.

Then Mommy related the story of the wrecked car and how she and Daddy had salvaged the doors and inserted them into the wall to create windows. The memory of those healthy and happy days put a pleasant lilt into her voice, and I felt captivated and thrilled by our Mommy's happiness in this special moment. Looking behind me to see how Grandma was enjoying the conversation, I saw through the open front door that she was back at the table under the trees, patiently peeling apples as Gene helped her. In the meantime, Mr. Hagan was delighting in Mommy's story. He appeared amazed by Mommy and Daddy's ingenuity.

In the gentle lull following her story, Mr. Hagan turned to Daddy with a look of seriousness.

"Mr. Warren," he said, "if you don't mind me asking, what did your doctor diagnose?"

Daddy remained silent, so after a moment Mommy spoke. "We have not been able to see a doctor."

"Well, I am gradually getting a little better each day." Daddy repeated his usual affirmation for perhaps the thousandth time. It would have been too difficult for him to confess that he owed so much to the one doctor available that he was embarrassed to ask for more credit. He and Mommy were still, little by little, "hacking away" at the mound of outstanding bills for Grandma Warren's cancer treatment the year before.

For a couple of minutes, we sat in silence. Then Mr. Hagan said, "I have a dear friend in Atlanta, a well-respected doctor, whom I need to visit. Arthur, how about you and Mrs. Warren accompany me to Atlanta Monday and let my doctor friend take a look at you? There would be no charge."

I listened for Mommy's response, knowing that she would not accept his kind offer. I remembered all the times when Daddy had driven his truck to deliver Government assistance to neighbors from the Relief Office at the courthouse in Ellijay. He would park his truck in our yard, where the neighbors waited, but Daddy refused to let us take even a bite of the luscious-looking food the other hungry children began devouring.

"My family does not accept Government charity," he would say to Colleen and me. He spoke that as a moral law, and we would quickly and proudly back off and watch our friends partake of the food, knowing we were pleasing our parents in doing so.

Mommy's response now was different, however. With only the slightest glance at Daddy, she meekly said, "That would be mighty nice of you," and Daddy smiled. The look on Mommy's face spoke gratitude more clearly than words could.

Her acceptance of Mr. Hagan's offer threw me off-balance for the rest of that afternoon. My Daddy, who was too proud to accept any government sustenance for us, was now taking free help from a stranger. How could this be? Was it because our situation was so desperate now, with Daddy having been sick so long? Or was it because Mr. Hagan's generous offer didn't come with a label announcing to the community that our family was accepting charity? I couldn't understand or feel comfortable with this idea that my parents would be willing to accept charity if it could be given to them privately, in order to preserve our reputation as proud citizens of our community. I finally decided that, whether or not I could understand my Mommy's and Daddy's response, I would just be grateful that Daddy would finally have the medical care he desperately needed.

After we were settled in our beds that night, our "family conference" took on an upward tone.

"Mr. Hagan seems like such a nice man," Grandma said.

In the darkness from my parents' bed, Mommy said, "Yes. It seems like a miracle that Arthur will now get to see a doctor."

I could not hear even a touch of tiredness in her voice. It was as if she had become younger and healthier, all in a day.

"It's not like I'm accepting charity, because Mr. Hagan already said he'd hire me to work for him," Daddy said proudly, in his weak voice.

Ahhh.... The mystery of Daddy accepting Mr. Hagan's offer so readily became clear to me: he didn't see this as charity, since Mr. Hagan had said he would soon be hiring Daddy to work. A rushing wave of love flowed over me, with a deeper understanding of my bull-headed mountaineer heritage. May wisdom guide me in the use of my stubborn spirit, always, I prayerfully thought.

Soon all was quiet except the katydids outside. I noticed their chorus was more rhythmic and musical tonight. I felt myself slipping into sleep with a tinge of impatience to get the hours of sleep done with, so that I could skip to the school bus in the morning with a light heart.

Chapter 16

Life after Mr. Hagan Returns

The Monday after Mr. Hagan's kind offer, while Colleen and I were helping Grandma get breakfast ready in the kitchen, Mommy was in the front room, busy trying to find what she called decent clothes for Daddy to wear to see the doctor in Atlanta.

As we poured milk and put out the biscuits, we heard Gene say to Mommy, "Can I go, too?"

"No," Mommy said, "you must stay here and help your sisters and Grandma. Mr. Hagan is taking Daddy to a doctor who we hope will make him well. Little boys are not allowed in grown-up people's hospitals. And in any case, you are a first-grader now, and you must stay in school."

Grandma said to Colleen and me, "Little Gene doesn't know he would look odd to be barefoot in a big city." She shook her head as she wiped her hands on her apron. "November is going to be here soon, and you children will need to have shoes for winter. Lord knows when we will have enough money to buy them. Look at your shoes, Colleen, and Odean's too, holes in them, and they will soon be letting your toes out onto the upper leather."

Grandma's voice trailed off. None of us had time to worry about shoes today with all the bustling around. As soon as Daddy woke up, Grandma turned to the fry pan on the stove, cracked an egg in it and concentrated on frying it just the way he liked. She fiddled with the egg, trying to get it just right. This was a new habit she had developed over the summer, in response to Daddy's illness. In earlier years, he would have gulped the egg down with a biscuit without taking any notice as to how it was cooked, because his mind would have been on getting out to his daily work in the fields, or cutting wood for the fire if it happened to be winter. Now his appetite was smaller and more fragile, and Grandma tried to make each dish something Daddy would at least try to eat.

Later that day, when Colleen and I came home from school with Gene and began our chores, we kept anxiously glancing up the hill to see if Mr. Hagan's car might be coming, bringing Mommy and Daddy back home with news of Daddy's physical condition. We had to rush to get apples picked and to help Grandma pick a mess of beans from the pods that had dried in the field after the frost. We would shell the beans for the next day's dinner. As soon as we got the apple and bean picking done, Grandma went inside to prepare our supper, while Colleen and I got the cows milked, and the pigs, mules, and chickens fed and watered. As the sun started to get lower in the sky, all three of us rushed inside to eat supper while it was still light. The less we used the lamp, the better, since it was almost empty of oil.

As soon as supper was over, I was washing dishes on the porch when I looked up to see Mr. Jones's old pick-up truck coming over the hill. Mr. Jones had the only telephone in the area, in his country store, so on rare occasions he could bring us news from a relative outside our neighborhood of a few square miles. Wondering if he was about to deliver alarming news, Grandma, Colleen and I breathlessly waited for him to get out of his truck and tell us. He took pains to push in the emergency brake, even though the red clay ground in our yard was level. He then took his time opening the truck's front door and stepping down. I thought his body movements were the slowest I had ever seen.

"Howdy," he said, once he faced us on the clay, and we were thankful that he quickly got to the reason for his visit. "Mamie called and asked me to come and tell y'all that they will be staying in Atlanta with the man who took them to the doctor and they 'spect to be home Friday."

Grandma nodded and tried to smile. "Henry, I really appreciate you coming and telling us this news."

"Ahh, Miss Effie, you'd do the same for our family. I remember so many things y'all did for us when we was growing up. Your dad too – Uncle Dock. I remember once I was throwing rocks and hitting the windowpanes of an old vacant house just to see them bust. He was passing and he saw me. He stopped and got out of his wagon and walked toward me, and I was so afraid he would tell my dad and I would be sure to get a whooping. He never told Daddy, though. He just gave me a good talking to and I never beat up the property of anyone else again."

I wished Mr. Jones would stop rambling and get to more of the news about Mommy and Daddy in Atlanta. I was sure that Grandma was as anxious as I was, because she had stopped taking dry clothes off the clothesline and now she just stood politely smiling and nodding at him as she hugged the mound of clean laundry.

Finally he cleared his throat and changed the subject. "I'm awful glad Arthur is going to get some medicine and with it the Good Lord can heal him. They're with the man who bought the Anderson farm, ain't they?"

"Yes, he seems like a nice man. . . ." Some of the bundle of clothes dropped from Grandma's arms and she bent to retrieve them.

At this point I could tell that their conversation was going to last a while, and small talk was not interesting to me. I wanted and needed to hear about my Daddy. I slowly walked toward the house, though staying within earshot long enough to hear that Mr. Hagan had settled my parents into a nice hotel near the doctor's clinic, so that he could take them back and forth daily for Daddy to have tests. They expected to have the results and the doctor's diagnosis by Friday.

Colleen had stayed on the clay area with Grandma and Mr. Jones. As I approached the porch steps, she called to me and Gene, "Grandma wants us to go to the garden and pick a mess of beans since Mr. Jones's beans are all dried up now."

I turned to follow Colleen around the house to the back garden, and Gene came too. That mountain expression "mess of beans" meant that we would pick what we would estimate to be a full black pot of green beans to give to him and his family of four. To show appreciation to a neighbor for a kindness extended, it was a common gesture to share vegetables, if one happened to have a plentiful supply of a particular one, and the neighbor hadn't had as much luck with their own garden. Mr. Jones thanked us warmly for the beans, and then he climbed back into his truck and slowly drove back up the hill in the dusk.

That week seemed endlessly long to us, since we could only imagine what was going on with Mommy and Daddy in a strange place and in even stranger and perhaps painful circumstances. Grandma had moved over to my parents' bed in the front room to sleep with Gene, but he was restless and cried during the night, because he had never spent a night without Mommy and Daddy. As always, Grandma was our safety shield. Her constant presence gave us a sense of security and happiness, much more than the community or church ever could.

Friday finally came, and we were delighted to see Mr. Hagan's big brown car crawling over the hill, making a long shadow at sundown. As he turned into our yard his face shone with a big smile, and then I glimpsed Mommy and Daddy's smiling faces also. They came as quickly as they could out of the car to grab the tightly entangled bunch of three kids meshed together like a walking octopus with arms, each of us wanting to be the first to give them a hug. It was easy to see that Mr. Hagan was enjoying our emotional moment of being together at home once again.

I noticed that my parents were wearing new clothes, which I assumed Mr. Hagan had bought for them. Later, I learned that as Mommy and Mr. Hagan had gone from store to store while Daddy rested, Mr. Hagan, now aware of their sensitivity about charity, had written a list of each item Mommy felt they needed, with the comment that he would take the amounts of her purchases from Daddy's future salary. As it turned out, however, Mr. Hagan would later claim that he had lost that list, and he never allowed them to reimburse him.

After hugs and delighted giggles, Daddy said, "I got good news from the doctor. He thinks with his treatment and a lot of medicines I will be as good as new. And the best news of all is that Mr. Hagan has hired me to help him get organized in building his chicken farm."

The following weeks were filled with excitement as we watched Daddy's health improve. I have always thought that Mr. Hagan's promise of the first and only salaried job Daddy ever had gave a tremendous boost to Daddy's health. Although the doctor had not found cancer, he had diagnosed a serious liver condition, along with kidney problems and malnutrition. During all the years that followed, in spite of the doctor's diagnosis, Mommy staunchly held to the belief that Daddy had been healed of cancer through the many prayers of his friends, combined with the excellent care of Mr. Hagan's friend, the doctor. We never argued with her about the details of Daddy's illness. All of us simply rejoiced with her that we now had our healthy Daddy back and had found a dear friend in Mr. Hagan.

Chapter 17

Emerson

The following spring, almost every afternoon on the narrow mountain road, our old school bus would meet an empty lumber truck coming from Mr. Hagan's farm. Then followed the slow process of the school bus backing up until it came to a wider place in the dirt road, to allow room for the two vehicles to ease safely by each other.

Mommy kept busy preparing Mr. Hagan's house for him to move into when his furniture arrived, and although Daddy rested as much as he could, he did start accompanying Mr. Hagan, and even chauffeuring him to Ellijay and Jasper for a variety of errands. Mr. Hagan seemed to enjoy talking with my Daddy about the area and asking him questions about farming. He also wanted to find out as much as he could about his own parents, who had passed away. My Daddy hadn't known his mother and daddy, but could tell him who had known them.

Grandma would be home each day cooking an enormous evening meal. Mr. Hagan had asked my parents and Grandma if he might buy groceries for all of us, and Grandma had agreed in return to cook for Mr. Hagan, in addition to her family.

"I would so love to enjoy Miss Ethie's delicious cooking that I have heard so much about from the neighbors," Mr. Hagan had said. "I could walk that lovely pathway up the creek and take my dinner back to my home each evening."

Grandma had said, "Oh, you should eat the food for supper, while it's hot, and not hold it over for the next day's dinner."

We had laughed and Grandma had smiled and said, "Oh, now I remember! What we call supper, you call dinner."

"Yes," Mr. Hagan had said, "and that half-mile walk to your house and back to mine is just the amount of walking my friend Dr. Roper suggested last week that I take each day."

In the meantime, the construction of the chicken houses was well underway. My friends and I would sometimes get off the school bus on Burnt Mountain Road and go straight to the Hagan farm. Some of the carpenters were the dads of my friends. It was exciting for all of us to see and smell the fresh sawed lumber, since none of our families had money to buy new lumber. All the construction with which we were familiar was done with old boards that came from buildings too far gone to repair.

One day, as we arrived at the construction site, Colleen walked up toward where Daddy and Mr. Hagan were sitting on the porch of his house, while I walked closer to the new chicken houses being built near the creek bank. Breathing in the smells of the lumber, I rubbed my hands up and down the smooth surfaces of one of the chicken houses. It was hard to believe boards could ever look like new. As I stood there, in the afternoon light, it struck me that the difference between these fragrant, fresh boards and aged, weathered ones was like the difference between a baby's soft face and an elderly person's dry, wrinkled one. With a happy and new awareness, I realized that this was the first time I had ever had this thought. I was excited to form new ideas like this one. I looked forward to a day when I could write such ideas down on paper, and share them with other people.

As I daydreamed about my future writing, I listened to the peaceful sound of the water flowing in Turkey Creek, beside the new structures. Three other spring streams joined the one that flowed from the mountain stream by our valley, to create this larger creek. I had always enjoyed walking on its mossy banks. I smiled to myself as I remembered how, when I was little, I had often wished I could turn into a stream so that I could one day see the big ocean.

The sun was now going down behind the mountain on the opposite side of the creek from the chicken houses, and as I looked past the long, freshly built structures to the house about fifty yards up the hill, I saw that Colleen was standing with Mommy and Mr. Hagan on the right side of his car, as Daddy sat inside in the passenger seat. It looked as if a family conference was going on, and I thought, what an unusual place for a family talk. I walked up into the yard, and stood beside Colleen.

Mr. Hagan turned and smiled at me as he said, "Hi, young lady. I saw you were observing the workmen. Do you approve of the men your father has chosen to work for me?"

"Yes, I do," I said. "I like seeing some of my friends' parents having a job working on the buildings. I was also enjoying the smell of new lumber."

Mr. Hagan had an important-looking book in his hand. It looked like a Bible, although I assumed it wasn't. He placed the book on the hood of his car, and then turned to talk again to my family. Walking a little closer, I read the name of the author: Ralph Waldo Emerson.

"Arthur," Mommy said, "we'd better get home so I can milk the cows before dark."

"Yes, yes. Let's all pile in the car and I'll take you home," said Mr. Hagan. So we jumped into his big brown Buick, Mr. Hagan and Daddy sitting in the front, and the three of us wedged inside the back seat. People didn't worry about seat belts in those years.

Once we had driven the short journey in style, and arrived home, Grandma and Gene came out to greet us. Gene jumped into Mommy's arms, and started to tell her about school and all the things he'd been up to.

Mr. Hagan said, "Miss Ethie, thank you for all those delicious dinners. I don't get to thank you often, since you're usually out doing chores when I come. I'm always excited to smell the appetizing aroma when I pick up that huge tin box." Grandma set this tin box each evening in the warming closet attached to our stove.

Grandma smiled, and Mr. Hagan continued, "I am thoroughly enjoying those big pieces of ham and the flaky biscuits, along with the green beans and tomatoes and all the other vegetables. I feel as if I'm a child again, eating my own Grandma's good food."

Grandma beamed as she answered, "You are most welcome and thank you for buying all those good groceries. It makes cooking easier and it's a joy not to have to skimp."

In conversation later that evening, I learned that a family conference really had been going on that afternoon beside Mr. Hagan's car. Mr. Hagan had suggested a plan for the carpenters to build a new, small house on the property, which he could live in. He asked my family if we would consider moving into the main house. We would have it to ourselves, and Mr. Hagan would be able to come over each day from his living quarters to share my Grandma's meals.

I wondered if Mr. Hagan liked the idea of being included in our family. His children were grown and married, since he had married young. He did not talk about why his wife had not joined him yet in his retirement on the farm, although he had mentioned earlier that she might. We were curious, but not presumptuous enough to ask questions; that would have been considered very poor manners. Being such a private man, and a relatively well-off "furriner," even though he had been born and raised in our area, Mr. Hagan inspired a good bit of suspicion in our community. But from the first, I never doubted Mr. Hagan's goodness. He was an unusually generous person, kind to anyone in need, and showed such genuine concern for my family, that I felt filled with gratitude and love.

As I realized instantly, to live in the house on Mr. Hagan's farm would give us much more space and comfort. It would also mean that Colleen and I would definitely be able to finish high school.

One spring evening, the day before we would be moving our furniture to the Hagan farmhouse, Daddy and I were walking from our old barn to our two-room house. This would be our family's last night to sleep inside those familiar walls.

Daddy and I were holding hands affectionately as we walked. I was enjoying the feeling that, while just a few months earlier, it had been necessary for us to hold Daddy's hand to steady him, now he no longer needed our support. I still felt reluctant, though, to let go of his hand.

"Daddy, what do you think healed you, medicine or prayer?" I asked him.

We stopped, and he gently released my hand.

At first he looked serious, and then his face muscles lifted into a smile, as he said, "I bargained with God and told Him that if He would let me get well so that I could see my children finish high school, I would promise Him that I would never take my little copper still and make corn liquor again."

I thought about all the fun I had had as a child, slushing my small bare feet in the white fermented mash as Daddy stirred. He would also let mounds of it "accidentally" overflow the big wooden box containers, so I could play in the extra mash. I loved the memory of us being out in the woods together; with the moonlight making ghostly shadows as deer and other animals rustled the leaves. Sometimes when Daddy would hear these noises, he would look toward the sound and softly say, "That might be the law!" When he said that, I would rush to hold onto the leg of his overalls. I could never tell which was the strongest emotion I felt – fear or the thrill of adventure.

"Daddy, what would have happened if it had ever been the law coming to your still?" I asked now.

He smiled as he let his shoulders shake, as in a mocking chill. "Your Mommy and Grandma would have taken my hunting rifle and killed me?"

"Well, you told me not to tell them I helped you with the mashing. Remember you told me that, as you washed my feet and legs in the spring branch? And I'm glad I never did."

I looked up into his face and smiled. I figured my height as a masher to have been just to the top of his hip, whereas now I stood almost even with his shoulder.

As Daddy and I neared the kitchen, the lamp in the window welcomed us with its soft light. We heard the happy sounds of Mommy, Colleen, Gene and Grandma making practical plans for our move.

"It's going to be a little sad, us sleeping in different bedrooms," Mommy was saying.

"I'll be glad!" said Colleen. I knew how happy she was to move, because she often spoke of how much she wished she had her own room, like her friend Dora, who had a room all her own where she could have her own personal sewing box, since she was the only child in her family. Colleen and her friends didn't care much for books. They felt they should be doing more practical things, like learning how to keep a home with husband and children.

I figured Colleen had made my decision easy, and I was happy. Mommy had told me earlier that I would be sleeping with either Colleen or Grandma, and even though I was now sixteen years old, I wasn't yet ready to leave Grandma's warm, comforting body.

As my Daddy and I stood together on the big flat rock that had been the step boosting all our feet and our ancestors' feet into the kitchen since before the Civil War, he looked down at me, and a mischievous wink briefly closed his right eye.

"It's going to be such a bother opening and closing the screen doors at the Hagan place," he said.

Remembering all the times I had heard him stand on that rock and say, "I wish someday we could have enough money to put up screen doors to keep all these damn flies and bugs out," I said, "We're just going to have to get used to it."

The move to the Hagan house lifted our standard of living way above what we could have imagined. Daddy gained regular income from chauffeuring Mr. Hagan on business trips to and from Birmingham, Alabama. He also helped him with repairs on the house and chicken farm. Their shared love of the mountains and Mr. Hagan's nostalgic admiration for my family's life style led these two people to become the best of friends.

Many times I heard Mr. Hagan say to Daddy, "You love and take care of your little mules and work them just the way my Daddy did his."

He also started a gentle habit of inviting Daddy to sit with him and share a couple of his beers most every evening, while they watched the sun set behind the mountain on the opposite side of Turkey Creek from the house. That mountain, named Old Rocky Top, was smaller than the surrounding ones, but it was special to us because it was in the direct path of the sun as it left our sight each evening among billowy red and orange clouds. Their conversations consisted mostly of swapping mountain stories that Daddy knew and some vintage ones that Mr. Hagan remembered hearing from his father.

In the meantime, Mommy made her first-ever weekly salary, tending to Mr. Hagan's chickens, and Colleen and I worked along beside her in the evenings after school and on weekends. Those part-time hours brought in a small but regular income, allowing us to continue high school.

I liked to rush through my work with the chickens so that I could spend time "cleaning" Mr. Hagan's living room, which was filled with books. Mr. Hagan's quarters included two large separate rooms – a bedroom and a living room – built in the yard about thirty feet from his farmhouse, where my family lived. Mr. Hagan's new rooms would probably not be classified as a house, since he did not choose to have a full kitchen, or even a kitchenette. He often remarked, "It's so nice not to have to bother with cleaning a kitchen." He had the carpenters build an attractive sheltered pathway from his quarters to our kitchen, where he continued to enjoy the meals Grandma prepared for all of us. I recall that my parents and Grandma admired the wisdom of his plan for both closeness and independence. He had moved into his new home every item that belonged to him, leaving the house open to our own items and way of living.

Daddy would say, "Mr. Hagan is a very wise man; he knows two families living so close together must make special plans for their daily habits or they will get hurt feelings. He also has the money to do it his way. Our family would have had to just let fellow family members, who had a need, move straight into our crowded house."

It was an absolute necessity, in my mind, that each and every one of Mr. Hagan's wonderful books should be taken off the shelf and carefully dusted. Since those books covered the four walls of his living room, by working a few hours each morning, I could touch every book at least once a week.

I lingered longest with the books of Emerson, flipping through the pages, perhaps an hour at a time, as I would try to understand him. I could feel Emerson's passion for life. He seemed to understand the depths of things and to articulate what I felt in my heart.

The day I read these words of Emerson, something clicked in my mind: "We animate what we can, and we see only what we animate. Nature and books belong to the eyes that see them." I liked the idea that a person can bring the world to life, through the power of imagination. I wrote this quote on a piece of a brown paper bag, and many times in the following days, while I was working, I would take that sweat-soiled crumpled piece of paper from my pocket and study it.

It struck me that Emerson was right. During all my years of dreaming about finding a better life, I had been creating the possibility of this life through my own vision of it. I might not have thought of it in this way, but it was true. Looking at the world around me, I had animated what I saw, and I had seen what I had animated. Through dreaming, in a most sincere and prayerful manner, about a life I could live, I had been helping to create the possibility that my yearnings would come true.

That thought was confirmed when I spoke to Mr. Hagan about the feeling I got from this Emerson quote.

"Even though I am not religious," Mr. Hagan said thoughtfully, "I see you're taking that quote so seriously and indeed I think you could say, it's a confirmation of the teachings of Jesus, who proclaimed to His followers, 'It is done unto you as you believe.'"

Oh, how I loved my conversations with Mr. Hagan! I felt that he was like a warm and caring uncle. He was the first person who had ever listened to my ideas with such attentiveness, and who spoke to me like an equal in the realm of thought. From time to time, as I was immersed in my "cleaning," Mr. Hagan would notice with affectionate interest my habit of lingering over the books. He might say something like, "See something good in that one, Dean?" and then he would proceed to go on to tend to his business in town or with some of his old neighbor's children, with whom he had grown up. The fact that Mr. Hagan always honored my desire, in high school, to change my name from "Odean" to "Dean" gave me additional proof of how thoughtful he was.

The truth is Mr. Hagan was not one of our kind of people. He was "citified." Even his old friends tended to be educated, well-off people like the President of the bank, or the doctor who had taken care of Daddy in Atlanta. Most all of his other childhood friends were no longer living in Appalachia, and, as far as I knew, none of them but Mr. Hagan had wanted to return to the mountains. Two of his other friends, whom Daddy had known, had died young, some years before Mr. Hagan had returned to the area.

As Daddy and Mommy told us in one of our family conferences, Mr. Hagan had let them know, confidentially, that his marriage hadn't worked out. He had hoped his wife would come with him, yet this hope had not been realized. Yet, apart from this conversation Mr. Hagan had had with my parents, he never again mentioned his wife, and we never mentioned her either. Even now I feel a surge of guilt as I write this, because I am betraying Mr. Hagan's privacy and the confidence of my parents. I have a feeling that Mr. Hagan would understand, however, because he was also a man who applauded honesty in writing. I like to think that, over seventy years after my discovery of his secret, he would grant me permission to reveal it.

My life during my first year of high school was filled with tremendous hope and promise. My precious friendship with Mr. Hagan opened my eyes to a new world of ideas beyond the Appalachian hills. Talking with Mr. Hagan about great writers like Emerson gave me a valuable sense of companionship. To my family and my neighbors, I may have seemed like a dreamer, yet to Mr. Hagan my dreams made sense. I wondered if he too was someone who took refuge in books and conversations about philosophy. His life, while it had been easier than mine in some ways, had held its own disappointments and challenges. Looking back, I often think that Mr. Hagan would have been better suited to teaching than to handling the cares of running a farm. For both of us, the world of ideas was consoling in its shimmering clarity and beauty.

Colleen and her friends, meanwhile, had started to date boys and even to think about marriage. Getting married and having a family had been the pattern of lives in my community for many generations. This way of life continued to have no appeal for me, however. The very idea of marrying and having one baby after another, as I had seen happening to my former classmates, seemed to me to be as depressing as entering an old shack after basking in bright sunlight.

Glen, my good neighbor and childhood friend, was one of the boys who made a number of different approaches to ask me for a date. I tried to ignore what he was really asking, or to change the subject.

Somewhat bashfully, he finally asked, "Dean, I would love to take you to the County Fair on Friday, would you go with me? My brother Wes is borrowing Daddy's pick-up and we could ride in the truck bed and feel the wind blowing in our faces."

I felt sorry for Glen, in his awkward stumbling. For a couple of seconds, I wanted to grab his slumped body in the patched overalls and tell him yes, but I stifled that urge and said, "No, Glen, I can't, because we're getting a house ready for a truck load of baby chicks and the old school bus is bringing them in boxes. I'm going to need to put them to bed."

Bedtime for the baby chicks was a tedious job. I had to go among the piles of chirping, fluffy baby chicks and shuffle their tiny warm bodies to make sure that they were not piling into heaps so that the ones on the bottom would be smothered. I was so glad I could speak the truth about that night, and I hoped I would not be hurting Glen's feelings.

I did go out with Glen some months later, and he would become the first boy I kissed. Although I thought he looked handsome in his Army uniform – he was on leave before he went overseas – I did not respond to his kiss with the enthusiasm he must have desired. I realize now that I was a "slow bloomer," with a cautiousness about sexuality that had been encouraged by my Mommy's and Grandma's and neighbors' stories about all the terrible things that could happen to a girl once she opened up that door of sex.

Glen was killed in the early summer of that year, on his first day in active combat on the beach of Normandy, on June 6th, 1944. I was horrified to think of that gentle boy having to die violently like that, so far from home. The only good to come out of his awful death would be that his family would be able to use part of his government life insurance money to buy a good farm on rich creek bottom land. The "bottom land" was perfect for growing corn and vegetables, and yielded cash crops to the lucky farmers who owned a parcel nestled in the valley. I knew that Glen would have been glad to know about his parents' greater physical comfort, in spite of their grief.

One evening after Glen's death in Normandy, I overheard a tender conversation between my Mommy, Daddy and Grandma, in which they counted over Glen's good qualities and their fond memories of him as a boy. As I sat reading inside my bedroom, I could hear them talking quietly on the screened porch just outside my window. Those porch conversations on summer evenings were a common occurrence, even a tradition, in my family all the years of my girlhood. The katydids led the night birds' chorus as we would watch the lightning bugs flicker in the dusk. The background for this orchestra was the soothing sound of the water flowing over the rocks in the creek bed.

Mommy said, "I miss seeing Glen coasting his old beat-up bike down the hill when he'd come and sit here and talk with us. You remember he had found that old bicycle in Mrs. Leach's junk pile?"

"Yes," said Grandma, "I remember, and how we did love little Glen's sweet and polite ways from when he was a child. He often told me how much he liked my apple pies, and he seemed to enjoy talking to us old folks. But I always knew when he came to sit with us that he had hopes Odean would come out of the house. She never did join us, though."

"I knew he had special feelings for Odean," said Mommy, "but she never really dated any boy around here much. Since her teenage years, she has had her heart set on getting away from our mountains, and I don't think anyone is going to stop her."

Daddy put in, "Aw, Mamie, you never can tell, she may change her mind and marry a young man around here, even before Colleen does."

As I listened to Daddy's hopeful idea about my future, I promised myself for the hundredth time that I would not get stuck in a marriage, especially if it meant staying close to home. Much as I loved my family, I wanted more than ever to live in a different way. I yearned for a life filled with books and ideas, and conversations just like the ones I was lucky to have had with Mr.

Hagan, as we sat on his porch, a book of Emerson's essays on the table between us.

Chapter 18

The Shiny Red Tractor

School meant the world to me. However, after working part-time on Mr. Hagan's broiler farm and going to high school for three years, since the start of eighth grade, I surprised everyone by deciding toward the end of my tenth grade year to leave school temporarily for one year, in order to work full-time in the broiler house. I had the idea that I could study independently, with the help of Mr. Hagan and his library. I felt sure that I would be able to keep up with my classmates, and in any case I could go back to school the following year for the eleventh grade, which was then as far as our high school went.

My reason for taking off a whole year had nothing to do with school, which I continued to love; it had to do with a fire-engine-red Farmall tractor that had recently been placed in the window of the combined pick-up truck and tractor store. During the spring of tenth grade, each time I had gone to town with Daddy, I had seen him stand and stare at that valuable tractor. I wanted so much to purchase it for him, yet I could not earn a quarter of the amount I needed with my part-time hours. I felt as if Daddy had been so supportive of me in my pursuit of education that I wanted to be able to give him something equally important.

I spoke to my parents and my Grandma again and again, but they remained vehemently opposed to my plan to suspend my education. They refused to listen to my explanation as to why I had changed my plans from school to full-time work. I brought out the fact that Daddy would be so much less tired if it wasn't necessary for him to follow behind the mules as he worked to keep the plow in place. If he only had a tractor to do much of the manual labor, he could stay healthy. I worried that if he continued to work so hard, he would get sick again.

On the day I planned to ask Mr. Hagan if I could work full-time, I decided to bake a cake and take it over to his living quarters about mid-afternoon. I found him pulling weeds from his prize dahlias. He greeted me with great joy, as he smelled the warm cake. I had also brought a jar of the rich milk that he liked. Many times he would say, "Oh this delicious unpasteurized raw milk, just like my mother had. I lived in Birmingham much too long."

He looked at the spread I had placed before him in his living room, and exclaimed, "Wonderful, wonderful, Dean! You will make some man a wonderful wife someday." He added, with a smile, "But I am so glad that you want to further your education now."

With that remark I could sense that the answer would be a definite no, but I continued anyway.

"That's what I wanted to talk to you about." Now my voice croaked and trembled as I spoke. "Mr. Hagan, would you please let me work full-time for a year, so that I could buy Daddy the tractor in the window of the tractor store?"

"Of course not!" Mr. Hagan was adamant. "Don't even think of it! As much as you love school, you must not drop out one year before you graduate."

I made my voice as stern as his had been. "I wouldn't be 'dropping out' of school, though," I said, "because I know I am going to go back and finish my final year. Why doesn't anyone understand me, and how much I want to see my Daddy riding that tractor instead of walking behind the horses and plow? Even when he stares at it in the window, I don't think he has ever considered the possibility of owning a tractor. I can make that dream come true if you will hire me full-time. I have already figured it out on paper to show you that I will make enough money in one year to buy it for him, and then I will be happy to complete high school."

I handed him the paper, but he just grasped it with annoyance and crumpled it up before tossing it onto the table. At that moment an intense flash of lightning and a blast of thunder jolted his living room, and I ran off to see if my family was safe inside our house. A typical summer storm was blowing swiftly through.

That entire summer, I tenaciously continued to plead the value of my decision to work for one year and buy the tractor for Daddy before I returned to school to graduate. At times, I just plain argued my point to Daddy, Mommy, Grandma, Colleen and Mr. Hagan. I am still not sure how I won – maybe I just wore them all down with my stubbornness – but win I did.

Come September, I went to work full-time, my heart filled with a mixture of heaviness and happiness. Each morning I would hear the old school bus rumbling down the hill with laughing voices inside, carrying Colleen and Gene to school. That sound would echo for hours in my mind, while I filled half-gallon glass jars and turned them upside down to release water to the thirsty baby chicks. Each time Mr. Hagan issued me the bigger paychecks, though, the heaviness lifted, as I experienced the weekly thrill of seeing my bank account expand. That money permitted me to make my first tangible investment and to realize my dreams for a better life my family could begin to enjoy.

After I stubbornly held to my decision to delay my high school graduation by a year, a number of surprising events materialized for me. First, the sweetest gift, which I shall never forget, was the special kindness extended to me by Colleen in between her scoldings about my decision.

After her days at school our evenings usually went something like this:

"Colleen, would you please show me your assignments in English and literature so that I can follow along with you and get an idea of what to expect next year?"

She generally responded with her usual parental-type conditions. "Alright, but first you must study my math assignments, because you don't like math, and remember, your poorest grades have always been in that subject."

I obediently did as she advised. Each day I raced through the math so that I could get on to literature. I had the attitude toward the algebra problems that I had about tending the chickens: Rush! In the afternoons I rushed so I could return to Mr. Hagan's porch, where we would sit and talk books. There the hours flew by until Mr. Hagan would insist I must go on across the yard and into the family house and get some sleep, because my morning hours of work with the chickens commenced at dawn each day.

Mommy and I shared many happy conversations during that year, much as we had enjoyed sharing the reading of *Gone with the Wind* at the stream a few years earlier. Although she was quiet on the subject of my schooling, I felt she sensed that my plan for purchasing the tractor was sincerely only a temporary detour from high school, and that I would continue with school the following year.

Colleen generously shared many books she had checked out of the county library. That library, which had expanded its collections over the years, now had shelves filled with books by great authors, as well as lighter books by authors like Faith Baldwin. Electricity had just come to our neighborhood, so even in the middle of the night I could slip into the kitchen to read and write. Many nights I sat for hours at the kitchen table, and when I saw daylight peeping from behind Kerns Mountain, I would leave for the broiler houses and spend four to five hours feeding and watering the chickens. Since I was so fond of reading Faulkner, I tried to write like him, even copying some complete sentences. Luckily, I didn't get published! I had never heard of the word plagiarism.

By early March, I had saved enough money to buy that new tractor for my Daddy. One bright morning I saw the tractor store salesman in a big truck, pulling a shiny red tractor over the hill toward our house. The noise of an unfamiliar motor brought Daddy out of the barn, and he came rushing across the road. His smile was even brighter than the sun rising over the mountain when he saw that red tractor come to a stop in our yard.

On the first day he used the tractor, I felt tremendous joy in seeing him get on it and take off, turning the soil.

"This is the prettiest little thing that I have ever seen," he yelled to Mommy and me as he made a graceful turn at the corner of the field nearest to us.

The smile that lit Mommy's face stretched her generous mouth, as she and I shared the special joy of seeing Daddy enjoy his gift. My joy was doubled when I saw her broad smile, as she rarely had reason to express that much happiness.

"I remember he used to say you were the 'prettiest little thing he ever saw,'" she said.

"But no more the prettiest," I said, smiling back at her.

The pungent smell of soil being turned in springtime is still sharp in my memory. Daddy could now rapidly bring up the dirt from its quiet calm of winter rest as he sped along on this machine. In less than an hour he had turned the same piece of ground that ordinarily would have taken a full day.

Much as the early Native Americans worshipped the earth, Daddy always spoke of God's earth as being alive and holy. He felt it was our obligation and pleasure to cherish it for its life-giving qualities. Now he sat on his new tractor and smiled as he looked over the upturned soil of the shining field he had plowed so quickly and so well.

As I immersed myself in this tractor project, and in Mr. Hagan's book collection, Colleen finished school and graduated. After graduation, she bought a wooden frame with her own money, to display her diploma. Two new firsts for our family: a high school diploma and enough money for something as unessential as a frame. Colleen would announce with smiling eyes, "I am going to always keep this diploma on my bedroom wall!" Throughout her long life, it would indeed remain right on her bedroom wall, where she could see it before she closed her eyes for sleep each night.

In the spring of my "tractor-buying year," I also had the happiness of buying a beautiful old foot pump organ from a neighbor. The story of this second big purchase is one that my daughter Jeriann has always loved. Many people showed up at the neighbor's sale of various belongings, and the house was crowded. My Daddy and I had gone to the sale together, but we soon became separated. Knowing that Daddy, the musical one in the family, really wanted the organ, I focused on trying to buy it for him. Unbeknownst to Daddy and me, however, we wound up bidding against each other. Together we raised the price to $25.00 – a lot of money in those days – for this big old organ, which sat in my parents' house for many years, and is now a beloved instrument sitting in Jeriann's living room in California.

I have always felt glad to be able to buy special objects like these. That tractor and that organ both contributed to my Daddy's comfort and happiness. It was a great pleasure to be able to give something back to him and to my family, after all they had done for me.

My life started to become more complicated, however, during the summer before my eleventh and final grade of high school. The complication came out of the rumors that started to swirl around my relationship with Mr. Hagan.

It was Colleen who first informed me one afternoon that my cool attitude toward boys of my own age, and my constant refusal to date anyone, had caused our friends to think I was "stuck up."

She and I were busy washing half-gallon water jugs for the baby chicks outside what we called "number one chicken house." Colleen had a dishcloth and soapy water in one tub, and I was bending over the rinsing tub that sat beside hers. We did this job together daily and sometimes we talked, but most of the time we were silent and busy with our own thoughts.

Colleen could not resist adding, "Dean, people are talking about you and Mr. Hagan too. I overheard some of them discussing you today, saying things like, 'All Dean wants to do is sit and talk and read with that old city man with money.'"

I was alarmed to hear Colleen say that, but I shrugged my shoulders and said, "I really don't care. What if I *had* rather sit and read and talk with Mr. Hagan?"

"Odean, if people gossip about you, it may ruin your life."

Even though I knew she meant to be kind, as she cautioned me, I was not receptive to her warning. As I finished my rinsing, I just laughed and rushed on over to Mr. Hagan's porch.

I could see he was reading our favorite author, Emerson.

He looked up at me and said, "Dean, listen to this!"

I sat down on his doorstep and listened to Emerson's words, as Mr. Hagan so eloquently read them: "'Nothing great was ever achieved without enthusiasm.'"

The essence of those words suddenly seemed to penetrate and light up my consciousness and body with the purest joy of being, such as I had never felt before. I became so sure that the only way to live fully would be to let gratitude, hope and happiness spread through my thinking, and to let my anger fade away. I felt that Mr. Hagan was encouraging me, with Emerson's words, to be my enthusiastic self and not to worry about what others thought.

Mr. Hagan's gentle way of accepting and reaching out to everyone, especially to newcomers, was unusual in our community, and increased our neighbors' suspicion of him. He was welcoming of an elderly man, for instance, whose family had moved to our community, and whose son Jesse was rumored to be a "queer." I wasn't sure what that word meant, but I was glad that instead of making fun of Jesse with mean snickers, as other people felt privileged to do, Mr. Hagan would be kind to him. Although Jesse was in his thirties, and a wonderful musician, in some ways he appeared to be much younger and more open than his peers. He liked playing ball and other games with boys, instead of talking with people his own age, although he was fond of older people and simply adored my Grandma. He also liked books.

Realizing that Jesse read at about a seventh grade level, Mr. Hagan searched through his collection of books to find appropriate ones for him. Whenever Jesse came over, Mr. Hagan gave him a special selection of books, which Jesse would accept with a smile. He seldom took advantage, however, of Mr. Hagan's kind offer to sit and read with Mr. Hagan and me. I suppose he was reluctant because he felt he might be a bother to Mr. Hagan. It seemed Jesse had developed that attitude because most people didn't have time for him or didn't care to make time.

My Grandma was as accepting as Mr. Hagan was. Whenever she asked Jesse to play our family organ, she would invite Mr. Hagan to come listen too. He was a most appreciative audience, which delighted Jesse and all of us.

Looking back these many years later, after having seen so much national progress in the area of appreciating individuals who have different orientations, backgrounds, and life styles, I see Mr. Hagan as an early messenger who demonstrated this sense of open-mindedness and acceptance in his personal life. He was able to foresee the very real necessity for future generations to move in this important direction. I am grateful that I was privileged to have the special friendship of a man who lived many years before his time.

Our community was far less open-minded than Mr. Hagan, however, a fact that soon became sharply clear in a personal way. A couple of Sundays after I had ignored Colleen's warning that my "character" was in danger of being destroyed, I saw Preacher Murphy and two deacons of the church standing on the porch and talking solemnly to Mommy as I returned to our house at dusk, after settling the baby chicks in their bedding places for the night.

Before they noticed my presence, I heard these words coming from Preacher Murphy's mouth: "Mamie, our church members are very concerned that you and Arthur may not know, and if so, are unable to warn your daughter of the jeopardy she is causing to her character. We expect our older children to set the highest examples among the younger neighborhood children. All the church elders have been praying for Jesus to show your daughter the way from her sinful behavior."

I was too shocked to speak. I turned and walked around the house to enter by the back door. There I met Grandma, whose face was pale and drawn.

She spoke just above a whisper. "Honey, it looks bad for you to stay in Mr. Hagan's rooms so much and read."

"But Grandma, I haven't done anything wrong!" I cried.

"I know, but if people think you have done something wrong it is just the same as if you did."

Her face showed agony. Perhaps she was remembering what she had endured in her own young life from neighbors gossiping about her pregnancy outside of marriage. She had never spoken to anyone about that chapter in her life, not even my mother. To my mind, though, that difficult period had actually produced positive events. Because of it, she had Mommy and our precious life together. Yet to Grandma that time in her life must have remained a tender and vulnerable memory.

Mommy came inside to stand beside us without speaking for a few minutes. She began to cry as she said, "Dean, I know you are a good girl, but you must stop reading with Mr. Hagan. It looks bad to the neighbors."

Knowing how much my family valued appearances in the community, I didn't protest.

"I understand, Mother," I said, and as soon as the words left my mouth, I realized that this was the first time I had ever addressed my Mommy as "Mother."

I walked toward my room, trying hard to hold back the tears until I could close the door behind me. I was glad that Daddy and Mr. Hagan were gone to Birmingham and that Colleen was out on a date.

Later that evening, settled in my bed, I thought about my situation. In less than a month, I would be starting back to school, and my final year would be finished in ten months from that day. I began to feel comforted by the soft moonlight passing through the window and lingering over me.

I spoke into its presence. "In less than a year I will be free of this bondage to the opinions of a small community, and I will live in a big city where no one will care about my affairs."

Those changes that had been so positive for my family – living in Mr. Hagan's house, and earning a good living – had not protected me from the stranglehold of our community. I resolved to spend my last year of high school studying hard and being grateful for the good things now being enjoyed by my family, even as I got ready to grab my future independently in a new place.

Under our Christmas tree the following December, I would find a gift from Mr. Hagan. Wrapped in newspaper, it contained a large black and white poster for me, containing those words of Emerson's, "Nothing great was ever achieved without enthusiasm." With the poster came a card that read, "Dean, may you always grow in prosperity, and love with enthusiasm," and it was signed, H. Surrounding the poster was a large picture frame made of tan fabric. That gift thrilled me as much as any I had ever received.

Although sadly I lost Mr. Hagan's gift in one of my moves, I now have a copy of that profound message of Emerson's. It hangs on the wall just over my computer, and I look at it now each day as I write my memories.

Chapter 19

One Year of Confusion

The week following the preacher's visit, I got through my daily work in a daze, as I tried to come to terms with people's image of me. I came to feel that I was being perceived as some kind of fallen woman, like Mary Magdalene, the figure of womanhood considered most shameful by the preachers. During the entire week, while Daddy and Mr. Hagan were in Birmingham, our home was enveloped in quietness. I do not remember Mommy, Grandma or Colleen laughing or even smiling. I did not believe that they thought there was any truth to back up Preacher Murphy's worry about me, but since my family held to the firm belief that gossip was as ruinous to character as fact, they were utterly devastated.

Once, after supper, I couldn't help having to listen to yet one more of my family's fearful conversations, in whispers so that Gene would not hear.

Mommy softly said, "I wonder who all have been talking about this."

To which Colleen said, "Everybody, I bet."

Looking very sad as if she were about to cry, Grandma whispered, "Oh, children, don't say that."

Without saying a word, I left the table and went to my room to read. Soon I fell into a tired state of dozing and half-waking. Most of the time, I was awake enough to hear a whippoorwill outside my window continuously repeating his name. "Whippoorwill, Whippoorwill." I paraphrased its call to fit my own longing: *Yes I will. Yes I will. Yes I will get away.*

When Daddy and Mr. Hagan returned from Birmingham, I waited to find a good time to tell Mr. Hagan the situation. I could not possibly tell Daddy. Mommy had said to me, "Your Grandma and I have decided we will never tell your Daddy about Preacher Murphy's advice, because it would make Daddy so angry that he might become violent against whoever has been spreading these rumors. He has great pride in how decent his girls are turning out to be." So, I don't reckon they ever did tell him.

Mr. Hagan, however, had to be told. After finishing my morning chores with the chickens that August morning, I saw him sitting on his porch reading, and I stopped to talk. Briefly, and with my voice choking as I made an effort to control my fury, I told him about the preacher's visit.

"Preacher Murphy said my character is being ruined because I stay here with you and read. So Mommy feels it best that I no longer read with you."

I expected Mr. Hagan to share some of the anger I had been carrying around inside me that week, which I had tried to express in this one distressed, blunt statement. Instead, to my surprise and disappointment, Mr. Hagan seemed most concerned that Mommy had been subjected to worry and stress.

He stood up and said, "I must find your mother and apologize to her for being careless. The preachers say, 'Never give the appearance of doing evil.'" He looked at me with a kind of sorrow. "When I moved back, I hoped I would find the goodness and neighborly unity that I remembered as a child. I have found these qualities here, Dean, but I have also found suspicion and a quickness to judge."

As he stood on the porch next to me, he held the book he had been reading and closed his eyes for a moment. Although I was too young to feel empathy as deeply as I have learned to feel it in later years, I did get the distinct feeling that he had experienced

216

heartache in somewhat the same manner as I was experiencing it now. Since there had been no physical contact between us, he didn't have the burden of having done any wrong, only the pain of knowing that he was not trusted. Looking at him, at that moment, was like seeing his enthusiastic face fade off a movie screen, and then reappear, emptied and flat. I could not help but feel he had given up on our close relationship, out of obedience to our community. I understood, and yet I felt bitterly disappointed.

He opened his eyes and turned to go to Mommy, who was coming from the barn carrying a fresh pail of milk.

As he rushed toward her, he called back over his shoulder, "Dean, I dislike the preacher's choice of words. Remember, 'character' is what you are; 'reputation' is what people think about you."

After this change in my life, I began to look forward to school starting again. I would sorely miss my days of rushing through chores to read books with Mr. Hagan, but at least I would have a chance to continue my education. I would also be outside the circle of the preacher and our neighbors.

The last Monday of August 1947 was a balmy, beautiful day. I was trembling with excitement as I stood with Gene, a fifth-grader now, as we waited for the old school bus. I could sense my parents' and my Grandma's great joy in seeing me keep my word and return to finish school.

No family member expressed more delight than Mr. Hagan. The early morning sun shone upon his graying hair like a bright white halo, and his smile lit up his face. He was a picture of unselfish happiness that I would never forget.

The bus came into view, and slowed to a stop. Gene jumped into the bus ahead of me, and I followed.

As I put my foot on the first step, Mr. Hagan said to me, "Happy journeying into a future of expanding your quick and eager mind."

I smiled and said, "Thank you, Mr. Hagan!" I thought that remark was so rare, and so like him. Even though I still felt the new and painful distance between us, which Mr. Hagan had accepted and I had had to accept too, I loved the feeling of making him proud.

The old bus was filled with many voices as friends greeted each other again. Gene took a seat beside a close friend, Roy Anderson. I could hear the two of them reviewing and laughing about all the fun they had had frog gigging – spearing – during the summer. I sat alone, which had been my habit in previous years. For a few minutes, though, I felt as if I might cry, because it was the first time I had ever gone to school without Colleen. Still, I was happy that she had found a job working at a small café in Ellijay. As I looked out the window at the trees still green from summer, I felt the promise of this year ahead, filled with education that would help further my success in life.

When the bus had almost reached the top of the hill, I looked back toward our house. My Mommy, Daddy, and Grandma had gone back to their chores, but Mr. Hagan was still standing in the same spot, watching our bus go out of sight. He seemed to be lost in thought, even as he waved and cheered me onward.

Once I entered the high school, the smell of books was as comforting as it had been all the years before. I felt more than one year older than I had been the year before, however. I had definitely learned a lot about life through working and making a salary, and also through reading so many of Mr. Hagan's books. Instead of feeling I might be behind the other students, I actually felt more confident than I had expected I would, as I took a seat in the first row, directly in front of the teacher's desk. I was pleased to sit there, because most of the other students were laughing and talking in the two back rows, while a few stragglers, including my old friend Esther, were filling some of the desks in the middle.

"Hi there, Dean, we thought you'd dropped out of school," Esther said.

"I just stayed out and worked a year."

"Yeah, I heard you had a good job and you were making money. Why did you quit?"

"I want to get a diploma so I can go to evening college in Atlanta next year."

She looked at me as if she thought I might be dreaming, and then she turned to talk to someone else.

I busied myself reading my schedule of courses. I knew I would love learning to type, and the shorthand would be a requirement to land a good secretarial job once I got to Atlanta. English would be a joy. Civics would be a new course for me. I thought I would enjoy geography, because I had spent a lifetime dreaming I would go to many places, and history would be very interesting, but math would be a challenge. All in all, I felt a sense of great hopefulness welling up inside of me as I eagerly considered this array of courses.

At supper that evening, after Gene had told all of us about his new class, and what he and his friends had been up to at recess, I had a chance to describe my first day of eleventh grade. I was especially eager about my English course, because of the books we would be reading and the writing I would now have a chance to do.

When I had finished, I asked, "Did anyone miss me here today?"

Mr. Hagan quickly answered, with a teasing remark, "We hardly noticed you were gone."

All eyes sparkled and danced as our voices joined in a little chorus around the supper table, and the clatter of silverware followed with its own form of practical music, feeding hungry bellies.

That final year of high school went by quickly. My classes and my part-time work for Mr. Hagan filled my days. I started to feel almost breathless with the excitement of my upcoming graduation as a member of the Class of 1948, when I would finally be able to leave the farm and go to Atlanta to find a job. All my energy was focused on this goal. At my request, Mr. Hagan had already begun to put me on the mailing list of some colleges in Atlanta that offered evening courses.

However, my parents and Grandma resisted my plan to go to Atlanta, offering ideas for how I could be happier staying close to them. Each time I talked about leaving, one of my family members would counter my plan with all the persuasive powers at their command.

Mommy would often say, "You are so young, Dean, you could do that some years from now. We're luckier than most people around here, because we can make our money working right where we live, here at home."

Mommy's biggest tug on me was the idea that I could help Gene at nights with his homework, as Colleen had helped me. I felt guilt overwhelm me whenever she mentioned this.

"No one in our family has ever left," Mommy would add. "We have always stayed close by to help each other out."

Finally my Graduation Day came, and my whole family celebrated with me. For that special day, and a happy week or so afterward, all of us put aside our tug-of-war about my future. Mr. Hagan beamed, and Grandma made a special graduation dinner.

Gene wrote me a card of congratulations in his best hand. Mommy and Daddy looked joyful in the knowledge that their second child too had achieved this important goal of a full high school education.

Yet the question of my yearning to move to Atlanta started to hang in the air with even greater intensity over the course of that summer.

One of the most emotional talks I had was with Daddy. One afternoon, he asked me if I would like to go with him to the Andy Spring. This was Daddy's favorite spot. As he often declared, "That spring has the best tasting water that has ever sprung from the rocks of God's earth." Right by this special spring was a stump he frequently sat on as he considered the many problems that had tangled his life. We called it "Daddy's praying stump." That peaceful stump could be reached by a walking trail about two miles from our house, even farther into the mountains. Years before Daddy's birth, a family had built a shack and had lived there. The only evidence of human life in that green place now was a pile of rocks from a fallen chimney and a bed of March flowers that still flourished among the wildflowers in springtime.

On this warm summer day, Daddy started the subject that seemed to be on everyone's mind.

"Honey bunch," he said, "we have such a good life together here, why do you want to break up our family by going to Atlanta where so much meanness is going on? You know you wouldn't be safe there in a big city like that. There are all kinds of people in such a place that could do you harm. Here at home everyone knows you and cares about you."

I described my plan to him in the best terms possible. "But Daddy, now that I have got a high school diploma, I could get a college degree in time by working as a secretary there, and evenings I could further my education. Mr. Hagan has already got me in touch with some colleges that are not too expensive."

I could not convince him, though, with all the persuasion in my power, and he could not convince me either, even with the beauty of this peaceful, green place around his praying stump.

Over the course of the following year, Mommy and Daddy's earnestness to keep me safe started to wear on me. I could feel them pulling down my soaring aspirations to go to college. My Grandma's pleas, however, had the most powerful pull. She would peer over her tiny spectacles as tears welled up in her eyes.

"Almost every night when I hear H. V. Kaltenborn reciting the news, he tells about people getting killed in Atlanta," Grandma would say. "Dean, you are so young, couldn't you just stay a few more years and not break our family up now when we have got to where we can live easier? You know that now I draw a little old age pension check that comes in every month and that will help us out some." Her head would hang down as she continued, "And last month the doctor said I have a bad heart and could die at any time."

Whenever she reached this point of talking about her weak heart, I would hug her and then take off to sit on my rock at the bank of the creek, where I would cry my own heart out.

I didn't know what to think about my Grandma's health. I knew that my parents had taken her to a doctor in Jasper. At the time, though, we had all simply rejoiced that we now had enough money to pay a doctor. Mommy and Daddy had not mentioned that the doctor had believed her heart to be so frail. I thought the doctor had just suggested that she take some medicines for her high blood pressure and come back to see him in six months. Since Grandma never lied, I wondered if her fear about her health, along with the worry she felt about me living alone in Atlanta, colored her thoughts about the seriousness of her condition.

Those conversations with Mommy, Daddy, and Grandma continued all through the winter and the following spring and summer. After each session I felt weaker, more bewildered, and less able to make that move to get myself out and on my own. I felt smothered by my family's concern, even as I felt grateful to them. I thought that if I stayed home much longer, I would not be able to breathe.

At least one chance to escape presented itself to me that year. A girlfriend of mine, Gladys Miller, came up with the idea of leaving home secretly and getting a ride to Atlanta. Knowing how much I too wanted to live and work there, she let me in on her plan.

"Dean, I want to talk to you about something that's a secret," she said, as she glanced nervously around our yard. Then she motioned me to follow her to the swing connected to a huge limb of our big maple tree. She whispered, "My boyfriend Allen has a temporary job driving the ambulance. He is going to Atlanta in a couple of weeks and I am going to slip away from home and go down there with him. Will you come with me?"

"I'll think about it," I told her, and I did consider her invitation, but somehow her plan just didn't seem right for me. She was very disappointed when I told her of my decision not to go, and I felt disgruntled with myself for turning down this opportunity to get away.

Unfortunately, as I soon discovered, when she and her boyfriend, the ambulance driver, approached Marietta, they ran upon a roadblock. A roadblock was a method revenue officers used periodically to search vehicles coming from the mountains and heading toward Atlanta. They searched the ambulance – which doubled as a hearse in our community – and found gallons of corn liquor Allen had been intending to sell in Atlanta. The officers swiftly arrested Allen and put him in jail. Then they brought Gladys back to her home, because they believed her when she told them she was innocent and hadn't known anything about the illegal alcohol.

I felt badly for Gladys, and glad I hadn't decided to go with her and Allen to Atlanta, yet I still yearned to find my own way there. I would be more careful when I went. I would have a much better plan than theirs had been.

During that year, Colleen announced that she was going to marry her boyfriend Charles, who lived in Rome, Georgia, a much smaller city than Atlanta but about the same distance from Ellijay, in the opposite direction. She and Charles had met in the little café in Ellijay where she had been working during the previous year. I was very happy to see Colleen looking vibrant with joy because she loved Charles. Always practical, Colleen said she and Charles had decided to wait for a few months before marrying, so that they could save money.

As I listened to my sister's excited plans, I commenced to consider a significant value of marriage I had overlooked before. It struck me that getting married could offer a smoother way for me to obtain my freedom from my family. This fresh possibility of escape started to occupy my daydreams, as I watered the chickens or scooped chicken feed from my wheelbarrow, distributing it into the receptacles placed all along the floor of the broiler houses. I decided to think seriously about marrying. It seemed to be my only hope.

I began to visualize myself happily married, living in Atlanta, working as well as attending college, and I became more eager about this new vision each day. The only missing piece was a husband. Whom could I choose? The only young men I knew were contentedly working on their families' farms, which had come down to them through the generations. If Glen had lived, I had a feeling he would have been like them, happy to stay put.

After Colleen had married Charles, I finally made the decision to get more friendly with a former neighbor, named Johnny, who had lived a few miles away from us during my early years, and who now had a job at the Ford plant in Atlanta. He often spent weekends with his older sister, who had recently moved to live with another sister in our area. Like Glen, Johnny had served overseas in the Army during the War, yet he had had the chance to make it home again. I had never talked much with Johnny; for one thing, he was about ten years older than I was.

Now instead of tending the chickens on Sundays, I asked Mr. Hagan if he could hire someone to take my place so I could go to church with my family. I didn't tell Mr. Hagan why church suddenly had an appeal for me: I knew Johnny would be there with his sisters.

These many years I have tried to erase the details of that quick courtship from my thoughts, so that now it is a blur. I cannot remember any touching romantic scenes. I cannot remember thinking any thoughts that were not laced with my desire to use Johnny as a way to get out. I did vaguely consider the fact that I would be kind to him and that we would somehow be friends, but mainly all my mental energy was thrust toward living independently from my family, gaining a college education, and making a lot of money, which would benefit my family and myself and hopefully Johnny too -- that was, if he left me alone to plan my own life.

Soon enough, Johnny asked me to marry him, a couple of days after Thanksgiving, and I quickly said yes. I began my secret plans for that very next weekend to be the time of my life-changing experience – my unromantic, matter-of-fact marriage. I had to figure out how to get away from my family's house long enough to become married without their knowledge. If they knew about my wedding ahead of time, I worried that they would have the power to persuade me not to go through with it.

On a Monday morning early in December, Mommy and I were in a chicken house watering three-day-old babies, who had awoken with the dawn and were chirping in a chorus, letting their whole world of the chicken houses know that they were hungry and thirsty. Mommy was sitting on a stool filling the half-gallon mason jars with water, and I was going back and forth from her watering station, carrying the filled jars to the small boards near the feeding troughs where the tiny chicks hopped about.

I knew I should be getting the word to Mr. Hagan that he, Mommy and Daddy should plan the chicken house schedule so that I would be off from the following Friday afternoon until late Sunday afternoon. Maybe because of Mommy's softness, I felt it easier to raise the subject with her.

"Mommy, Johnny and I are planning to go with his brother Joe and his wife Sally to spend the weekend in Chattanooga," I lied.

Mommy shut the hose off from pouring water in the jars and answered, "Alright, your Daddy and I can cover for you, and we will manage to keep things going."

So without telling anyone, I married Johnny on a Saturday afternoon in December, in Rome, Georgia. The small service took place at the home of his sister, led by her husband, a Baptist preacher. I was twenty-two years old.

When I returned to my family the next day, and told them my news, they surprised me by appearing pleased. I quickly realized how they saw this situation: they felt relief that now perhaps I would settle down, like Colleen, and cease dreaming impossible dreams. Johnny was someone who had a background similar to mine, and even if I moved with him to Atlanta, I would not be alone in that city.

The next day was a cold and rainy Monday. I could not put off talking with Mr. Hagan about my elopement and my upcoming move to Atlanta. He was not surprised, since my family had already told him the news, but he did appear to be profoundly disappointed in me. I knew he had wanted more for me than a hasty marriage to someone who had far less education than I did, and no evident plans for more. He had hoped I could find someone with as much eagerness to discover new ideas as I had. I realize, looking back, that Mr. Hagan had no trust in Johnny as a husband who would be able to bring me happiness. He was worried for me, clearly sensing that I had not thought this marriage through.

I tried to find the right words. "I do want you to know that, with all my heart, Mr. Hagan, I am grateful for the opportunity you gave me to work for you and help our whole family to live here with you. And I especially thank you for helping me save money to buy Daddy's tractor."

I hugged him as I started to cry. His arms were trembling as he embraced me.

"I wish you much happiness always, Dean, and I hope you will continue to be enthusiastic about learning. And don't forget about Emerson," he said with a voice that sounded hollow and weak, as if he had become, in one day, a very old man.

I rushed to get away.

Over the next couple of days, I tried to fill myself up with the goodness of my family's home. I enjoyed each bite of my Grandma's delicious meals; I helped Gene with his spelling and writing; I did as many extra chores as I could, thinking in advance of the added work my Mommy and Grandma would have in my absence; I relished my family's quiet talks by the fire. Each item in our home started to look newly precious to me, as I readied myself to go.

It was all so confusing. I felt grown-up, in a way, since I was now a married woman, and yet I had gravely disappointed Mr. Hagan, who could not understand my marriage.

The worst of it was, I started to become aware of the truth of Mr. Hagan's point of view, even as I tried fiercely to ignore the nagging worries I had about my marriage. I knew my family and Mr. Hagan so much better than I knew Johnny. I had no sense of what Johnny was really like, or how he lived in Atlanta. I had never seen him look at a book. He chain-smoked cigarettes, and he also drank more beers than my Daddy or Mr. Hagan ever did. I could not envision what my life with Johnny would be like.

Yet I consoled myself with the thought that at least I would finally have a chance to live in a big city and go to school. I was sure that Johnny would earn good money, and at least some part of my dreams could be realized. To this day, I still wonder whether I would ever have had the courage to leave home if I had not first taken the step to get married.

On the day I saw Johnny again, after those days at home, my worries instantly increased. It was as I walked into his sister's house that I had my first jolt of true awakening. There was Johnny, sitting with a bowl of his cigarette butts on the table beside him, and a couple of empty beer bottles. He looked drunk, although it was only the middle of the afternoon, and he didn't lift a finger to help his sister. As I went into her kitchen, hoping I could immerse myself in preparations for dinner and postpone having to stay in the same room with Johnny, I fought the realization that this marriage I had chosen might become a nightmare. I tried not to hear myself think that my past years had been a wonderful dream that could now turn into a horror from which I would not be able to awake.

That night, instead of going to bed with Johnny, I rushed outside through the back door and into a cold winter storm. I wished I could be at home again, still unmarried. I wished I could go talk with Mr. Hagan about Emerson and enthusiasm again. I wished I still had my Grandma's warmth and my Mommy and Daddy's sturdiness nearby.

As I stood on the wet clay, shivering, I could hear the roaring winds from the pines that I had so often heard in my childhood. That night they became a lonely, moaning winter chorus, singing, "Little girl, little girl, what have you done to your life now?"

Chapter 20

Heading to Atlanta with Johnny

On the following rainy Sunday afternoon, a few days before Christmas, I tried hard not to burst into tears as I hugged Grandma, Mommy, Daddy and Gene. Colleen was living with Charles in Rome, and training to become a nurses' aide. Amid the goodbyes and tears, Johnny walked up the porch steps and held his opened umbrella for me. I stepped under it beside him and we rushed through the cold wind and rain to his Buick. I was headed for Atlanta to share my new life with him in his home.

Once we reached Johnny's car he opened the passenger door, tossed my basket of belongings into the back seat, and ran around to enter the driver's seat. I waved to the blurred images of my family as they stood on the porch. As our car eased along the driveway to enter the road, I looked toward Mr. Hagan's rooms and saw him sitting at his desk, reading. I waved to him, but I knew I would be invisible, as I sat inside the car with the sheets of rain pouring down. I could understand why he hadn't said goodbye, but I still felt saddened and very hurt.

"Saying goodbye is always hard," Johnny said. "The saddest day of my life was the day I followed the hearse carrying my mother's body to her grave."

His remark caused me to consider that at least I would be seeing my family the very next weekend, and I immediately felt better.

In my kindest tone, I said, "Yes, Johnny, that must have been terrible."

We traveled in silence the three miles along the muddy dirt road and then turned left onto the graveled highway.

"Could you hand me my basket?" I asked.

"Sure," he said, and smiled. Looking at his teeth, I realized that his constant smoking must have turned them yellow. I felt a little surprised that I had not ever looked very closely at his mouth, and had never kissed him in a way that I would have noticed the taste.

With his left hand holding the steering wheel, Johnny reached into the back seat to get my basket and place it in my lap. Most of my belongings, except my work clothes, lay in this basket, hand-woven from poplar bark. It was comforting to let my hands caress its sides. Mr. Hagan had bought it for my birthday two years earlier from a neighbor, whose special trade was basket weaving. It was typical of Mr. Hagan that his first choice in any purchase would be to support the local merchants or craft-making neighbors. I even knew the exact poplar tree this neighbor had cut down to make that beautiful and useful container. Several times, when walking in the woods, I had sat on the poplar's tree stump and thanked it for giving its life so that I could have a pretty basket.

The first item I lifted out of the basket was a navy blue dress with a white collar. I had bought that dress to wear on the night of my graduation. It was the loveliest dress I had ever had, and wearing it to my graduation had been the happiest occasion of my life. I liked remembering that night, when I could almost taste the joy of my dreams' fruition. The last time I had worn it had been at my wedding. Not feeling the deep wave of happiness about my wedding that I had felt thinking about graduation, I quickly folded the blue dress and placed it on the seat between us.

Next I took from the basket a white blouse and a black and white checkered skirt. I owned a couple of other dresses, but I hadn't brought them, since we would be returning home in five days for Christmas.

Finally, I lifted a brown leather dictionary and held it near my heart. It was my graduation present from Mr. Hagan. I brought the book down from holding it in a sacred position and laid it in my lap. Then I opened to the front fly page and read the inscription: *Dean, I know how you love words. I present this to you with my best wishes, knowing you will never be at a "loss for words." Best wishes, HWH.*

Johnny, noticing my preoccupation with the book, said, "I take it that is a special book."

"It's a dictionary that Mr. Hagan gave me and I treasure it more than anything I possess."

"Oh," he said blandly. He just kept looking straight ahead as he drove, and said nothing more.

I wondered, not for the first time, if Johnny had listened to the gossip that had gone around in the community, about Mr. Hagan and me. Johnny's deliberate quietness and coolness, when I spoke of Mr. Hagan's gift, suggested to me that he had. The neighbors' interpretation of my closeness to Mr. Hagan was still a sensitive subject for me, and it pained me to the quick to sense that Johnny might misjudge my relationship with Mr. Hagan just as my neighbors had. I felt that, at a minimum, Johnny was devaluing the gratitude I held in my heart for Mr. Hagan's kindness to my family.

In those moments in the car, as I held the dictionary, I felt distressed and angry enough that I decided to hurt Johnny back. If Johnny had heard any of that gossip, I would make it seem as if there was substance to it.

"I don't really mind if the neighbors disapproved of me," I said. "Mr. Hagan likes me, and that is all I care about. And he's given me a lot of support."

Luckily, before I said anything more to Johnny, I thought what a terrible falsehood I was insinuating about Mr. Hagan. I was humbled, but not to the point of wanting to back up and clarify the nature of our friendship. I childishly let the remark remain, as I changed the subject to the weather.

"The rain has slacked a little, hasn't it?"

"Yes, a little."

I thought – how ironic! The bride and groom are speaking nothings to each other already, so as to bridge the widening gap between them.

Even though we had already agreed that when we returned for the weekends, I would stay with my family and Johnny would stay with his, I wanted to hear him say it again.

"I'm glad we're going to spend our weekends in different places, aren't you?"

"Yes, I am," he said curtly.

Looking back, I realize that Johnny might have been amenable to this plan of mine because our first week of marriage had been disappointing and baffling to him. I believe he may have been glimpsing that I was not that sweet and compliant girl he had thought he was marrying. For one thing, I hadn't wanted to go to bed with him. In the weeks before our marriage, I had been shy about physical closeness, and Johnny had seemed okay with letting me be as untouched as I felt inclined to be. I had learned to like him, in fact, in large part because he hadn't pushed me into more intimacy. Now that we were married, though, and I remained physically shy, he had started to feel hurt and irritated. I hoped that I would start to feel more open to Johnny, once we had created a home together.

Another surprise for Johnny had been my constant desire to read. Although my family had accepted my intense love of reading and privacy, Johnny was new to it. He had no similar love of books, or of wrapping himself in shimmering daydreams. He wanted to live in the real world, with a wife who would cook for him and go to bed with him.

The buildings we were passing now had a ghostly look, because of approaching darkness and the heavy rain coming down in buckets.

"What time is it and where are we?" I asked.

"It's almost seven and we're going to turn left and drive about twenty miles down Northside Drive and enter the city limits of Atlanta." He raised his voice slightly and looked perturbed, as if he might still be thinking about our conversation of a few minutes earlier, but didn't know just how to open the subject of Mr. Hagan again.

"How about lighting me another cigarette," he said instead.

I pushed the car's round lighter knob for what I thought was about the eighth time since we'd left home a couple of hours earlier, and I was not counting the times he had lit up his Camel cigarettes from the butts of used ones. When the lighter popped out, he rolled down the window and tossed his old cigarette outside, quickly closing the window because of rain, and then he lit a fresh cigarette. I was grateful for that brief instant of fresh air, since my eyes were burning from the smoke and my throat was dry.

"Oh, I would love a drink of cold water," I said.

"We're almost there, and I think there's a couple of Cokes in my place."

I imagined how good a cold Coke would taste once we arrived.

"You're going to love Atlanta," Johnny added, his voice growing a little gentler. "Even though I'm fond of my family and the mountains, when the weekend is over, I'm ready to get back to the big city."

He smiled as he turned to face me, the cigarette now stuck to his dry-looking lower lip and hanging there.

As Johnny and I drove down Northside Drive, I began again to cherish the memory of my childhood home and all the fun we had had in those years. Gazing out the window at the dark houses and storefronts, I remembered rolling our old house's car windows up and down with Colleen and our friends. I remembered reading on the way to the spring, and playing with Colleen in our outdoor play area. I remembered Grandma's delicious biscuits and her warmth as I snuggled up to her in bed. I remembered Colleen and me swinging little Gene between us, and his worry about his "pretty knees." I remembered reading with Mr. Hagan on his porch, and feeling filled with discoveries about life.

Soon Johnny fumbled in his shirt pocket for the almost empty package of Camels. This time I didn't need to push the cigarette lighter into its outlet, because he was again lighting the fresh cigarette from the butt of the one he was still smoking. He handed the short, still-lit butt to me, indicating that I crush it in the ashtray. The receptacle was so full, though, that my fingers, nervously pushing the hot butt into the ashy pile, caused an overflow of three stale butts and the hot one. I scrambled to retrieve them from the floor.

"Oh, let me have them and I'll just toss them out the window," Johnny said.

"I heard on the radio that it's very dangerous to do that, especially with the drought having been so serious last summer." I added, after a moment, "I know you said you're going to stop smoking, and I'll be glad when you do, because the smell of cigarettes kind of makes me sick and burns my eyes."

He glanced at me with a hint of exasperation. We rode on in silence a while. Meanwhile, he turned the knob of the radio to a station where country singer Roy Acuff commenced wailing, *"Death on the highway, death on the highway, and I didn't hear anyone pray, no, I didn't hear anyone pray."* He repeated the chorus over and over again, with his Smoky Mountain Boys joining in singing and fiddling. The song reminded me of my Daddy playing his father's fiddle at home when I was a child, and I started to feel so homesick that a knot began to form in my throat. I almost asked Johnny to stop the car and let me out so that I could run back home, but I was now already almost a hundred miles from all I had ever known, as we sped on to our new life. A strange feeling came over me – a sense of hopelessness, much as I imagined a very old person might feel when life no longer held any happiness or possibility of change.

Quickly I grasped the familiar, positive thought that I was finally getting out of the mountains. I held fast to that idea as we entered the city limits of Atlanta.

"We're almost home now," Johnny announced, as we drove through a very run-down and rough section.

"Is this near the Farmers' Market?" I asked, remembering dimly the other times I had been to Atlanta to sell vegetables with Daddy and Mommy. We had had eleven flat tires on one trip.

It then occurred to me that Johnny had never brought me here.

"Why haven't you brought me here before?" I asked.

"Well, it ain't much to see, and in a few weeks I'm planning to get a job in a cotton mill in Rome where my brothers work."

I was quiet with the shock of this statement. Johnny had never mentioned living anywhere but in Atlanta. Not to be in that city and not to go to college – I felt frightened by these thoughts. All that I had planned for seemed to be slipping away from me.

He spoke with extra warmth, to persuade me to look at this situation as he did. "You'll love living near my family. They just love you! Your sister is there too."

I finally found my voice.

"But Mr. Hagan has already got me applications for college courses here in Atlanta."

"Oh, well, they've got colleges in Rome as well," he said, as he gave me a long look and then added, firmly, "The Bible says that the man is the head of the household. Of course the man is supposed to be the breadwinner and make the decisions."

My heart sank. I didn't have the energy for any more conversation, especially about that old strict religious belief. I had not thought of Johnny as being particularly religious, but I knew religion could sometimes come in handy to support people's habitual ways of thinking.

When I had visited Rome a few weeks earlier, Colleen had driven me past several colleges on our sightseeing trip. I had not asked her whether those colleges had evening classes. Rome was considered a large town, but not a metropolis like Atlanta. It was a city situated in an important cotton farming area about a hundred miles southwest of Ellijay. The city had a large Government hospital for tuberculosis patients, where Colleen worked now as nurses' aide. In fact, my family would not have objected so much to my leaving home if I had joined Colleen in working at the hospital in Rome, as she had wanted me to do. I had known, however, that hospital work was not for me.

"Here we are."

Johnny pointed to a dirty brick building with unscreened upstairs windows filled with hungry-looking children, who were staring down at us.

We entered a musty smelling hallway with one very dim light bulb in the ceiling, which cast ghostly shadows of Johnny and me as our steps thumped on the squeaky boards of the floor. Johnny turned the key to let us inside; then he walked to the center of the room and reached to pull a string hanging from a light bulb in the ceiling. The bare light revealed a tousled, unmade bed on one side of the room, and a table with a hot plate and two chairs on the other side. It hadn't occurred to me until that moment that Johnny's apartment would contain only one room.

"I would get you something cold to drink," he said, "but I just realized, the ice man won't deliver ice until tomorrow morning. But anyway, there's some beer in the icebox. They're hot now, but I think I'll have a couple of them suckers anyway. If you're thirsty, I guess I can find you a Coke." He offered this doubtfully.

"No, I'm not thirsty. I'll get some water later."

"I'll show you the bathroom. It's at the end of the hall," he said, pointing to a door with a woman coming out. She was smoking a cigarette and wearing torn, dirty pajamas. "We share it with two other families," Johnny said, "but they're nice people."

"Howdy," the woman said, in between spasms of coughing.

I nodded and tried to smile as I quickly ducked into the bathroom.

When I came back to our room, we straightened the bed together.

"I started my period today," I said, without looking at Johnny.

It was the first of many lies I would tell my husband, and I was a bit pleased with the smoothness with which the words came out.

He nodded as if I hadn't surprised him with this news.

"I feel like a little walk and I need a pack of cigarettes, but I'll come in quietly so as not to wake you."

His remark had a hard-to-interpret neutral tone, as if he were carefully trying to figure out how I had taken his stance about a man being the head of the household.

He reached for his billfold, lying on the table, and softly closed the door behind him. After he left, I could not get to sleep. I was used to the quietness of the mountains, where you could hear the streams, the wind in the trees, the rustlings of animals, and the soft breathing of other family members nearby. Here all I could hear was loud talking and arguing from the rooms on either side of our apartment, and the noisy traffic out the window. However, I did pretend to be asleep, hours later, when I heard Johnny open the door. His belt buckle clanged sharply as he dropped his pants to the floor. I clung to the edge of the bed and turned away from him as he sank his body down beside me.

I lay there trying not to smell his stale, hot breath on my neck, which somehow reminded me of the uncomfortable sensation I had had when my fourth-grade teacher Miss Oden had often scraped her fingernails on the chalkboard by accident. I wondered how I would be able to find a way out of this suffocating situation, which I had just traded for the oppressive but loving one of my girlhood home.

After years of being preached to about how people's sins will find them out, I knew there would be punishment for my choice of a marriage to this person I hardly knew, in order to get off the farm. Maybe I was being punished already. I had refused to let my family or Mr. Hagan discourage me or hold me back from my dream of marrying and escaping to Atlanta, and yet how realistic had my dreams of life with Johnny been? I felt that, in rushing headlong into this marriage, and becoming Mrs. Johnson, I had thrown myself right into a concrete wall.

As I lay next to Johnny, however, I told myself that things might look better in the morning. I was determined more than ever to make my original dreams come true somehow. And so once again, I pacified myself by echoing that vow Scarlett O'Hara was famous for using when temporarily leaving an unsolved problem: "I'll think of that tomorrow."

Chapter 21

Dreams Realized, Dreams Lost

The next morning the noise from Decatur Street awakened me, along with Johnny's thunderous snoring. With my eyes still closed, I lay a few minutes listening to him. Groaning, he rolled over to face me. Immediately I slid out of the bed and made my way down the long, dimly lit hallway to the bathroom.

I raised my hand to tap on the closed bathroom door, but just before my fingers touched, I could hear retching sounds coming from within. They caused me to shiver, and I wanted to run, but there was nowhere to go. I felt a longing to be back in the mountains on familiar ground, where the air was fresh and the birds sang in the trees above me when I needed to use the bathroom outside. There the woods were a pleasant shelter. Here the only wood lay in the creaking floorboards.

The bathroom door started slowly to open, with a screech from the rusty hinge followed by a man's coarse, congested coughing. With my head hung down, I turned in the opposite direction so as not to look straight into the man's face as he came through the door. I had no idea of the correct protocol in such a situation, but it seemed good manners to look away. Certainly I hoped other people would respect my privacy in such a way, now that I was about to enter this same bathroom.

After I had used the bathroom, I tiptoed down the hall as quietly as I could, clutching my granny gown tightly to my chest, but with every step I took, the squeaky floor ensured that my return to the room would be anything but inconspicuous. I turned the knob to our door slowly and softly so as not to wake Johnny, but I need not have been so quiet. As the door opened, I saw he was not anywhere inside our room or kitchenette. Realizing that I was on my own, I felt anxious and uncomfortable. In spite of the fact that I had not been able to face Johnny in bed, he was the one person I knew in all of Atlanta. Without him, I felt as if I had become caught up into a frightening film, moving around among strangers in shadows.

A few minutes later, to my relief, Johnny returned, with a luxuriously thick newspaper under his arm. He grinned as he handed it to me. I could see it was a current copy of *The Atlanta Constitution* – a new one, not like the old ones Mrs. Leach had given us during my childhood to paste on our walls. I felt he was giving me a grand gift. I just knew that within the want ads of that paper, I would find a job.

I was so thrilled that I rushed to give him a big hug, which at first seemed to stun him, but after a moment he reciprocated my hug most tenderly. I felt tears of gratitude and hopefulness well up in my eyes as I reached to get my hands on that newspaper. Eagerly I began searching, and soon found a position for a file clerk in an insurance company.

Johnny came to glance over my shoulder.

"That address is across town from here." Johnny sounded concerned for me. "You'll have to take a bus from the bus stop that's just outside this building, and once you get downtown, you'll have to transfer to a different bus to get there."

I looked into my husband's face and felt a tenderness toward him that I had not felt in the first few days after our marriage. I realized that I had been so distressed by the agony of separating from my family, and the heartache of being wholly cut off from my friendship with Mr. Hagan, that I had taken my frustrations out on Johnny. I was embarrassed about my behavior now.

"Oh, I don't mind that it isn't close by," I said. "I'll love the bus rides."

I thought about how great it would be to have freedom in this big city. In the light of day, and with a possible job waiting for me, I felt one big step closer in my quest to make my dreams a reality.

After toast and coffee, Johnny walked me to the bus stop. As he left for work, he reminded me of the numbers of the buses I was to take.

I entered the line of hurrying passengers up the steps of the bus, watching closely their example of placing coins in the little box, which sounded so cheerful as it swallowed the nickels and dimes. The driver, a middle-aged man with the same lean build as my father, caught my eyes and gave me a big smile.

"Good morning, young lady, how are you this morning?" he said, and immediately I felt a warm glow.

Once I had gotten off at the right bus stop, I had to figure out which building housed the Fireman's Fund Insurance Company. Moving through crowds of people and cars, I had to conquer my worries because I needed to succeed, that morning above all other mornings. After a tense couple of minutes, I found the large brick building. Feeling great joy that I was on my own, and had successfully reached my destination in this big city, I started to feel more self-confident. As soon as I entered the spacious, high-ceilinged lobby with marble floors, I felt that my movements became as graceful and confident as the happy-sounding employees among whom I walked. The young, friendly switchboard operator, dressed in a soft blue suit and navy high heels, introduced herself as Jill.

The elevator man was so young, I thought he might be a college student, especially since he had a pile of books on the stool behind where he stood.

"Good morning. Your floor?" he asked.

"Number 2." My voice came out clear and strong.

The office door opened as I neared, and a good-looking, smiling woman greeted me. She wore a gray-blue suit with a paisley red and green blouse.

"Come right in, Mrs. Johnson. My name is Martha. I am Mr. Hawkins' secretary."

I immediately felt great warmth emanating from her as I returned her greeting. She seated me by her desk and helped me fill out my application, as we chatted a bit about my birth city of Ellijay and her birth city of Perry, which she said was near the Georgia state line next to Florida. I thought that she was almost a foreigner, having come from so far away, but I didn't say anything. I felt reluctant to leave her presence when her buzzer sounded, announcing that Mr. Hawkins was ready to interview me. I clutched my application and walked into his office.

"I see you are from the North Georgia mountains, the most beautiful part of the state," Mr. Hawkins said, as he pulled a chair out and motioned me to sit. His gesture was so nice, just like in the movies, and he was so polite, that I started to feel more comfortable. After we had had a few minutes of pleasant conversation, he looked over my application, and then he offered me the job. I could tell that Martha was glad for me, as she congratulated me on my way out.

I doubt if any new hire could have been happier than I was as I skipped through that huge majestic door of the Fireman's Fund Insurance Company and on to the bus stop at Peachtree and Fourteenth Street. All the while, a quotation from Emerson, which

244

Mr. Hagan had read to me one day, kept playing over and over in my mind: "Once you make a decision, the universe conspires to make it happen." To me it meant that I was on the right track. I felt connected to the Infinite, buoyed up and carried along by a positive current. A surge of gratitude for Mr. Hagan filled my being and my feet barely touched the ground as I rushed past the seasoned bus travelers slowly heading for the door of the bus. I hoped he would be proud of me for finding a good job in Atlanta on my very first day.

Soon I settled into a routine of work and weekend visits back home. I was experiencing a great deal of happiness, once I had consciously made a decision to think of Johnny as an older brother in whose presence I felt safe. Safety was a big plus here in my strange surroundings. I vowed to make every effort to ignore Johnny's habits of drinking and smoking. Sex was not a major issue, since drinking beer and watching the big new miracle of television seemed to be more exciting to Johnny anyway. When he did indicate a desire for sex, I went with the flow of letting it be. The entire act from start to finish took only a short period of time. During the minutes of intimacy with him, I am sorry to say, I kept thinking of how I could get back to even a minute or two of reading.

As far as I knew, most other women shared my feelings about sex. From bits of conversation I had overheard from Mommy's friends over the years, sex was something women just yielded to for the benefit of the men; of course, it was also necessary should a woman want children. Most people I knew did want children, who could look after them in their old age. There were no living facilities outside the family home then for older people in that area.

I realize, looking back, how little I knew of the joyful side of sexuality. Luckily, this knowledge would come to me in my second marriage. Although I could wish that my Mommy and Grandma had been able to give me a hint about the positive aspects of sex, I can understand how, to their minds, teaching children about sex as a necessary discomfort may have seemed wise, given how many of the neighborhood girls became pregnant in their teens. Whatever method helped to delay sexuality until marriage must have appeared to be a good thing.

All this time, I felt comforted by the idea of my family and Mr. Hagan continuing on and thriving. I pictured the farm as peaceful and prospering. I imagined Mr. Hagan contentedly reading his books, enjoying my Grandma's meals, and talking with my Daddy on the porch after supper. I felt secure in the knowledge that the chicken farm was bringing in a good income for Mr. Hagan, and that my family would continue to do well as they helped him make a success of it.

Yet one spring weekend, when I returned home, I was shocked to discover, out of the blue, that Mr. Hagan could no longer afford to own the farm into which he had poured all his personal resources. His finances had reversed to such an extent that he had decided to sell it and go back to Birmingham.

I almost couldn't believe it. How had this happened? My family confessed that they had noticed signs of Mr. Hagan's financial strain for a few months. The chicken houses had been falling into a state of disrepair, with leaking roofs and other problems. They had sensed that Mr. Hagan had started to have trouble making ends meet. Even so, once the news had surfaced of his major losses, my Mommy and Daddy had felt shaken. The change in circumstances meant that no income would be coming in to us from the farm, since the chicken houses would not be supplied with baby chicks.

That farm of Mr. Hagan's had served as such a life-changing benefit to our family. To have our home and my Mommy and Daddy's livelihood become vulnerable again was an unanticipated blow. It was clear that a drastic change lay ahead of us all.

"Mr. Hagan just didn't understand farming and I didn't feel comfortable to keep asking him for more money to fix things," Daddy said.

This financial crisis had also affected Mr. Hagan's health. Grandma was especially worried about the fact that Mr. Hagan was not coming to the family house regularly for food.

"Children, I think he is going to starve to death," she sadly declared.

I was, in fact, shocked to see that the healthy glow and excitement I remembered in Mr. Hagan's eyes were no longer there. He looked so haggard that I too became concerned.

In a family conference, we decided that if Gene and I could contribute some of our savings, my parents would take a government loan and offer to buy the farm from Mr. Hagan. Of course I wanted to help salvage the better living conditions we had enjoyed ever since Mr. Hagan had come into our lives. I knew how important it was to pull together. Yet I also realized what this new situation would mean for me: the money I had hoped to spend on college courses would have to wait while I made payments on the property. Once again I put my evening courses on hold for at least another year, when I hoped, with a possible job promotion, I would be making more money.

During the following spring and summer months, once Daddy and Mommy had bought the farm, they went back to their old job of peddling their fruits and vegetables at the Farmers' Market in Atlanta. They also sold produce for some surrounding farms, and brought back items for sale. Daddy explained his new plan to me on one of his and Mommy's trips to Atlanta.

"We can bring back staples and sell the goods to neighbors at a slightly cheaper rate than they could buy them at the country store. And the profit from the sales will pay for the gas for the pick-up truck to make regular trips to Atlanta, with some left over to live on."

"Besides all that," Mommy chimed in, "our trips will allow us to see you more often, Odean, and know how you're getting along down here."

My parents grew a bumper crop of cabbage, green beans and sweet corn that year. The apple trees on the farm hung heavy too. Grocery store buyers were excited when they could get fresh sweet cabbage, green beans and Yates apples. The private grocery store owners allowed that their customers were especially fond of the green vegetables. (I don't think there were any large food chains in Atlanta at that time.) It was a proud fact for the mountain vegetable growers that their vegetables were more flavorful because they were grown in the rich soil of the valleys between the tall mountains, or else from well-fertilized hillside farms such as ours had become. The compost from Mr. Hagan's chicken houses had fertilized the barren land of our hillside farm so that it had become rich in the proper nutrients for growing abundant crops, and the rains had come in plentiful supply.

My parents especially liked making their Farmers' Market trips to Atlanta on Thursdays, because then they could sleep over and wait in my apartment until I came home from work Friday afternoon, when I would ride back with them to Ellijay to spend the weekend. Each Sunday evening, I would take the bus back to Atlanta.

When Mommy and Daddy were in town, I would come home from work to prepare meals and make a bed for them on the floor. Soon, however, the husband and wife who managed our apartment building became so fond of my parents that they cleared a storage room and moved a bed into it so Mommy and Daddy would be more comfortable. They did not charge them for rent, but of course Mommy and Daddy supplied the couple with generous amounts of fresh vegetables.

While I enjoyed seeing my Mommy and Daddy on those Thursdays, and then each weekend on the farm, my marriage became more and more fragile. Johnny could not seem to hold onto work, and I found it discouraging to come home to a smoke-filled apartment, with my husband sitting in a chair watching television, empty beer bottles beside him. I began to avoid Johnny by making more and more dates with friends I now had at work.

One of my friends, Judy, sold tickets at the Fox Theatre next door to the insurance company. As we met most days for lunch at a hot dog stand, we discovered that our farm backgrounds were similar, which allowed us to have fun conversations about our childhood experiences. She and I also shared a love of movies, and she would often tell me about the most recent ones, starring famous actors and actresses, like Cary Grant and Katharine Hepburn. I loved having the chance to laugh and feel lighthearted for a while, and to enjoy imagining the beautiful mansions and the privileged lives shown in those movies. Those conversations with Judy touched on my childhood dreams of happiness, inspired by the healthy and wealthy people populating our newspaper walls.

One day, Judy came bouncing to meet me for lunch, looking radiant as she began blurting out her great news.

"I could hardly wait to tell you! My boss, the owner of the theater, is entertaining Dean Martin and Jerry Lewis next week. They'll be making an appearance to promote their new movie. My boss asked me to come along to the restaurant and have dinner with them. Can you believe it? I will sit next to Dean Martin, and

I am already in love with him." She giggled as the pitch of her voice rose higher and higher.

Although I was happy for Judy, I seemed not to be able to snuff out my jealousy that she could have such good luck. I so wished that I could be the one to sit next to Dean Martin, or at least that I could go along to the important dinner. After all, I had dreamed about such events all my life, and now one would be taking place right here in Atlanta.

One evening, a number of years later, after I had married my second husband, Jerry Brady, I was sitting ringside at the Fontainebleau Hotel in Miami Beach, with Jerry and some of his celebrity friends, including Dean Martin of the famous Rat Pack. Dean, Frank Sinatra, and Sammy Davis, Jr., in fact, were the star performers at the Fontainebleau that evening. Sitting between my husband and Dean, I felt glad that I had not met that movie star when he had come to Atlanta so many years earlier. Dean met me as a lady of quality and not as a paid escort.

I could not see into my future then, though, and all I could feel was that Judy would have a chance to step through the invisible door into a magical and glittering world. I was beginning to doubt that I would ever find such a way out of my own very real life.

Chapter 22

A Nicer Apartment

As the first summer of my marriage continued, I had two bright spots in my life. The first was my job at the insurance company. I did so love my job and all the people with whom I worked. The second bright spot came from a conversation I had with the office manager, Martha. I had casually mentioned to her the distance I traveled to work. A look of horror crossed her face.

"Dean, that address on Decatur Street must surely be the most undesirable section in the entire city of Atlanta. You are not safe there."

I told her something of my plight regarding my recent marriage and my move to this city, where I had known no one. She said nothing in response, and her silence embarrassed me, because company rules discouraged conversations about your personal affairs. I thought I had crossed a line.

The next day, however, I discovered that Martha had taken my problem to heart. As we entered the office building together and walked toward the elevator, she seemed eager to tell me her news.

"Dean, this morning as I drove to work, I saw a sign advertising an apartment, and it's just a block from here, on Fourteenth Street."

I sighed. "These apartment houses around here are so nice. I'm sure they would be too expensive for me, though, since my husband lost his job. He's only been able to pick up a few hours a week at a gas station. I'm sure we couldn't afford to live near here."

"We won't know until we ask," she said. "I could take you there during lunch. I have two sandwiches -- if you'd like, I'd love to share one with you so we could hurry and see the apartment today."

Her soft brown eyes expressed affection as she spoke. It felt good knowing that I had such kind friends, who really cared about me in the same way my family did.

I quickly agreed to look at the apartment with her, although I added that I had my own sandwich, which I'd brought from home. I felt inwardly grateful that my paycheck had allowed me the privilege of being able to be so self-reliant.

The apartment was lovely and not much more expensive than our first one, considering the additional daily bus fares I had been having to pay on my commute. The space contained a combined living room and bedroom, a kitchenette and a private bathroom. When the Murphy bed lay vertically inside the wall, and out of sight, the space could look quite large. One of the added attractions for me was that the Peachtree Art Theatre sat just a block away, on Thirteenth Street.

Since Johnny and I had no money to secure our deposit, Martha lent us the full amount, and said she would take only a small amount from my paycheck each payday until she had gained it back. The husband and wife who managed the apartment house on Decatur Street were sad when they learned of our upcoming move. They had become attached to us and to my parents.

After our move to the new apartment, my life settled into a new grace period, when I felt that all was going to be as good as I had so often dreamed it could be. I could hardly wait to show my new home to my parents the following Thursday, when they would be bringing their weekly truckload of vegetables.

My parents were glad about Johnny's and my new home, especially because it was in a safer part of the city. Once they arrived, I cooked dinner for them, using some of their delicious greens and fruit. After dinner, we took a bus to explore the Cyclorama, where you could see a huge cylindrical painting of the historic Battle of Atlanta.

I enjoyed pleasing my parents on each of their visits. Sometimes I would take them to a movie at the Peachtree Art Theater close by, or at another theater a bus ride away. Their amazement at the elegance of the big theaters delighted me. Even now I can hear the echo of their laughter at the antics of Laurel and Hardy and other comedians at Loew's Grand Theatre, where the premiere of *Gone with the Wind* had taken place. Loew's became a hallowed spot for my Mommy, just as it was for me. As we would stand on the sidewalk in front of the theater, she would talk with me about how the characters in Mr. Shepard's copy of *Gone with the Wind* had become so alive to her that summer when I was twelve.

Usually my parents and I left Johnny just where he wanted to be – slumped in an easy chair close to our black and white T.V., with a 12-pack of Budweiser beside him. It was embarrassing to have my parents realize that he would be passed out, usually in the same chair, when we returned later in the evening.

At times, I sensed my parents' concern about my marriage to Johnny. Once, as we sat in a restaurant on Peachtree Street, Mommy asked, "Honey, has Johnny ever hit you when he gets drunk?"

"No, he hasn't," I said, ignoring the times when he had angrily shoved me against a wall.

"That's good, honey, that's very good."

Daddy echoed her words, looking relieved. "Yes, that's good."

To them the minimal criterion of a good marriage was that a husband did not beat his wife. I am sure my parents remained worried for me, yet after this conversation they kept quiet about my situation, and did not directly express further concern for my happiness.

In the meantime, Johnny appeared to be getting a little tired of my parents' weekly visits. He started to visit his family in Rome every other week, so that he would be home for only two of my Mommy and Daddy's visits each month. He told me that he was seriously trying to find a job in Rome, where two of his brothers worked in the cotton mills.

"I'll get good wages, and the rent is cheaper in Rome than in Atlanta," he said.

Whenever he spoke about this plan, I would feel discouraged. I felt that as long as we stayed in Atlanta, I still had a chance to take college courses one day, and in the meantime I had a good job and friends I enjoyed.

One October weekend after my parents' visit, I stayed in Atlanta because I needed to work with Martha at the office Saturday morning. I felt she had made that request for me to be the one to help her because she thought I might need extra money to pay rent on my new apartment.

After spending the whole morning with me in the office, Martha said, "Dean dear, you are such a hard worker that we've finished earlier than I expected. Now you go and have a lovely weekend and I'll see you Monday."

She smiled and gave me a quick hug. Her perfume – Chanel No. 5 – reminded me of Mrs. Leach, as she would walk across her expansive green lawn, bringing Mommy and Daddy and me her delicious cookies and milk for our work break. As I skipped down the stairs to the lobby of my office building, I thought about how everything – at least, everything outside of my marriage – seemed to be unfolding so happily for me now. At least Johnny had a part-time job, and he had started to talk less about moving to Rome. With Martha's kind words and the extra money in my purse from my morning's overtime, I daydreamed about how I might soon begin my college courses. Maybe, sooner than I knew, I would even be able to start writing down the stream of stories I had carried with me for so many years. As I reached the lobby, I started to believe that I might have the privilege to become a writer. I straightened with pride as I made my way through the door into the brilliant sunshine of that Indian summer day.

As I walked along Peachtree Street, filled with these daydreams, I decided that I could not endure another afternoon of being in our apartment. Since I was not buying groceries to prepare food for my parents, or a Trailways bus ticket for home, I walked to the bus stop and waited for a local bus to go downtown. I thought how fun it would be if I might find a new dress in Rich's Bargain Basement.

Not only did I find a beautiful aqua blue dress marked way down, I also bought a pair of nylons. Once I had looked at myself in the store mirror, clothed in that dress, I could see that the one pair of nylons I owned were covered in too many bits of clear nail polish, which I'd used to stop the runs. At the cash register, as I counted my money to pay for the new hose, I turned and saw a fancy garter belt that I just had to have.

After my shopping spree, carrying my packages and bouncing with joy, I took the bus back to Peachtree and Fourteenth Street. The messy apartment smelled of musty cigarette smoke, urine, and beer, just as it had in the old place on Decatur. Johnny lay asleep on the covers of the bed, with his pants unzipped and wet; evidently he had not made it to the bathroom before his bladder had emptied in a puddle beside him on the bed. The little fan was wearing its life away moving from side to side, in an effort to send the bad air out the window.

Thinking about Martha's kindness, the fragrance of Chanel No. 5, and my lighthearted shopping spree downtown, I realized for the hundredth time how quickly our pretty new apartment had changed into a place of unhappiness. I emptied the ashtrays, and then I pulled the window shade so the neighbors across the courtyard could not see inside. The sound of the shade aroused Johnny, and he reached to pull me down on the bed. I recoiled from his pinching hands and dirty fingernails, but not before his grip had ripped my blouse and sent two buttons into the fan, which bounced them across the floor.

"Leave me alone!" I yelled.

He stood up and shouted, "One of these days, I'm going to leave you alone permanently." His face was blood red, contorted with fury. He lost his balance then, and sprawled to the floor.

I bit my tongue to keep from retorting, "Is that a promise?"

Rushing into the bathroom, I closed the door and listened to his angry mumbling as he opened and closed the refrigerator (no longer just an icebox, as in the other apartment). I could hear him fumbling with the beer can opener and then, after a moment, giving a loud burp. Again I heard stumbling, and then all was quiet. I supposed that he had dropped back onto the bed. After staying silent several more minutes, I opened the bathroom door a crack and peeked out. Sure enough, he had passed out again, and the room was filled with his snoring.

I crept from the bathroom to the closet where I had hung my new blue dress. I ran my hands over its smooth surface and pressed my nose into the soft folds to inhale its freshness.

Carefully, I took it off the hanger. That act brought with it a brief wave of pure ecstasy, calming my senses. With the feel and smell of the fabric's delicate newness, I became overwhelmed with the intense joy of owning something so beautiful, bought with my own money. It was difficult to pull myself away from that sensuous moment and to come back to my present reality. I just kept daydreaming as I breathed in and out, holding the dress to my face. Then I let my body fold up and ease to the floor of that tiny closet.

Another Saturday had passed, and my marriage was as unhappy as ever. I wondered how long I would be able to comfort myself with daydreams.

Shattered Dreams

On Christmas Day my whole family was together, except for Mr. Hagan, who had chosen to spend the holiday with an old friend in Atlanta. Although Mr. Hagan had sold the farm to my Mommy and Daddy, they still welcomed him as a special member of the family, and he still lived in his little house, coming to my Grandma's meals when he felt up to it. Although his health was fragile, I gathered that he tried to contribute a certain amount of money each month to my parents, in effect renting his living quarters on what had once been his own farm. My family's gratitude to him for all he had given to us now had a chance to be expressed in our love for him and our concern for his welfare. It was painful to see his new frailty, and to realize that he no longer had his old enthusiasm and energy.

Johnny had spent Christmas Eve with his sister, but he made an appearance at our house for Christmas dinner. My relationship with him since his drunken outburst that Saturday night had been even more tense than usual. As my family sat down to enjoy our dinner together in the early afternoon, I just hoped that Johnny would stay sober and show his best side.

Mommy was the first to express her gratitude for blessings during the previous year.

"I am happy we are blessed with Johnny being our new family member," she said, her voice trembling as she recited her well-rehearsed lines.

She glanced quickly at his face, and then just as quickly bowed her head. Mommy was not a good actress and certainly no hypocrite. Closely watching her, I could tell she still didn't really like him. When we raised our glasses, I was relieved that Johnny's glass contained water, the same as ours.

I missed Mr. Hagan on that visit, although I was grateful that I didn't have to watch his dismayed reaction to my husband. Walking past Mr. Hagan's porch on Christmas afternoon, and in the days following, I yearned for those conversations I had had with him about Emerson and the other authors he and I loved. I missed his encouragement and his nurturing spirit. He would always remain the most inspiring figure of my life, in spite of all that he had suffered. I decided that when I returned to Atlanta, I would take the steps that would make Mr. Hagan proud of me again.

A week later, Johnny and I were having dinner back in our apartment. Johnny was on his third beer.

As we shared one of Grandma's fried apple tarts for dessert, I asked him, "Tell me, what's your New Year's resolution?"

"I'm going to quit smoking and drinking," he said, as he looked sideways at me and then shifted his eyes back to his beer bottle. Knowing he didn't really intend to quit, I shrugged.

"Good! I'll tell you mine," I said. "Thursday evening of this week, I am registering to begin my college courses in the evenings, and I am so happy I want to jump up and down just thinking about it."

I skipped about on the kitchen floor. Johnny didn't pay any attention to me as he sucked on his beer with lowered eyes and concentrated on his cigarette ash.

My New Year's Resolution ran into a major obstacle, however, before I could even savor it. Wednesday of that week, when I returned home after work, I found Johnny slumped in the living room chair, drinking, in spite of his promise. Two empty beer cans were lying on their sides on the table beside him. He reached for a sheet of paper on the table and handed it to me. It was a letter from his boss, saying that he had been fired from his part-time job. This was the second time he had lost a job at a service station.

At first I tried to be hopeful that Johnny would find a new position somewhere. Day after day, however, nothing turned up, and days turned into weeks, weeks into months. Finally he found a weekend job in another service station, yet this only allowed him to make enough money for beer and cigarettes and sometimes a loaf of bread and a quart of milk. He seemed to settle for so little.

Unshakable sadness now began to plague me. I was still paying a hundred dollars a month to my parents, toward the mortgage on the farm, so Johnny's sudden lack of income meant I had to postpone my college courses once more.

After work, most days, I went for walks around Piedmont Park and sat on benches until dark, thinking about the mess my life had become. Sometimes I just kept walking, until I had become so tired I would have to go back to the apartment just to get off my feet. I would come home bitter and fuming, because I felt that Johnny was the reason I was being held back from my goals. We had never had a romantic or passionate relationship, but now his attempts to dominate me through threats and sex were fast wearing down my spirit.

I shared with Martha a few facts about my situation at home and how all joy had drained from me in my marriage; whatever happiness I could still feel was now only outside of my relationship with Johnny. Martha arranged for me to see a company doctor, who offered me good advice about how I needed to release some of the burden I was carrying around daily. He prescribed medication that would help with my depression.

However, I did not have sufficient money to continue with the prescription.

Seeing Johnny sitting in a drunken state each evening when I returned from work, I would usually ask with an edge in my voice, "Did you find anything in the want ads today?"

"No, I couldn't find anything again today," he would say. "I guess I'm lucky to have that weekend job at the gas station, since it allows me to have a little money to buy some groceries."

Glancing around and seeing that *The Atlanta Journal* had not been opened, I would tauntingly counter with, "Sure, you make enough money to buy beer and cigarettes. By the way, that baloney you bought where you work was spoiled."

"It tasted alright to me," he would say, gulping another swallow of beer.

It is clear to me now that Johnny and I had no knowledge of how to support each other emotionally. I had had no experience with a family member who drank as much as he did, and who appeared to have so little vision of how to live with integrity and effort. Even though all during my childhood we had been poor, each family member had pulled together, fiercely battling to survive. My impatience with Johnny fueled his attacks on my family. He would toss out any remark that he knew would touch on this sensitive issue. He would criticize my Dad for not getting a job in the cotton mills with a regular paycheck, as Johnny's brothers did. I would counterattack with my own prideful opinion.

"Oh yes, look at my Dad who has held onto property that's been in the family since before the Civil War, instead of letting the land go and renting a house in some slum district in town, like your family."

Seeing Johnny's rifles lined up in one corner of our small kitchen, I would resist the urge to slam them with a swift kick. I would let my foot scramble among them, though, so he could hear the clatter as I would leave, slamming the front door behind me.

"You better not kick my guns or I'll . . ."

His threat would be lost to my ears, since I would already be rushing down the stairs and out into the neighborhood, where I could slowly start to breathe again.

By that second winter of my marriage, I could actually feel myself turning into a hard, weathered woman instead of a young woman, still only in my mid-twenties. I felt worried, thinking about the bitter person I was becoming, but I couldn't seem to rise above it. My youthful spirit now surfaced only when I was interacting with my coworkers, who seemed so vibrant and filled with energy.

It was fortunate for me that my parents did not come to Atlanta in the winter, since they had no produce to take to market. Putting a rosy glow on my situation, for their benefit, was becoming harder and harder. When I went home to visit my family now, I went by bus and on my own.

Of course my parents and Grandma asked me what was happening with Johnny and me, and I let them know he was having a hard time finding work, but I didn't go into much detail. It was exhausting for me to have to keep a lie ready so they wouldn't be concerned. I was grateful that they did not keep pressing me for more information.

One winter afternoon when I returned from work, Johnny greeted me with excitement, saying he had something to tell me. I thought perhaps he had landed a job, but I was quickly disappointed in that wish. The joyful news he wanted to share was that he had found a gun in the pawnshop where his friend worked. He held it up for me to see.

"A real bargain in this rifle," he said. "I would love to keep it, but if we run too short with money, I know I can sell it to one of my brothers or their friends."

I stared at the rifle, glistening in the light from the overhead bulb. I was too angry to speak. As I walked into the kitchen, my eyes locked on the collection Johnny already had. I thought to myself, some women, in this situation, would have turned the rifle to point it into his face.

"I wouldn't do that," I said in a whisper, yet I honestly felt that I couldn't be too sure. Maybe it would take only a few more of his drunken, insistent requests for sex.

"Come here, little wifey," he would say. "You know, like the Bible says, it's your duty as my wife to satisfy my sexual needs."

Then he would stagger toward me, reaching to pull me down onto the couch or bed. I would jerk away, yelling, "Leave me alone!"

I didn't trust myself enough to be sure that one of those times would not lead to my breaking point.

Chapter 24

A Detour by Way of the Biltmore

The end of February showed promise of spring, with daffodils – my Great Grandpa Eli's "March flowers" – poking from the ground to cheer everyone. I could not feel cheered, though, since for me nothing had changed except that I was more discouraged with each passing month. The early spring flowers and dogwood that had thrilled me in earlier years now left me unmoved or even sadder. I hardly noticed the soft warm breezes caressing my face as I walked.

Reaching our apartment after one of my long walks around the park, I would already hear Johnny's snores through the door. The sound of his snoring would give me a slight sense of relief, because it meant that if I kept very quiet he might continue to sleep and I wouldn't have to talk to him. I would just tiptoe in and open the window in an effort to let in some fresh air.

Since Johnny was now home most of the time, taking naps during the day, the Murphy bed had not been back inside its closet for months, and the room looked very crowded. After spending time in the kitchenette, I would go into a corner of the living room to sit in a soft chair.

One day, sitting curled up in this chair, listening to Johnny's congested breathing, I felt more panic than usual. At first I tried to go back to my childhood way of dreaming myself into a better place. For a while, I pictured what it would be like to be Vivian Leigh escorted to a dance by Clark Gable. Soon the idea floated into my head that I could go on my own to Loew's Grand Theatre at Peachtree and Forsyth. The idea of walking into that special theater lifted my spirits so much that I went to the closet and took out my high heels, a new pair of hose, and my aqua blue dress, which I had hardly ever had an occasion to wear. Feeling the soft fabric of the dress and burying my nose into my clean nylon slip, for a moment I could no longer smell our apartment. I became intoxicated as I imagined myself moving inside a theater among people who were happy. All I could think was, "For a few hours, I will not be a hostage."

The little closet just outside our bathroom became a pretend dressing room. It was thrilling to imagine I was some kind of Cinderella who could toss off my shabby bargain basement clothes and dress in beautiful fabrics. I was happy to see myself even for one evening as an exciting young woman, instead of the desperate, angry woman I had become. In spite of the fact that I knew I was just pretending to be free, I felt a soaring relief. I pictured playing this game for a few hours, just as I had enjoyed building my castles in childhood out of moss and stones. Once again I would be living the dream I had held in my heart for years.

With each step in this dressing process, I found I could use that old mind energy that had been lying dormant; it could work now for me, as I looked in the mirror, much as it had when I'd gazed at the elegantly dressed women pictured on our newspaper walls. I enjoyed the feel of my slim legs as I smoothed my hose carefully, making sure that the seams of my nylons were absolutely straight. I thrilled at the way I felt in my blue dress and my high heels. Now I was ready to walk quietly past that snoring, dirty form of a man lying unconscious on the bed.

Standing at the bus stop on Peachtree Street, I got a thrill from seeing some heads turn and hearing a couple of young guys whistle from their car as they passed. I hopped onto the bus, filled with a glow of excitement. As the bus started down Peachtree, however, it struck me, why would I, in my pretty blue dress and my fresh stockings, want to go sit in a dark theater watching a movie that might not even interest me? I was dressed to be in the limelight. So I slipped out of the bus after just a few blocks, and found my way to the Biltmore Hotel, which rose up in front of me, eleven stories high, a grand brick structure. Approaching the entrance of the hotel, I remembered the newspaper pictures from my childhood, of Vivian Leigh and Clark Gable smiling and waving as they stood in front of the Biltmore, and I recalled hearing that the hotel's first owner had been Asa Candler, the druggist who invented Coca Cola.

Caught up in my childhood memories of Mrs. Leach, the heiress of Dr. Candler's Coca Cola fortune, I swept gracefully through the glass doors, and then I walked through the glittering lobby with confidence, as if I were about to meet someone and knew just where I was going. As I approached a dark romantic room off to the side, however, I slowed down. The room, filled with laughter and smoke, magically pulled me in, and I found myself drifting toward the most animated voices along one side of the bar. I hesitated, though, as I looked at the groups of people laughing together on stools and at little tables, with glasses of alcohol glinting in front of them. I had never been in a bar before, and now here I was in this dark, fancy one with its crowd of well-dressed strangers and its large, ornate mirror hanging behind an array of gleaming bottles. I started to lose my courage and to grow frightened by my own actions, which had brought me here.

Right at that moment, a handsome man sitting on a stool motioned to me to sit on the empty stool beside him. His smiling face was comforting.

"I'm William," he said, holding out a perfectly clean, manicured hand.

"I'm Dean," I said, as he cupped both hands around my extended one.

A delightful tingling went up and down my spine and even turned up my toes as William gently helped me on to the bar stool. I glanced around to see how the other ladies were sitting, and I did likewise, latching my high heels onto the steel circular rod that wrapped around the lower part of the stool.

"What would you like to drink?" William asked.

Not knowing the name of any drink, I pointed to his glass.

"I'll have what you're having."

As he turned and motioned for the bartender, I looked at his profile, and I heard myself exclaim, "Oh, my God!"

Startled, he stared into my face.

"What's wrong?"

"Oh, nothing. It just shocked me to see how much you look like Clark Gable," I blurted out, "even the mustache."

"So that must give me a head start in our beginning relationship," he said, smiling, and I realized he even had the Clark Gable charm.

Our fancy drinks were now in front of us. William raised his glass toward me and we clinked glasses.

"Here's to an exciting evening for us and beyond," he said.

My first gulp tasted better than I had thought it would, and the second gulp was even better, since it seemed to touch every fiber of my body with a relaxing sensation. The entire room and the mingling, jovial people took on a glow I had never experienced before.

"It's interesting how you said I look like Clark Gable," said William, "because I do capitalize on that bit of good luck. It helps when I teach Sunday school to teenagers, I will tell you. However, you should know, I'm about ten years older than Clark."

He smiled and touched his martini glass to his lips for another sip, showing his Clark Gable look-alike smile.

"You teach Sunday School?" I asked.

"I'm the pastor of a Baptist church outside of Macon."

"I practically grew up in a Baptist church," I said, "and none of our preachers looked or acted like you."

William leaned in closer.

"Well, I'm not a preacher tonight. Remember, we're pretending I'm Clark Gable, and we're experiencing our first night of magical living."

I couldn't think what to say to that. My daydreams were becoming real right in this magical room within the Biltmore Hotel.

"What brings you to this hotel?" I asked.

My Clark Gable sat back and winked at me.

"Well, I'll tell you. In addition to my work in the church, I work very hard as an automobile dealer in Macon. So I'm here in Atlanta at an important car dealers' convention. And I must say, I'm having unusually good luck tonight, to have a beautiful young princess come sit beside me."

He reached his arm around my head and brought my face tenderly against his chest. I thought I could hear his heartbeats, which I imagined to be both thrilling and sincere.

Everything William said after that made perfect sense to me. He offered comforting and reassuring words to my ears, even though the surroundings were so different from a Baptist church. His praise and keen interest added intensity to the rosy glow I felt from the martinis. I seemed to be experiencing that heavenly ether the preachers promised we would breathe if we were good and went to heaven.

Sometime later, we were waltzing around in his suite of rooms. I could scarcely remember how I had gotten there, but it didn't matter, because everything felt enchanted. The high ceiling and red velvet drapes made the suite look like a royal bedroom in a castle. My real life in Atlanta, in the apartment on Peachtree, filled with the Murphy bed and my snoring, drunk husband, seemed to be the dream, while this large, softly lit space with its cream-colored walls and freshly made-up bed seemed to be the entrance to a new and happier reality.

When I awoke in the hotel bed a few hours later, I saw light streaming through the open bathroom door, and the messy hair of the pretend Clark Gable, who was now sprawled on top of the sheets absolutely naked, and snoring with his mouth wide open. Embarrassed, I wanted to fling the sheets and the down coverlet over him. The next instant, I realized that Johnny must be awake by now.

I rushed to the bathroom, overwhelmed with anxiety and shuddering at the sight of my clothes tossed around all over the floor of the suite. After hastily cleaning up and brushing my hair, I flung on my clothes as the preacher-car salesman roused from sleep.

It washed over me like cold dishwater: I wasn't a heroine in a romantic movie. In fact, I could be classified as the lowest form of womanhood. All I could think of was that I had to get away.

William appeared to be thinking the same thing. As he pulled on his trousers, he said in an irritated voice, "I'll take you downstairs and get you a cab. Since I've been drinking, I shouldn't drive."

My head was whirling around, partly from all those drinks, but mostly from panic. As William made a half-hearted effort to escort me from the room, his hand was no longer in a waltzing position behind my back; it now hurriedly pushed me along.

Silently, we entered the elevator down to the lobby and then walked out the huge front door of the Biltmore, which was opened for us by a smiling doorman, who greeted us with a bow. Ignoring the doorman, William rushed on to the taxi stand. He jerked the door of a cab open and practically slammed me into the back.

Through the glass, I could hear his previously warm voice, now with no emotion, mumbling, "See you later."

"My address is Peachtree and Fourteenth Street," I said to the cab driver.

William had already turned to go back into the hotel.

The taxi ride took only a few minutes at that early hour, and I pictured Johnny waiting for me, furious and filled with questions about where I'd been. Once inside our apartment, though, I saw that Johnny was still asleep on the bed. The little fan was still desperately trying to push the combined smells of piss, beer and cigarettes out the window.

Nothing inside was different. But I would be forever changed.

Chapter 25

A Difficult Choice

Morning nausea began to plague me some weeks after that night of total foolishness. I tried to hide how I was feeling from Johnny. Once or twice, though, when I rushed to the bathroom to throw up, I told him I just had a virus, and inwardly I hoped I was right.

When the nausea and the odd feeling of fullness continued, I asked my boss for a day off work to see a doctor, and he readily granted it to me. As I took the bus to a gynecologist-obstetrician's office, I couldn't help feeling increasingly worried. Once there, I gave a urine sample and filled out a sheet of paper about my health. As I sat holding the piece of paper, the other women, in varying degrees of pregnancy, looked at magazines or talked quietly together. This was the first time I had ever been in a gynecologist's office, for an exam or a prescription for birth control.

The other women looked as if they felt comfortable there, and I realized that most of them might already have other children. I hoped my appointment would go smoothly and I would discover that I had just been imagining my changed physical state, and could be free to go home, relieved and still just my ordinary self. I vowed that if I could win this freedom, I would figure out a way to make my life better. Something had to change, and I would figure out how to change it.

A neat, smiling lady about the same age as my mother came to the door of the crowded waiting room. She was dressed in a pink jumper over a starchy white, immaculate blouse.

She called, "Mrs. Johnson."

As I arose, she smiled and motioned to me. I walked, with shaking knees, toward her. She must have noticed my anxiety, because instead of walking ahead of me, she placed her right arm around my shoulders, holding in her left hand the sheet of paper I had filled out. As we walked, she talked in a gentle voice.

"I am Mary Jordan, and I volunteer a couple of days each week in the organization known as the 'pink ladies.' Perhaps you have heard of us."

"No, I haven't," I said in a soft voice, "but I'm very glad you're here."

I began to feel a little more comfortable as she patted my shoulder and led me inside an open door to a chair where I seated myself. She assured me the doctor would arrive soon. She turned back and smiled as she neared the door, and she smiled again as she closed the door behind her.

Feeling the lingering warmth of her loving pats, I thought of my Mommy and Grandma and how they had comforted me so many times. Oh, how I wished one of them were here with me now. That yearning dissipated, though, as I pictured how they would look at me, how their faces would register their disappointment and their disapproval of the awful sin I had committed. I took off my clothes and put on the paper gown the volunteer had given to me, and I sat on the examining table to wait for the doctor.

After a few minutes, a kind-looking doctor appeared, in a white coat, with a stethoscope showing in his pocket. After introducing himself as he sat down on a stool in front of me, he reached for my hand to feel my pulse. Afterward he gave me a pelvic exam, as gently as he could. Once the exam was done, he said I could put my clothes on again, and he left the room so that I could have privacy.

As he walked back into the room, he looked into my eyes with a warm glance and said, "I have good news, Mrs. Johnson. You are going to be a mother. It looks as if you have a fine, healthy baby growing inside you."

The words of the doctor echoed in my mind. I could barely listen to anything else he said, and I walked out of the clinic as numb as if I'd jumped into freezing cold water. This could only be the car salesman's baby. Johnny and I hadn't had sex in well over three months.

After somehow catching the bus and getting off near our apartment, I walked slowly along the street. I felt like a criminal. I thought a criminal would have a better chance for a good future than I would now have.

Johnny had no clue as to the difficulty I continued to face each morning in getting to work. Usually he would still be sleeping. If he were awake, his attention would be focused on that snowy box, the television. If I couldn't help vomiting, I tried to cover the noise by flushing the toilet and running the water simultaneously. My efforts to eat breakfast and get dressed mingled with two prayers. The first prayer was for me to be able to die, and the second was a prayer for strength to get through the day.

In my anxiety, I started to talk to a young, single neighbor about my pregnancy. Diane worked days at an advertising company while she took college courses in the evenings. I had often told her that she had a most wonderful life. She would smile and say, "Dean, don't despair, you'll have this kind of life soon." Her bright and confident reassurance each time I saw her had never failed to lift and encourage me.

I asked Diane at first about possible remedies for nausea, and she suggested some simple over-the-counter drugs, which proved helpful. I could not bring myself to talk to her, though, about how I really felt about my pregnancy or my marriage.

During the ensuing weeks, I wrestled with possible ways to solve my predicament. Could I pretend to my husband that during one of his drunken stupors, I had become pregnant by him? That would mean raising a child with a man I could not possibly love anymore. Could I give this child up for adoption? What reason would I give to Johnny and my parents for such an act? Even if somehow I could keep my pregnancy and the birth wholly secret from everyone in my life, I had no knowledge of how to give up a baby, and I doubted I could do it.

I knew that to return to my childhood home, pregnant and divorced, would not be possible, because of my parents' religious beliefs. They took the Ten Commandments literally and seriously. They would believe that I had broken two of the Ten Commandments: I had not honored my father and mother's teachings, if I had gotten myself into such a mess, and I had committed adultery.

Daddy had always made it clear that if a daughter of his ever got pregnant out of wedlock, he would never allow her to come home again. Each time I remembered his words, they pierced a little deeper into my heart.

Even worse, I was certain that if Johnny discovered this baby was not his, he would take after me with his hunting rifles and kill me. There was no way in heaven I could ever breathe a word that the baby's father was someone other than Johnny, someone I had known for a few hours at the Biltmore Hotel.

An abortion appeared to be just as difficult to face. If I were to have one, I would never be able to tell my parents or

Johnny. This action in their eyes would break a third and very grave Commandment: Thou shalt not kill.

I finally told Diane my whole story one day as we sat in the garden while she did her homework. I told her that I had fallen so low, I wondered if I could ever pull out of the mess I had created for myself. I shared with her my desperation and the hopelessness I felt about following through with this pregnancy.

She reached out to hug me, and expressed her heartfelt concern.

"I have a policeman friend who might be able to help you," she said. Her voice became a whisper as she spoke about how her friend might help.

Diane arranged for me to meet the policeman in her apartment a few days later. He was a tall, strongly built young man, who did not give the appearance of being connected with anything illegal. I was instantly certain that his kindness in helping came from pure compassion for me, a woman in a dreadful situation. Many years later, during the Roe versus Wade conflict, I often thought of him, and I could well imagine the side he would have been on.

Handing me a folded piece of paper, he said, "I give you this number with my best wishes that all goes well. But I do ask you to please never speak to me again should you see me on my beat."

During our conversation, I sensed that Diane and her friend were both maintaining a careful distance from me, since their voices were low and they avoided looking into my eyes.

I gave the policeman my promise and expressed gratitude to both of them. Due to the atmosphere of secrecy in which they offered help, I felt that any more communication between us could, in some way, jeopardize their future, and so I refrained from any further contact with either of them.

When I dialed the telephone number, a man answered. With a nervous voice, edged in hostility, he asked how I had gotten his number. I gathered that he must be the doctor. Frightened, I lied, telling him that a girlfriend, a former patient of his, had given it to me. Then I panicked, thinking he would ask for my friend's name, but he didn't. Neither did he ask for my own name. Instead, he asked me to describe how I looked and what I would be wearing. He said I should be at his door at 3 p.m. the following day for our first meeting. Then a click indicated that he had hung up.

The "doctor" lived in a basement of an old run-down building on Ponce de Leon Avenue, near a downtown area called Five Points. This section of Atlanta was at that time filled with homes that had once been beautiful, but were now dilapidated. Following the directions given to me by the policeman, I went down a flight of stairs into a hallway with plaster walls stained by dampness. Only one dim light bulb hung a couple of feet from the ceiling. I wished I had brought a flashlight. I couldn't see any name or plaque, just a bare door in need of paint. After I knocked, I saw an eye peeping through a tiny hole. According to the written instructions, the man would introduce himself by saying, "I am the doctor," and it was not necessary to say my name.

The door opened about a foot, and a man said, "I am the doctor." With that he let me in and motioned to me to sit at a kitchen table, covered with a greasy tablecloth, as he took a seat across from me. He was a short man, with only a few wisps of graying hair on his head. His cold, piercing eyes never left my face as we talked. He mostly mumbled his instructions, with a lighted cigarette dangling from his dry-looking lower lip. Sitting at the table, as I listened, I had cupped my chin in my hands with my elbows resting on the table, when an eerie scream came from a nearby room. I jumped and my elbows slid on the oilcloth.

The man flashed a sarcastic grin.

"Change your mind?"

I shook my head.

He came back to our discussion, naming the price. "I must have $400.00 in cash placed in this hand before I do the procedure," he said, holding his right hand in front of my eyes.

I nodded, and then he asked when I wanted to have it done.

I chose a date that would be a week later, because I knew Johnny would be spending that week with his brother in Rome. The "doctor" nodded in agreement with that date and let me out the door.

I had no idea how to come up with $400.00. I had no savings, because any extra money went toward my monthly contributions to my family's mortgage payments on the farm. My greatest purchase in many years had been that aqua blue dress; ordinarily, I just felt lucky to have enough food for Johnny and me to eat. Finally, after much anguish, I contacted my boss at the insurance company, who kindly loaned me the money without asking questions.

The procedure was agonizing. I held my breath through most of it. There were no kind words or touch for support. The doctor had one assistant, a large middle-aged woman who wore a mask over her nose and mouth. I guessed that she wore the mask so that her face would not be visible to patients, rather than as a protection from germs. Her fingernails had rims of black dirt inside.

The only conversation occurred when the "doctor" muttered a few directions to the assistant, who said nothing and never even glanced at my face or the upper part of my body. Although it was a hurried process, it seemed to take an eternity, and I believed it would surely end my life. My bleeding was severe.

Afterward, as I lay on the operating table fighting back tears, the assistant said bluntly, "You'll be spending the night here. I'll show you to your room."

I was thankful that Johnny was far away in Rome, and would not wonder why I had disappeared, yet I also could not help worrying that something might happen to me in this godforsaken place, out of sight of any normal community.

A young woman, perhaps in her mid-twenties, with her black hair in a bun, appeared in the doorway. She was wearing an apron.

Leaning a broom against the wall, she asked, "Which room?"

The assistant answered by pointing to a room across the hall. When the young woman escorted me to my room, I saw that it held a bed, a table, and a straight-backed chair. On the table was a tray.

"That's your dinner," she said, pointing.

Then she walked abruptly out of the room.

I looked at the tray, which held soup, crackers, and a pitcher of water. I had no appetite, however, and instead of eating, I crawled into bed.

I could hear a television blaring and people arguing on the other side of the wall. A dim light shone weakly on a bedside table. I pulled the sheet over me, but quickly flung it away from my face because the smell was so musty, as if dozens of women had been under it, each one suffering as I was suffering. I was too hot in any case to need covers. I could hear someone in the bathroom, and I was alarmed that they would come into my room, but I soon became aware that the bathroom was a shared one, with two doors.

Exhausted, I fell asleep. Sometime later, I awoke to a scratching and scrambling noise under my bed. In the faint light, I saw a large rat scamper across the floor.

I tried to stay motionless because the blood flowed more profusely with each move I made. I could feel my strength ebbing away, and I started to long for an ending to this horror. I honestly wanted to die. Feeling so alone, I wondered should I be dead in the morning, what would happen to my body. The "doctor" didn't even know my name. How would my parents and Grandma even know what had happened to me?

Morning in the basement began with the banging of pots and pans and the smell of coffee. Turning from my side to lie on my back, I felt more blood gushing from my body. Struggling against weakness and shooting pains in my lower abdomen, I made a couple of attempts to get out of bed, but each time dizziness forced me to lie back down. With my body half off the bed and one foot on the floor, I prayed for strength to walk. A few minutes later I was able to raise myself slowly to a standing position. Trembling and nauseous, I grabbed hold of the table and the chair, and somehow I managed to get to the bathroom. The toilet had been left unflushed by the person who had used it earlier, but I was grateful just to have been able to reach the bathroom.

While there, I heard a loud knuckle-knock on the door to my room, and through the door of the bathroom I could see light burst into my room from the hall.

A coarse voice shouted, "Here's your breakfast!" as someone opened the door to my room wider.

At first I couldn't tell if the voice was a man's or a woman's. Quickly I glimpsed the same woman from last night, still wearing the mask, as she briskly entered my room carrying a tray. With one hand, she lifted the soup and crackers tray from the night before, while with the other hand she set the breakfast tray onto the table in its place. Her cough rattled with phlegm like a heavy smoker's cough. Needing more air, she raised her hand with the dirty nails to lift the white mask slightly as she breathed in, and then she pulled it back down again to cover her mouth as she walked out.

I washed my hands and face carefully. Luckily they had given me a clean towel to dry off with. Then, holding to the wall and again reaching for furniture to steady me, I managed to get to the chair at the table.

Poking her head back in the door, the woman called, "Hurry and eat your breakfast. The doctor has got a man picking you up in a few minutes. He'll take you to Peachtree Street, where you can get a bus."

"I live at Peachtree and Four-- . . ."

Impatiently, she flung her hand back and forth in front of her face.

"We don't need to know your address. The bus will take you there."

She slammed the door behind her.

I looked down at the tray. She had brought me toast, scrambled eggs, grits, and coffee. Even though the smell of it made my nausea flare up, I pushed as much of the food down as I could, knowing I would need strength for the ordeal of getting home.

Soon a nervous young man appeared at the door.

"Ready?" he asked. "I'm double parked."

I reached for the shopping bag with the items I had brought and followed him. I was amazed I could even walk, given my soreness and weakness. The young man didn't even look over his shoulder as he reached the car. He looked over my head as I ducked into the back seat with my bag.

At a bus stop corner on Peachtree Street he stopped, and looking quickly into the rear view mirror, he said, "Here you are."

As I got slowly out of the car, he stayed in the driver's seat. He shot me a quick glance from the corner of his eye, and then he drove off.

I leaned on a garbage can near the bus stop, and soon a bus arrived. All seats were taken and the aisles were filled with standing passengers. After gently pushing my way through the other passengers, I headed toward the rear door so that, at my stop, I could hurry out. Getting near to the door, I held to a pole. A young African American man, sitting in the rear of the bus – which at that time in history was the designated section – stood up and moved a couple of steps to stand beside me.

"Please take my seat," he said.

A panting "Thank you" came from my mouth as my heart flooded with gratitude.

I looked into his kind eyes and tears welled up in mine. His was the first caring face I had seen in two days. I wanted to reach out and hug him, but I knew that if I did that, the bus driver would have us both arrested for "indecent behavior."

Stepping off the bus at my stop, I breathed a thankful prayer as I walked carefully home. I had a moment of pure and sudden appreciation for being alive on this beautiful May morning. The trees were green again, and flowers brightened the walks. The air was warm and fresh. I looked forward to being able to wash more carefully, and lie down for the rest of the day, as I recovered. The apartment would be wonderfully quiet without Johnny in it. I could open the windows and let in the fragrant air.

As I approached the entrance of my apartment house, however, to my great surprise and dismay, I saw my Mommy and Daddy pacing around their old pick-up truck parked outside the building. I had the strange thought that somehow they had discovered what I had just done, although I knew they couldn't possibly have known. Their faces were filled with grief, and then another worry hit me like a blow: was my Grandma alright?

As soon as they saw me, they rushed to hug me.

"Where have you been? We have been so worried," Daddy said.

Mommy added, "We got so worried, we went to where you work, and they said you had got off for three days."

I tried to compose my face, so that I could come forth with yet one more lie for my trusting parents.

"My friend Judy had an operation, and she had no one to take care of her."

"Oh, that was good of you," my Mommy said. "You look tired, Odean. I'll make you a cup of coffee, and I brought you some of Grandma's good biscuits. She sends her love."

So it wasn't Grandma then. The relief was like a blast of clean air, and in my happiness that instant I almost forgot about the "doctor" and the assistant, the pain of the procedure, and the rat scurrying in the dark. Maybe none of my family would have to learn about what had just happened to me. Maybe they would never have to know how my life had crumbled. I promised myself that I would build it up again somehow. I didn't know how, but I felt at last the inkling of a sense of hope.

Pausing at the entrance to my apartment building, Daddy said, "Odean, we have to tell you something. We've got bad news."

I searched his eyes and his face. "Grandma's alright, isn't she?"

"Yes, your Grandma is alright."

"What then?"

"It's Mr. Hagan." Daddy put his hand on my shoulder. "He died of a heart attack last night."

I could scarcely believe that such sadness could be added to the bewilderment and pain I was already feeling that morning. It seemed impossible that right as I had been going through that terrible day and night, Mr. Hagan – my beloved, kind, and encouraging mentor and friend – had left the earth. Somehow I managed to get through the following days, leading up to the funeral, although I felt like only half of myself. The only thing that could give me comfort was that Mr. Hagan would never know what my marriage had been like in Atlanta, and what I had just chosen to do. I held onto my secret from that day until now, as I write this book.

Chapter 26

Goodbye to Ellijay

Early morning light filled the sky over Kerns Mountain one Sunday morning at the farm the following October. I slipped out of bed and eased my way onto the front porch to feel the sun's brilliance and to store its energy and warmth inside me. I was often dizzy still, after the procedure the previous May, and I could not get my energy back. I hadn't gone to a doctor, because I felt sure I could not have opened up about my abortion. I could not imagine a doctor who would treat me, knowing what I had done illegally.

Once on the porch I remained very quiet, not because I would disturb anyone, since I knew that by sunrise Mommy, Daddy and Gene were already tending to the outside morning chores, and Grandma was busy inside making breakfast. Colleen and Charles were here on a visit; Colleen was helping Grandma in the kitchen. I loved listening to the birds, and to the sound of my Grandma humming to herself as she prepared the biscuit dough. I loved the smell of our wood fire smoke mingling with the fragrance of grass and fallen leaves. I wanted to absorb the sense of security and safety that had enveloped me all my childhood.

That sunny morning looked just the same as many autumn Sundays had during all my years on Route 2, Ellijay, Georgia, but I knew that this day would be different. The following Tuesday, I would be boarding a bus heading for Miami. This was a secret known only to me. As in recent years since graduating from high school, I could not face telling my family the truth of my plans, because I worried that they would somehow find a way to stop me from attempting to find a better life for all of us.

After several months of looking for a job in the cotton mills in Rome where his brothers worked, Johnny had despaired of the search. Another brother, Phillip, who lived in Michigan, had encouraged Johnny to go back to Michigan with him. On a recent visit, he had become worried about Johnny's possible alcoholism, and he believed he could help Johnny find a job at the automobile factory where he worked. I had encouraged Johnny to listen to Phillip, especially because I knew that Phillip did not drink. So a week earlier, Johnny had accepted Phillip's invitation, and Phillip had driven him up to Michigan. Johnny hoped I would follow him north as soon as I could, yet I knew that once I left Ellijay, I would finish packing up our apartment, and then I would say goodbye both to Atlanta and to my married life.

The warm, familiar scent of my Grandma's coffee brewing and biscuits baking invited me inside and made me nostalgic. The biscuits had that "brown crust smell" that let me know Grandma's delicious breakfast was nearing completion. Soon Mommy, Daddy and Gene would be eagerly coming inside to fill their stomachs with the everyday miracle of my Grandma's meal.

I began to think about all the years when Grandma's milk gravy, biscuits, and a small serving of scrambled eggs had made a family feast. Grandma would never have described her meals as "gourmet," but anyone who ate them knew what a gift they were. Every time I had been home from Atlanta that summer, I had been reminded of the comfort my family had given me throughout my life. At the "eating table" my eyes would pass from one family member to the next as my heart poured out a silent flood of love and gratitude for each of them. I tried not to think too much as my eyes fell on Mr. Hagan's vacant place. I still missed him keenly.

As I sat there watching the sun easing a bit higher over Kerns Mountain, I recalled that my parents were not the only ones in our area who, out of fear for their daughters' safety, had tried to hold them close. Parents weren't always wrong. I remembered what had happened to my friend Gladys in her own effort to escape, and I realized that my decision a few years earlier to stay home and not to go to Atlanta in an ambulance-hearse with her and Allen had been one of many near misses I had experienced during my young life. I remembered my fear of Luther, and of the pilot snakes that had struck at me in the crawl space under our old house, as I had tried to reach our hens' eggs. I remembered lying in the bed at the "doctor's" in Atlanta, and almost fainting in the bus afterward. I remembered worrying that Johnny would figure out about my pregnancy and my abortion. After all that, I was grateful simply to be alive on this mild October day. I hoped that when I was finally in Miami, I would have lucky chances and no additional frightening surprises come my way.

On the day Johnny was to move to Michigan, as he stood outside our apartment building waiting for his brother to come by and pick him up, he had said, "When I get a couple of paychecks, I will send you a ticket to come and join me. O. K.?" When I gazed at him without responding, he had again repeated the question, this time looking straight into my eyes. Since he was already drunk, I considered that it might be dangerous to be honest. He would probably have come back angrily with one of his assertions, like the one he often liked to use, defining marriage: "and God said a couple should stay together until death do them part."

Having just received the diagnosis from my insurance company's doctor of "pernicious anemia needs immediate attention," I hadn't had the energy to take on both Johnny and God. I wondered if he was thinking, as I was, that it might be near impossible to find any two people in a union of marriage who were as mismatched as we were. So as we stood on the sidewalk, I vaguely nodded yes. To my relief, Phillip arrived before I had to say anything more, and Johnny and I embraced swiftly. Then

286

Johnny was inside the car waving as he and his brother turned at the end of the block.

Back inside the apartment, I had glanced at the chair where Johnny usually sat and watched television, as I opened windows to let in fresh air. It was ten o'clock in the morning. I started to clean the entire apartment from top to bottom, scrubbing the kitchen and the bathroom tiles, washing the sheets and coverlet, even washing as much as I could of the windows. For the first time in months my energy had seemed to increase with my brisk movements until I had finished cleaning the whole place to my satisfaction. The apartment looked new and pretty again, ready for other people, who might have a greater chance at happiness.

With a feeling of relief, I had stood at the window and looked up at the evening stars. With all my heart, I had wished Johnny a happy life now, free from me. Perhaps he would find a wife who would not have her head in the clouds, dreaming impossible dreams as I did and always looking for sparkling champagne in some imaginary castle. Perhaps his future wife would just sit down and share a beer with him.

It had felt good to be on my own for a whole week, since Johnny had left with Phillip. For the first time in my life, I could now enjoy the freedom to make my own decisions. I sincerely wished all good to unfold for Johnny, as I breathed easier, knowing that I would never live with him again.

Each day of the summer and fall since the abortion, I had been planning this change in my life. The urge to get away had been intensified by the fact that I had so little money. Without Johnny's knowledge, I had been slowly paying back my $400.00 debt to my boss, with a certain portion taken out of my salary each week, so Johnny and I had had a significantly smaller amount to spend for necessary items. It had started to become difficult for me even to raise the $1.50 necessary for a round trip bus ticket each Friday between Atlanta and Ellijay, yet I knew that if I didn't go home each weekend, my parents would likely have had to make the journey to Atlanta most Fridays or Saturdays in that old sadly neglected Dodge pick-up truck that kept getting flat tires. Daddy never intentionally neglected the truck; it was just that a hungry mule braying at the barn for food got more immediate attention than did a silent pick-up truck parked in the yard. One time, in the early summer, Daddy and Mommy had had seven flat tires on their way to see me. After that ordeal, they had arrived at my apartment exhausted, even to the point of being ill.

Each time my parents visited me in Atlanta, I became tense about every extra penny I had to spend to care for them. I made sure to have enough food to give them, plus a few dollars left for gas money to help fill the tank in the truck for their return to Ellijay. It had now reached the point where I could not tell who was toting the most painful albatross around their necks – theirs for me or mine for them. I felt that the seven hundred mile distance between Ellijay and Miami would allow all of us to have breathing space from the loving but stifling attachment that had held us together all my life.

Once Johnny had gone to Michigan, I had to decide which city I would choose. I did not know a single person in any other big city besides Atlanta. As I was working late on Wednesday evening, to catch up on some filing in the office, I decided that I would make a definite decision that very night as to where I would go: Miami, New York or New Orleans. Taking dice from my boss's desk, I told myself that if one of the pieces of dice landed with one dot up, I would go to Miami; if it landed with two dots up, I would go to New Orleans; and if it landed with three dots up, I would go to New York. When I tossed the die, I almost couldn't look at it at first, as it lay on the desk. I felt that my future lay in that little white cube.

Holding my breath, I looked, and saw that it had landed with one dot up. My bus ticket would be for Miami. Immediately I felt a calm sense of relief, as if I inwardly knew the die had chosen well for me.

A sense of took hold of me after this choice had been made, and those office papers to file seemed to move through my hands and enter precisely into the correct manila folders with little effort on my part. As I rushed to complete my filing, I thought about Emerson and Mr. Hagan, and how they would say that for such a harmonious movement of my hands and body to take over meant I was definitely in tune with the Infinite. Thinking of them, soon I closed up the office and practically danced my way the entire block to my apartment. Two days later, I took the bus up to Ellijay for the weekend, to say my inward goodbyes.

"Breakfast is ready," Grandma said now, as she came onto the porch and patted my shoulder. "Honey, I thought you were still in bed. Have you been sitting out here long?"

"I needed to think," I said, giving her a hug around her waist.

"Are you lonely now being down there in such a strange and different place?" she asked, but before I could answer she hurried inside, scolding herself. "I smell something burning! I must have turned the coffee pot up instead of down."

I was glad Grandma hadn't been able to wait for my response. Answering her questions did not used to be so complicated, I thought, as I joined the family for our last meal together before I would leave.

After our hearty breakfast, we all remained seated around the table with Colleen and Charles. It was fun to hear the two of them talk about their future and their plans to buy a small house in

289

Rome, where Charles worked driving a Merita bread delivery truck. Colleen was enjoying her job as a nurses' aide at a hospital there, where she would continue to help patients for the next forty years. She and Charles seemed to be happy, with no longing for anything else. I was glad for them, but I knew I could not be as contented as they were, in the life they had created. I could feel the big wide world beckoning to me.

Grandma said, "Let's go sit on the porch and talk, since in a few hours Odean will be gone again."

We seated ourselves on Mr. Hagan's porch, where our conversation turned to that dear friend, whose presence we still felt.

"I'd like to go and place some of Mr. Hagan's dahlias on his grave if the frost hasn't gotten to them yet," I said.

Mommy nodded. "Yes, that's a good idea. Yesterday I saw the last two huge dahlias."

"I'll get the pick-up unloaded and ready for us to go to the cemetery," Daddy said agreeably, as he stood up.

All during the summer months, since Mr. Hagan's death in May, each time Daddy had gone to town, he had stopped at Mr. Hagan's grave and pulled any weed he could see coming up through the "the red old hills of Georgia! so bald and bare and bleak," in the words of Henry Rootes Jackson. With that poem coming to mind, I remembered that I had memorized it in my high school English class with Mrs. Ruth Hamrick. She was married to Mr. Hagan's childhood friend, who had become president of the local bank.

Soon Daddy appeared at the edge of the porch.

"You ready to go, Hon?"

"Yes. Just give me a minute to get another one of Grandma's half-moon pies."

As I walked down the hallway to the kitchen, I met Grandma and told her how much I wanted one of her little apple pies. She smiled a big smile and lifted her small specs with one hand, as she reached for me with the other. We shared perhaps the four hundred and forty-nine thousandth heart to heart hug. With reluctance I released her warm body. Then I followed her as she limped to the kitchen, showing signs of her painful arthritis. She handed me the biggest half-moon pie on the platter.

"You know, Odean," she said, "I miss cooking for you and I long for your sweet hugs when you are gone all the way to Atlanta."

With effort, I held back the tears and breathed a silent prayer that I could have the strength to go on as planned.

Standing under the oak in the little Methodist churchyard, as I looked down on Mr. Hagan's simple tombstone, I smiled at the memory of my friend Gladys telling me that the Methodist people were strange and would not go to heaven. In my teenage years, I had joked with Mr. Hagan about how I believed Gladys knew that as a fact. He and I had enjoyed a good laugh over that. I had never shared with him the fact that my parents also believed that only the Baptists were God's chosen. Although my Mommy and Daddy had inherited that strong belief from their forebears, they had been respectful to Mr. Hagan, even as they had always been worried about his salvation. He had been such a good man and so important to our family's welfare that it must have been a bit confusing to them that such goodness could come from a Methodist.

As I walked past the large rock beside his grave, I remembered that during his funeral, I had been bleeding profusely from the abortion a couple of days earlier. I had not been able to remain standing, and had had to sit on that very rock. I felt again the tension I had felt then, afraid that if I fainted they would rush me to the hospital, where the doctors would see the evidence of a botched abortion and my secret would be revealed for all to know.

Now I reached for the last two dahlias – a red and white honeycombed one, and a large-petaled white one – which Mommy had so carefully placed in a vase filled with water. I silently thanked Mr. Hagan for his influence in opening my eyes to the grand possibilities out there in the world. I doubted whether, without his influence, I would have had the courage to go forward in seeking to develop my dreams into reality. I remembered how, early on, he himself had escaped the constraints of those mountains and years later had returned and settled happily there again. Would that happen to me? I was unable to imagine such a fate.

Near sundown, I finished my goodbyes to my family and boarded the Trailways bus back to Atlanta. As I hugged my Grandma, I don't think I have ever had a more prayerful wish than the one I had then: that I would soon find a successful job in Miami, which would allow me the opportunity to help give her and my parents a happier and more comfortable life than they had ever known.

As the mountains became smaller to my view out the window of the bus, however, my heart started to feel hollow and numb. I became more aware of my weakness and dizziness. The emotional turmoil I had experienced during the weekend had rendered me so exhausted that I fell asleep and did not awaken until we had traveled the entire one hundred miles.

Warren family as taken by Charles Lankford, my sister
Colleen's husband, in back of their home in
Rome, Georgia in 1951

Chapter 27

Greyhound Journey

Early Monday morning, I was back at work for my last day. Knowing that I would not be at the insurance company again, I had many silent goodbyes to extend in thought to my co-workers, all of whom had been so kind to me that year, especially Martha, the office manager. I had written a note expressing gratitude to Martha and a more formal letter to Mr. Hawkins containing my apology for the short notice. I would place those letters on their desks after they had left their offices that afternoon. In my letter to Mr. Hawkins, I asked him to please recommend me for a transfer to the company's Miami office. I knew that my sudden departure from his office could very well hinder the Miami office from accepting my transfer. However, since I still owed Mr. Hawkins the $400.00, I hoped this debt could factor favorably in his recommending me for a transfer.

On the morning of my big journey, the local bus let me off in front of Macy's, further down Peachtree Street. The driver barely glanced at me while I maneuvered Johnny's ancient brown suitcase out the back door. Quickly he closed the door behind me and looked straight ahead as the bus lunged forward on its designated route.

The bustling lunch hour crowd was trying politely to avoid bumping into the suitcase, now swinging by my side as I turned onto Lucky Street. I started to talk to myself in a soft mumble, to distract myself from thinking about what I was about to do. I didn't want to get emotional, so I calmly described my actions as important steps toward my dream.

"I'm beginning a long journey that has played out in my head most of my life. It is only a matter of minutes now before I purchase a ticket to Miami. I'm going to travel a distance of seven hundred miles 'into parts unknown.'"

I tried to remember where I had read that phrase, 'into parts unknown.' That was the way I was; when I read a nice-sounding group of words, they immediately became my own. It was my habit now, in conversations, to try to find ways to include sentences containing more and more beautiful words. As I looked for the bus station, I began to consider that, in the future, I should remember and give authors credit for their phrases and sentences. I thought of how, when I wrote my own book, I'd want people to give me credit for my polished phrases. As soon as I thought this, I realized I had spoken of my book as "when" and not "if."

I heard myself speak again. "I may become an author soon."

My steps took on a faster pace along Lucky Street, and soon the Greyhound bus station came into view. Feeling sure that this word Lucky was a good omen, I entered the rambling old building, lively with loud speakers constantly announcing bus arrivals and departures in a strange-sounding voice, which seemed to come through the walls.

Once inside the station, I became a bit startled, wondering why I was not more nervous or sad now that I was really here, near the buses, and my getaway was in progress. I concluded that I had imagined the events of this departure over and over for so many years that the actual steps came naturally to me. I had already created this story in my mind, and now I was inside it.

After buying my ticket, I caught the delectable smell of food coming from the nearby cafeteria. I had eaten only a small bowl of cold grits before I had left the apartment. I had had no bread for toast, because I had decided not to buy a whole loaf right before my journey, for fear of wasting it. I was drawn to step in line with the other customers, thinking that I might get a small piece of corn bread for a few pennies. Placing my saucer with the corn bread on my tray, I just could not pass by the cheapest item – black-eyed peas. I pointed to the peas, and the attendant at the bar dipped a couple of tablespoons into a cup.

"Would it cost more if I had some of the broth?" I asked.

"Yes, it would be a couple of pennies more."

"Just a little soup, then," I said, and she poured almost a tablespoon of the broth over the peas.

I moved along to the cashier, who weighed the peas and broth together. The price was 11 cents for the peas and 3 cents for the corn bread – a much higher price than in the little café near where I worked. I paid with some coins in my change purse and found a table in a far corner, a little apart from the other diners, because I didn't think they would want to talk to me.

As soon as I placed my spoon in the cup, I could see a little white dead worm floating in the liquid on the peas. After spooning the worm out and onto the saucer beside the bread, I continued to devour the delicious peas and corn bread with a glass of water.

"Bus for Miami now loading at Gate One," announced the loudspeaker.

I toted that beat-up case to the bus, with Johnny's dog tags still fastened on it, and pushed it into the long storage compartment underneath, alongside the other passengers' nicer luggage. As I looked at those smooth leather suitcases, I remembered my Dad's worried comments from perhaps my seventh or eighth year.

"Odean has warped her brain from seeing too many pictures of all them rich movie star people pictured on the walls."

"Yes, Arthur," Mommy would say, "but she has such a good time looking at the pictures, and she's learned to read that way."

Thinking of Mommy's habit of always trying to put in a positive comment, I almost started to cry. Instead, I pushed that memory out of my mind, because I needed to think clearly as I was starting to climb the stairs into the smelly old bus.

What a sight I must have been: a forlorn, shabbily dressed young woman, who had the common sense needed to farm, but so little knowledge of how to succeed in the outside world. Although I had held a job in Atlanta for a year, I had almost never had money to buy clothes, after my monthly payment on my family's farm and other expenses. So, apart from my cherished aqua blue dress and the pair of hose I had worn to the Biltmore Hotel on that regrettable night, my wardrobe largely consisted of my dress for graduation, one pair of rundown shoes, two secondhand skirts, and two blouses.

Picturing my pretty blue dress now folded carefully in my suitcase, I looked forward to wearing it in Miami to a successful job interview. I bounced with new energy as I walked down the aisle and selected a seat near the rear of the bus. As I settled in, I placed my old hand-me-down crocheted purse on the seat beside me. This had been a gift from Colleen, given to her by someone in the little church in Rome where she and Charles were now members. Inside that purse was the dictionary from Mr. Hagan, and a loving letter I had written to my parents explaining why I couldn't say goodbye in person. In the letter, I explained that soon I would have a great paying job, because I had gotten a promotion and a transfer. The part about the promotion and transfer was more of a hope than a truth, but I felt deeply that it would soon become true. I planned to mail the letter when we reached a bus stop near Miami.

The fumes in the back of the bus reminded me of some of my last memories of Johnny, one being his beer breath as he pulled me toward him. A few weeks earlier, before he had left for Michigan, he had bought himself another suitcase – not a new one, but a pretty good one – in a pawnshop. That had been the weekend when he had proudly announced that he had bought a 6-pack of beer instead of his usual 12-pack, so he could have enough money to buy the upgraded suitcase.

As soon as my body relaxed into the cushioned seat, I realized how exhausted I was. However, I didn't immediately close my eyes to sleep, because I didn't want to miss the experience of the journey.

A few minutes later the loudspeaker announced, "Final call, leaving for Miami, Florida," and our driver closed the door.

For a short time, we moved slowly as we started and stopped for traffic lights. It was lunch hour, so the streets were crowded with people. Through the open window came the clanging and banging of garbage cans and voices yelling. My last view of the city as I looked back was the imposing Biltmore Hotel. I was glad our next turn left it out of sight, and I hoped that, in time, it would also be erased from my memory. As we picked up speed, cool, refreshing breezes coming through the open window touched my face, and the sounds from the streets died away.

Our speed seemed very fast, once we left the hillier regions around Atlanta. The flat land of central Georgia allowed for much faster traveling than I had ever experienced before on the sharply curving mountain roads of my home. I felt as if we were flying. This sensation reminded me of many cold, gray days in my house, poring over the newspaper photos of Amelia Earhart preparing for flight.

Curled up on my bus seat, I started to slip into a dozing state, where those photos and other fragments of memories lapped over me. My mother's voice came to my ears as a faraway echo, repeating her puzzled, frustrated thoughts about me.

"What is wrong with Odean? Why can't she be like her sister and other children in the neighborhood who stay content being with family and helping with the daily chores?"

I thought sleepily about how my family's particular concern had always been the salvation of my soul. I pictured how sweet my Mommy and Daddy and Grandma had looked in church, all those years sitting on the hard wooden benches, looking straight into the face of the preacher in the pulpit, because they felt he had received the words he was saying straight from God.

I felt tears sting my eyes. I made an effort to pray, but I couldn't get comfortable praying to the God of my childhood – a stern, vengeful figure who watched your every move to judge it as either good or bad. I had sinned so many times by now that surely I was outside God's jurisdiction and in the devil's domain. Then again, I didn't completely discount the possibility of a little help from God, since I had always heard that God helps those who help themselves. If I were to find myself in a bind, maybe I could bank on that.

Drying my eyes, I stepped into the aisle to smooth the wrinkles from my sweaty, crumpled skirt. Some of the old dream energy started to rise up in me. I vowed to leave self-pity behind and to fight obstacles as they arose. I had started this Miami adventure on my own, and I could follow it out to a good conclusion. I could finish this change that I had set in place.

After a while, I awakened from what seemed like a short doze. Having no watch, I couldn't be sure how long I had slept, but looking outside at the passing scenery, I could see that twilight was beginning to blend trees and buildings into a dark blur as we sped on.

Settled back in my seat, I began to review the only four independent decisions that I had ever made. The first had been my decision to delay my senior year of high school so that I could buy my Daddy that fiery red Farmall tractor. I felt very good remembering the joy he had had in owning it and how much easier it had allowed his farming to become. That had been a successful decision. The second independent decision I had made, my marriage, was so painfully sad that I hesitated to linger on it. I knew that I must always keep uppermost in my mind that this marriage, mistaken though it had been, had changed my life. I knew now that never again would I marry without knowing my husband well, and for sure I would know without a doubt that I loved him. I admitted to myself that marrying to change my life had been a desperate decision and not a responsible one. I had painfully learned a lesson never to be forgotten: I was the only person responsible for change in my life.

The third decision, to go to bed with the car salesman-preacher at the Biltmore Hotel, meshed together in my mind with my pregnancy and abortion, and this set of choices too felt so raw and distressing, I could not think about them for long.

The fourth decision had been to leave.

I dozed off to sleep again. Long hours piled on top of each other, with the monotonous drone of the motor being the only sound, since the few passengers seemed to be sleeping or, like me, thinking. As I remembered events of my childhood and girlhood, my thoughts turned into "never again vows."

Never again would I see Mommy, pale and trembling, trying to convince the tax man that we would have enough money by tomorrow to pay on the late taxes so we wouldn't lose our home. I'd make sure there would be enough money.

Never again would I have to see my Grandma writhing with pain from an illness that could be cured. She would be able to go to a doctor.

Never again would I see anyone in my family suffer or come close to dying because we could not afford the medicine.

Never again would I make a choice that would so negatively affect my life or the life of others as my marriage to Johnny had done.

As we approached our next stop, and the bus slowed, this litany came to an end. From out of nowhere, joy enveloped me with the memory of my parents' determination that their children must each graduate from high school. I just knew I was now on my way to being a big success, and my parents and my Grandma would be so proud of me.

The driver broke the comfortable silence. "Macon, Georgia. This stop is Macon, Georgia."

A man and a woman entered the bus and took a seat about three empty rows in front of me. As the bus started up again, I could hear them softly talking to each other. Their voices added a touch of warmth to the darkness surrounding us, and I fell into peaceful sleep.

"Pompano Beach, Florida. This stop is Pompano Beach, Florida. We will have a thirty minute rest stop here."

Rising out of my curled-up position made me remember the pilot snakes and rattlesnakes whose curled bodies had many times straightened to strike at me in the grass at home, especially when I would be cutting long, green ragweed for the mules, using Daddy's sharp pocketknife. I thought about what a tough little ragamuffin I'd been.

I straightened my body with pride. Reaching down to put my shoes on, I felt how swollen my feet had become with all that sitting in the warm air of the bus. My legs were as numb as two sticks of stove wood. They clumsily moved my body out of the bus and onto the first gritty ocean sand I had ever walked on.

Instead of the pungent salty smell of the ocean I had read about, however, it was the luscious, appetizing aroma of biscuits, fried bacon and ham that wafted to my nose. The biscuits smelled just like Grandma's. I tried to ignore how much I longed to eat something, because I knew I had to save my money as best I could. Staggering from weakness, I held on to a light post and then walked over to a bench.

Soon the loudspeaker announced that my bus would be leaving in ten minutes. I had to mail that letter before I returned to the bus. Spotting a mailbox, I quickly pulled it from my purse and kissed the envelope. Then I looked to confirm that the 3-cent stamp was still on it. I wanted to make sure that my parents got the letter so they would know where I was and that I was safe. I had timed it so that the letter would reach their mailbox a day before I would be due to arrive in Ellijay on the Trailways bus for my usual weekend visit.

Once again, settled in the bus, I began thinking of the bus driver's comment as we pulled out of Pompano Beach. "A couple more stops until we arrive in Miami," he had said. "First up is Palm Beach and then . . ."

I hadn't heard the other name, because my mind had become stuck on Palm Beach. Mrs. Leach's winter home was there! I couldn't help remembering how Mrs. Leach had wanted to adopt me. If she had, I might be heading to such a winter home myself right now. Yet the thought of my Mommy and Daddy and Grandma at home, receiving my letter, sobered me, and cut off my daydream. Fumbling to open Colleen's old purse, I carefully counted the money I had, which was one ten-dollar bill, a five, one single dollar and twenty-two cents. Even before I counted it, I had been pretty sure of the amount of cash I had. For the first time, I realized how little it was: $16.22. It hit me suddenly, and for the first time, that a lack of funds could turn out to be one of the main obstacles I might encounter in Miami. I began to realize that hunger pangs would not be dismissed with my often repeated phrase, "I'll think of that tomorrow," because my stomach and not my brain was in charge of hunger.

"This is Miami, the end of the line," the now familiar voice of the driver announced.

"This is not the end of the line for me," I thought, determined. "It is the beginning of a bright, new life."

Descending the steps from the bus, we passengers, perhaps six of us, sleepily walked around to the side of the bus to collect our baggage from the storage underneath. The fresh soft breezes gently touching my face were comforting. The aroma of salt water from the ocean was pungent.

I became aware that beside me was a strange object that looked like a long brown pole towering above the bus station building. It had a slim, brown trunk that appeared to have roots in the ground. It had no branches or leaves that I could see, however, until I peered to the top and saw a large round dark mass of something that appeared to be limbs mingled together at the very top.

"What is that?" I asked a man waiting beside me, as I pointed to the towering pole.

At first, he looked stunned at my question, but a smile quickly stretched his mouth.

"It's a palm tree," he said.

As I kept staring upward to the top of the tall tree, I saw bright stars twinkling at me. They were the same stars I had loved in Georgia, but I wasn't in Georgia any more.

27014749R00171

Made in the USA
San Bernardino, CA
07 December 2015